YOU GET A PASS

"Pass on, human," the Shade said in a low, pleasant voice. I was hearing her in my mind; I wondered what Buck heard or if he heard anything. "Leave me to eat, and take pleasure in there being one fewer enemy to your sort in the universe."

"Let's get 'em, Buck," I said. We went for the Shade.

The Shade was a thing of the Waste so that wasn't a choice here, but we sure could've gone back the way we came. Her hands were anchored in her prey, and I didn't think she could get loose in time to grab us if we cut past her and her victim in the direction we'd been going.

Thing is, the Shade was the enemy of all life. The Beast might well be my enemy, but if I'd been by five minutes quicker the Shade would've had me instead.

The Shade's face was as smooth as marble. Her hands were withdrawing, but they wouldn't be clear before I could hit her.

The perfect mouth opened and a three-forked tongue extended. The tips touched my cheeks and the underside of my jaw. I was hooked as sure as I ever had a crappie in the pond at the bottom of the big field. The Shade's right hand was lifting, already clear of the Beast and reaching for my chest.

I triggered my weapon.

BAEN BOOKS by DAVID DRAKE

THE RCN SERIES: *With the Lightnings • Lt. Leary, Commanding • The Far Side of the Stars • The Way to Glory • Some Golden Harbor • When the Tide Rises • In the Stormy Red Sky • What Distant Deeps • The Road of Danger • The Sea Without a Shore • Death's Bright Day*

HAMMER'S SLAMMERS: *The Tank Lords • Caught in the Crossfire • The Sharp End • The Complete Hammer's Slammers, Vols 1–3*

INDEPENDENT NOVELS AND COLLECTIONS: *All the Way to the Gallows • Cross the Stars • Grimmer Than Hell • Loose Cannon • Night & Demons • Northworld Trilogy • Patriots • The Reaches Trilogy • Redliners • Seas of Venus • Starliner • Dinosaurs and a Dirigible • The Spark*

THE CITIZEN SERIES with John Lambshead: *Into the Hinterlands • Into the Maelstrom*

THE GENERAL SERIES: *Hope Reborn* with S.M. Stirling° • *Hope Rearmed* with S.M. Stirling° • *Hope Renewed* with S.M. Stirling° • *Hope Reformed* with S.M. Stirling and Eric Flint° • *The Heretic* with Tony Daniel • *The Savior* with Tony Daniel

THE BELISARIUS SERIES with Eric Flint: *An Oblique Approach • In the Heart of Darkness • Belisarius I: Thunder Before Dawn° • Destiny's Shield • Fortune's Stroke • Belisarius II: Storm at Noontide° • The Tide of Victory • The Dance of Time • Belisarius III: The Flames of Sunset°*

EDITED BY DAVID DRAKE: *The World Turned Upside Down* with Jim Baen & Eric Flint • *Foreign Legions*

°Omnibus edition

To purchase these titles in e-book format, please go to www.baen.com

THE
SPARK

DAVID
DRAKE

THE SPARK

This is a work of fiction. All the characters and events portrayed in this book are fictional, and any resemblance to real people or incidents is purely coincidental.

A Baen Books Original

Baen Publishing Enterprises
P.O. Box 1403
Riverdale, NY 10471
www.baen.com

ISBN: 978-1-4814-8359-9

Cover art by Todd Lockwood

First paperback printing, November 2018

Library of Congress Catalog Number: 2017037363

Distributed by Simon & Schuster
1230 Avenue of the Americas
New York, NY 10020

Pages by Joy Freeman (www.pagesbyjoy.com)
Printed in the United States of America

To Lynn Bessette
A fellow Arthurian Enthusiast

A MAP OF THE TERRITORY

This one is different.

In the late '80s, on a whim, I turned themes from Norse mythology into Adventure Science Fiction. The result was *Northworld*. Normally I use Adventure SF as a synonym for Space Opera, but *Northworld* was something else again; like nothing else that I'd written or, to the best of my knowledge, that anybody else had written.

The Spark is another whim, but a very different one.

A twelfth-century French writer, Jean Bodel, referred to the three literary tropes, "matters," that everyone (here meaning every writer, I believe) should know: the Matter of Rome, the Matter of France, and the Matter of Britain. These Matters are basically structures in which one can tell stories.

The stories which fall into the Matter of Rome include various forms of the *Alexander Romance*, which is full of remarkable literary inventions (I definitely hope to do something with it, though probably as embellishment to other stories rather than using the plot directly), and the whole cycle of stories about Virgil the Magician, a character based on the poet Vergil but as surely a fantasy construct as Paul Bunyan. Avram Davidson did a series of stories about this Virgil, and I used some of the mythos in *Monsters of the Earth*.

There are many other medieval tales in the Matter of Rome: those above are just two of my favorites. That's the beauty of the Matters: they give a writer (now or a thousand years ago) any number of very different hooks on which to hang stories.

The Matter of France covers Charlemagne and his Paladins. Again, this is a treasure-trove for a writer. One of the earliest Chansons de Geste, *The Song of Roland*, belongs to this Matter, as do the huge, discursive *Orlando Inamorato* and *Orlando Furioso* of the Italians Boiardo and Ariosto. Poul Anderson in *Three Hearts and Three Lions*, and Quinn Yarbro in *Ariosto*, have done extremely different modern takes on the Matter; and one of these days I'm going to try something in that area also.

The Matter of Britain involves King Arthur. From the eleventh century it has never ceased to be a major source and subject for writers. *The Spark* is one more example of that.

The background of my plot comes from the Prose *Lancelot*, a large work by (probably) three French authors which appeared in the early thirteenth century. The tenor of *The Spark*, and some of the specific business, come instead from the slightly earlier Arthurian romances of Chretien de Troyes.

The *Lancelot* is realistic in the sense of being non-fanciful. It may not make any historical sense, but there are no marvels to be found in it. Chretien is full of marvels and wonders, and *that* is the feel which I'm striving for.

The tone of *The Spark* is partly that of Chretien (who was, after all, writing romances), but I also drew from *The Idylls of the King*. There are various kinds of 'realism.' The human sadness of, say, *Merlin and Vivien*, is every bit as true as the stark violence of *The Dragon Lord*, my first novel (which is also Arthurian).

Finally, I adapted some of the business from English folktales. I think Chretien would have approved. (The writers of *Lancelot* would not have.)

I said that *The Spark* used the same basic technique as *Northworld*, but to a different end. *Northworld* came from very harsh material, and when I wrote it I was just starting to climb up from the place I'd been since Viet Nam.

I'm a much more cheerful person now than I was in 1988, and the Matter of Britain, even at its darkest, is much less bleak than the sleet, snow, and slaughter of Norse myths. *The Spark* isn't set in an ideal world, but it's a world *striving* to be ideal. That's a *world* of difference.

What really matters isn't where a story comes from or what category it falls into but rather whether or not it's a good story. I hope that you find *The Spark* to be a good story.

Dave Drake
david-drake.com

But he by wild and way, for half the night,
And over hard and soft, striking the sod
From out the soft, the spark from off the hard,
Rode...

—*Pelleas and Ettarre*
Alfred, Lord Tennyson

CHAPTER 1

Arriving at Dun Add

Neither my dog Buck nor me had ever been more than a day's hike from Beune before, so I didn't realize we were approaching Dun Add. There was a group of about a dozen of us by now, folks coming together on the Road as we got closer to the capital, and some of the others had been here before.

Dame Carole lived in Dun Add, as a matter of fact. She was in her fifties and had been making a pilgrimage to religious sites with six people; six servants, I suppose, though one was a priest and Duncan was a man at arms. A rich woman might want protection anywhere on the Road, but from what Duncan had said to me they hadn't gone far enough out from Dun Add that trouble was likely.

Duncan pointed to the trees on the right side of the Road and said, "See how the Waste changes? It's gotten reddish, you see? We're near Dun Add."

"I see something," I said. I didn't see red—it was

1

all sort of gray/green/brown. What to me had been medium-sized broadleafed trees for at least the past ten days, however, was now brush that mostly wasn't as tall as I was. "I wouldn't have known what it meant, though."

Folks didn't see the Waste the same way, probably because there was nothing really there. Everything you see on the Road—and the Road itself, I guess—is in your mind. That doesn't mean that it isn't real, but everybody has a different reality.

Buck whined. He was feeling something different too. It made him jumpy, or maybe he was feeling me be jumpy.

I was going to Dun Add to join Jon's Company of Champions. Beune is a nice place but it's a long way from most everything—except for Not-Here, which in long past times spread over Beune too. Not-Here still wasn't very far away.

If you haven't been anywhere but Beune, then you know you're going to be over your head in any real town. I sure did, anyway. Going to Dun Add, the Leader's capital, couldn't make me any more lost than I'd have been in someplace smaller, and this is where I had to be to become a Champion.

George was a farmer on a place called Wimberly. He must've been doing well because he was travelling to Dun Add just to see the place. He'd brought his daughter Mercy along, calling her Mike and dressing her in boy's clothes. Mercy was fourteen and, well, well-grown. Despite the loose clothing.

I guess George was afraid of what the men they met on the Road might do to his daughter, but the truth is that Mercy was *way* ready to be done to. I don't figure it had been any different when she was back on Wimberly. For myself, I called her Mike in public, and after the first time, I saw to it that she never got me alone again.

It seemed to me that Dame Carole knew that Mike was a girl too and that she was a *lot* more interested in Mercy than I was. I didn't like to think about that—Carole was so old, for one thing!—but it was none of my business.

On Beune we keep ourselves pretty much to ourselves. Besides being the way I'd been raised, it seemed like a good way to be.

You don't need an animal to walk the Road, you can wear polarized filters. I've seen good ones of mica, though a Maker of any skill can build better ones out of raw sand. Seeing through an animal's eyes works a lot better, though, and most people can manage the trick even if they don't know the animal real well.

Carole had a fluffy white cat. Cats are supposed to be great, slipping along instead of ramming through rough patches the way dogs do, but they're no good in a fight. You can't control what they're going to do, and if you've got to fight your beast as well as your opponent, you're probably going to get the blazes knocked out of you.

Heyman, one of two merchants on the way to Dun Add, had a sleek gazehound that his pair of bearers used also. Heyman traded in textiles. He didn't talk much, not with the likes of me anyway, but his bearers said that some of his fabric had been woven in Not-Here.

Rilk, the other merchant, carried a pack heavier than I'd have wanted to heft on a long trek. It was pottery that he'd turned and fired himself. Nothing fancy, just undecorated earthenware, but I liked the

shape of some of his mugs. If we'd been back on
Beune, I'd have bought a couple.

Rilk had a mongrel named Sachem. There wasn't a
lot to choose between him and Buck, though Sachem
was a good few years older.

I never saw the point of fancy breeds, but maybe
that was sour grapes. You weren't going to get hounds
like Heyman's on Beune; and if you had, I wouldn't
have been able to afford one. I'd sold the farm to a
neighbor to get enough money to buy food for me
and Buck on the way to Dun Add.

"Oh Pal...?" Mercy called, walking over close to
me. "Is it true that we're getting close to Dun Add,
the way Carole says?"

"She ought to know, Mike," I said, nodding toward
Dame Carole. She glared back like she wanted to slip
a dagger in me, though she must see that I wasn't
doing anything to encourage Mercy. "Duncan here
tells me the same."

Mercy looked like she wanted to come closer yet,
but I clicked my tongue to Buck and we stepped
out a little quicker. Seeing through Buck's eyes, the
Road was a stretch of poles laid edge to edge on the
ground; in grays and browns, of course. We'd been
pacing along comfortably; speeding up was clumsy and
more tiring, so I backed off after I'd put the girl a
step or two behind us.

"Pal, I wonder if we'll see each other in the city?"
Mercy called. "You know, it's all new to me and I'd
like to see it with a friend."

"I guess you and your dad can hire a guide, Mike,"
I said. "For myself, I don't know anything about the
place. I'm going to be real busy besides."

Duncan stayed quiet until Mercy had taken her disappointment back to her father. Then he chuckled and said, "*She* thinks she's old enough, lad."

"That's between her and God," I said. I grimaced because I sounded like a right little god-bothering prig, which I'm *not*. But you shouldn't be trifling with fourteen-year-old girls unless, I suppose, you're fourteen yourself and you're inclined that way. I hadn't been inclined, and now I was twenty.

"Your choice, lad," Duncan said, shrugging. "Carole settles as soon as we step onto the landingplace, and I'll pay you back right off."

He grimaced much the way I just had. "I have to do it then," he muttered, "because like as not I won't have it in a couple days. I used'a tell myself it'd be different this time, but by now I don't guess it will be."

Duncan wasn't a bad fellow. He'd helped me a lot when we stopped at way stations.

It was my first time any distance on the Road. Before I met Duncan—and the rest of Dame Carole's crew—I'd been sleeping rough. I knew the innkeepers weren't giving me fair quotes, but I didn't know what *was* fair, so I couldn't beat them down. Duncan got me in at better rates than any lone traveller was going to get, because he made it sound like I was another of Carole's guards.

The lie bothered me a bit, but Duncan said that if we were attacked he bloody well expected I'd fight too—which I surely would. I guess it was all right.

Duncan had gotten an advance on his wages before they set off, but by the time I fell in with Dame Carole he was stony broke. I loaned him money for ale or whatever the waystations had; but not too much. He'd say things when I cut him off, but I think in his heart he was just as glad I was doing it. Like I say, Duncan wasn't a bad fellow.

A couple more branches of the Road had joined ours since Duncan said we were getting close, but nobody was on them. I wondered where they went... and wondered if I'd be sent along those ways after I'd joined the Company of Champions.

Two of Dame Carole's attendants had gone a bit ahead. The younger one turned and waved his hands. "We're here, milady!" he called. "We've arrived!"

"I forget how many times I've come back this way," Duncan said with a sigh. "It stopped being exciting a long time ago."

"It's exciting to me," I said. "I guess I'm afraid, too. A little afraid."

It was more than a little and Duncan probably knew it; but I'd come to Dun Add because it was the only place where I could become part of making the universe safe for human beings. Making it the way things had been thousands of years ago, before the great collapse. Jon and his Champions were doing that, putting down bandits and monsters from their capital in Dun Add.

People talked about Jon's dream even as far off as Beune. The more I thought about it, the surer I was that until it had been done, it was the only real job for a man.

There was nothing holding me on Beune after Mom died; Dad had been dead these past ten years. I sold the steading to Gervaise, my neighbor to the south, and spent three months preparing. When I decided I'd done everything I could to get ready, Buck and I set off for Dun Add.

And here I was. I took a deep breath and walked from the Road onto Dun Add, the capital of the human universe—

If there was going to *be* a human universe again.

The first thing I did on the other side of the foggy curtain was sneeze. Bright light does that to me, and it was cloudless noon on the meadow outside the landingplace of Dun Add where the Road entered.

Buck always likes to come back to Here, though he never balks when I tell him it's time to get onto the Road again. Now he started wagging at the new sights, and there were surely plenty of them.

The first thing I saw was the castle up the hill straight ahead. It took me a moment to realize that it *was* a building, not just a higher part of the hill. I'd seen pictures, sure, but I hadn't really appreciated what it would be like to be close to something that big, something human beings had made.

"God save me," I muttered. I suppose I looked like a hick from the back of beyond as I stood gaping at the castle, but in all truth that's what I was.

"I was in the Commonwealth army for a couple years," Duncan said. "Even though I've lived here, it hits me still every time I see it. There'd been a small fort on the hill for I dunno how long, but Jon built it to what you see now. It's because so many branches of the Road come together here. The hinterland's more than big enough to support the court too."

He'd stayed beside me, probably figuring how Dun Add was going to strike me. I'd been luckier than I knew to have met Duncan on the Road.

"You were one of Jon's Champions?" I said.

Right away I was sorry that I'd sounded so disbelieving, but I really was. It was like Duncan had told me that he could flap his arms and fly like a bird.

He gave me a wry smile and said, "A Champion? No, lad, that's not for the likes of you and me. But Jon needs regular men at arms too, and I was one of those. There's only a hundred and fifty Champions all told, and that's if the Company was at full strength— which I don't know that it ever has been."

I cleared my throat and said, "Ah, Duncan? You say the Champions aren't for you and me. Why is that, exactly? Back where I come from, Beune, I'd heard that the Leader takes warriors from all over to fill his Company."

"Oh, Jon takes warriors from anywhere, you bet," Duncan said with a snort. "What he doesn't take is any *body*. You have to have great equipment even to try. My stuff is good enough to see off a couple bandits on the Road."

He waggled his weapon and shield, a modular unit. It didn't impress me, but I hadn't seen it in use. And I hadn't been into it in a Maker's trance, either, which I thought might show me more.

"For the Companions, though," Duncan continued, "you need the best there is and that costs money. If you're the lord of a big place like Mar or maybe the son of the top merchant on Castorman, you can afford it. *I* couldn't, and I don't guess Beune runs to that kind of money either."

He frowned, staring at my equipment. "Now that I come to it," he said, "where did you come up with this hardware, lad? I've never in my life seen anything looking like that."

"Well..." I said, trying to keep my voice steady. I knew it looked rough. "I made it myself, on Beune. I've used it, and it works."

That was true, but I'd have to admit that neither trial had been much of a test. A half a dozen bullies had arrived from Kleruch, that's the node with the most people in our neighborhood. They tried to shake down Gammer Kleinze, who keeps what passes for a shop and tavern on Beune. I ran them off, but none of them had a shield and only two had real weapons. I kept my weapon at twenty percent power so I didn't have to recharge.

The other time was when something from Not-Here landed in a patch of scrubland near the boundary with the Waste in the north side. Jimsey, who had the nearest farm to it, called me over.

The thing, whatever it was, didn't have a real shape but it was the size of a barn. I jabbed it a couple times, then hit it full power. That punched a hole clear through and into the Waste beyond, but I had my heart in my mouth when I did it. If the thing had come for me, it'd have been all over. My weapon takes about five minutes to recharge because I'd rebuilt it from a miner's rock drill.

The thing turned and oozed back into the Waste. None the worse for wear, as best I could tell, but it must not've liked the jolt I gave it. I'm not sure it ever knew I was there; if it had eyes or anything like that, I didn't see them. Where it'd been browsing, not only the plants were gone but all the soil too, and a layer of the limestone bedrock had crumbled to a calcium dust.

"What do you mean you made it, hey?" Duncan

said, a little sharper than I'd heard him speak before. "Are you saying you're a Maker, then? Or are you just playing silly buggers with old Duncan, hey?"

I spread my boots a little farther apart and straightened my back. "Sir!" I said. "I'm a Maker, yes. I'm pretty much self-taught, but out on Beune we learn to make do. My neighbors have been bloody glad to have me around, and I've made stuff that peddlers have taken away to sell on, too."

"Well, I'll be," Duncan said, relaxing again. Our dogs relaxed too. They'd picked up the smell of trouble when Duncan thought I was mocking him. They were both ready to mix it if that was the next thing that happened. "Sorry, lad. I'd taken you for a warrior."

"I *am* a warrior," I said, "or anyway that's what I've come to Dun Add to be. There's no law against being both, you know."

"Maybe not," said Duncan, "but I never heard of it happening."

"Well, I don't know that I have either," I said. Duncan was the closest thing to a friend I had nearer than Beune. Even if I never saw him again, I didn't want us to have parted on bad terms. "It's two different ways of looking at the things that the Ancients left. Not everybody's a warrior, and I guess there's fewer still that're Makers."

I coughed and added, "I don't claim to be any great shakes. But I'm good for Beune."

"Just remember you're not on Beune now, Pal," Duncan said. "You're a good lad, but Dun Add is a big place."

He sighed and said, "I'll get your money, now, and be right back with it. Bless you for your kindness to an old man who hasn't always been a good friend to himself."

Duncan walked over to Dame Carole. There was a line of people waiting from before we arrived, being checked in by a clerk. I guess a place like Dun Add has to have a notion of who's come in, though it's not something that you think about in Beune. Nobody much does come to Beune, of course.

It seemed to me that the clerk was doing just fine, but he had an overseer with a plush hat, puffed sleeves, and a pair of bright red galluses holding up his tights. The overseer waited till the clerk had gotten the particulars into a notebook, then snarled at both the clerk and the traveller and snatched the notebook away. The overseer made more marks, then slapped the notebook back into the clerk's hands.

There was no chance I was going to forget that I wasn't on Beune anymore. Every moment I stood looking at Dun Add, I more and more regretted leaving home. Buck whined like he was wondering why we'd left too. I rubbed him behind the ears.

The landingplace was grassy, though it'd been tramped pretty bare except around the edges between the kiosks. I thought those might be something to do with the government like the clerk and his boss, but when I looked closer they were all selling something or trying to.

Some hawked clothing—"Town clothes! Don't look like a rube on the streets of Dun Add!" and some were jewelry booths—"Show her that you care, bucko, and she'll show you that she cares!"

But the most of them, twenty or more, were dram shops. Some fancier than others, but at a glance I wouldn't expect anything better to drink than the cheap-jack clothes and the trashy baubles from the neighboring hawkers.

I didn't mind being taken for a rube. I was one, right enough. I wasn't a bloody fool as to spend my money on the shoddy I saw here, though.

A river, bigger than I'd ever imagined, lay to the left. More of Dun Add stretched along the shore than was down here by the landingplace, though that may have been because of rules. The first hundred yards from here toward the castle was by paths through the woods.

Beune isn't very big, and the streams back home wouldn't float anything more than a rowboat. Some of the ships on the Dun Add waterfront had sails on two masts for going back upstream against the current. I'd heard of ships that big, but seeing them made me blink.

The rafts were what really interested me. They were made by pinning together the trunks of full-sized trees, all softwoods that I could see. Some were still loaded with the bales and casks they'd carried from the interior, but others were empty and had been winched to an island in midstream.

I couldn't tell whether the island was natural or if it'd been built on pilings, but I could hear the scream of a circle saw driven by a wheel out in the current. The rafts were being turned into boards and timbers to build Dun Add even bigger than it was already.

At least they'll have room for me, I thought. I smiled, but there wasn't a lot of laughter in my mind.

Duncan joined me again. Dame Carole was still well back in the line, and not looking best pleased about it, either.

"Here you go, lad," Duncan said, counting five silver pieces into my palm one at a time. They had the face of Jon the Leader on one side and on the other a dragon with its tail knotted to fit in the space.

"They're fresh from the mint here," he said, which I could tell by looking at the coins. "And this—"

He added a brass piece, a little larger than the silver.

"—is from Castorman. In Dun Add it passes at about three to one against the dragons. We can have it weighed out in a jeweler's booth, if you like?"

"No, I trust you," I said, putting the coins into the suede pouch I hang inside my waistband in the front. I still had enough of the small change that I'd brought onto the Road that I wouldn't have to break a silver piece right away.

We don't use money a lot on Beune. Mostly it's barter or what amounts to the same as barter: doing a favor for a neighbor because he's done a favor for you, or he will do when you need one.

I needed minted money to go on the Road. Gervaise had to really scrape to come up with what my farm was worth, or something close to it. I think in the end he was getting money from folks who knew me and were doing me a favor. They didn't want me to leave Beune, but if they had cash they helped me with my dream by paying Gervaise for a cask of next year's cider or a sheep in the fall, to slaughter or to raise.

To the right of the landingplace was a plain that was even bigger but with only a dozen or so people on it. They were too far away for me to catch details beyond seeing that most of them were men, but I suddenly realized from the shimmer that some of them were warriors fighting. I started walking in that direction, barely murmuring goodbye when Duncan headed back to his employer.

This was what I had come to Dun Add for: to be a Champion of Mankind, to fight other warriors not for my own sake or even for the Leader's sake. I would fight so that scattered humanity could unite instead of being ground to dust piecemeal.

Buck caught my mood and growled at the back of his throat. The black bristles along his spine had risen, though he didn't know what it was that'd made me feel this way.

"Mind how you go, buddy!" a voice said closer to me than my thoughts were. "Nobody gets off the landingplace until they're checked in with the Herald of the Gate."

Called back to today, I blinked at the pair of stewards. They wore blue tunics with a dragon embroidered on the left breast; they carried wooden staves. One of them had set his staff crossways in front of me, but it was the other who'd spoken.

"Oh!" I said and backed a step. "Sorry, I was looking at the Champions instead of paying attention to where I was going."

The fellow with the outstretched staff butted it and laughed. "You *are* new if you think those're Champions," he said.

"All right, I'm new," I said. Being new didn't give a fat man with a bad shave the right to sneer at me, and I was just about in a mood to remind him that I was armed and he wasn't.

"If you don't watch your tongue, Platt," said the other steward in a weary voice, "somebody's going to feed you your teeth. It might even be me."

He looked at me, met my eyes and said, "Two of those fighting are Aspirants, kid. One's named Newell and he's been here a few years. The other fellow arrived in the past couple months, but I didn't catch his name. They're training for seats in the Champions' Hall, but they haven't passed the test yet. The other two, the nearer pair, they're just a couple warriors from the army, getting in a little exercise."

"I figured there'd be testing," I said. That was true, but if Newell had been an Aspirant for years it sounded like the testing was more formal than I'd expected.

What looked like shimmering around the fighters was the way they slipped out of Here when their shields went on. It was like being on the Road, only it was just you and you could engage it anywhere.

I guess it sounds funny, but I'd never seen what a warrior looked like with his shield on. I was the only person on Beune who had a shield, and I was inside when I engaged it. All I knew was what my neighbors told me they saw.

From what I've heard, different warriors control their shields in various ways. With me I take the grip in my left hand and switch it on with my thumb. I tighten my fingers to narrow the shielded segment or spread them for wider coverage.

The real problem is that I built the shield from what was basically an umbrella, which I beefed up really a lot. It'll stop a weapon stroke—the two thugs I ran off Beune both hit me square before I knocked them down—but moving with it on is really hard. I figure it's got a lot more inertia than a shield that was meant for fighting, though I haven't tried one to be sure.

I could've asked Duncan to let me handle his unit. I guess I was embarrassed to, because he'd want to try mine. I know my shield and weapon—I made them, after all—and I know they've got quirks. Somebody who wasn't used to those quirks, well, he'd laugh at me. Duncan wouldn't have laughed out loud, but I'd have known what he was thinking.

I watched the warriors spar a little longer, then looked back at the line. It'd gotten down pretty short; Dame Carole and her crew were through, Duncan among them. I suppose he was off to a tavern, which made me a little sad. I had no right to feel responsible for a man who was older than my father had been when he died.

I nodded to the steward who'd been polite to me and headed back to the clerk and his overseer. Dun Add was waiting for me, but I had to get through the official before I saw any of it.

CHAPTER 2

Finding My Place

I reached the line just as the clerk processed Rilk, the last person from the group I'd arrived with. The old potter hadn't set his pack down while he waited, I guess because he struggled so hard to lift it again.

I'd helped him mornings on the Road and I'd have helped him again here, but I'd been off watching the warriors. I felt a little bad about that, but Rilk wasn't my business either except because I tried to be courteous to other people.

The clerk looked about as beat down as Rilk did, but in his case it was the weight of overseer on his back, the Herald of the Gate as the steward called him. "Name and business," he said. He didn't raise his eyes, which meant he could see my trousers and sheepskin boots; and maybe the wooden closure of my belt that Jimsey had given me after I chased the creature back into the Waste. I'd just knotted the leather before then.

"I'm Pal of Beune," I said, standing straight. "I've come to Dun Add to join the Company of Champions."

The clerk looked up then, his eyes opening wider. He was young, not much older than me, but I could see the strain at the edges of his eyes.

I don't know what he might've said next, but he didn't have time to. The overseer jumped like I'd goosed him and shouted, "Are you mocking me, hobby? Do you think I'm just another yokel that you can jape? I'm the Herald of the Gate, and if you think you're so funny you can just take yourself back into the Waste!"

"Sir, I'm not mocking you," I said, keeping my voice as calm as I could. Right now I was bubbling with anger and fear too. I didn't know what I'd done wrong, but it sounded like I might not even get into Dun Add. "I'm not the kind that does that sort of thing."

For a moment it looked like the Herald was going to bust. I guess he didn't know how to take me. That could happen even back home where most folks knew me or at any rate had heard about me. It's too bad when people figure there's got to be something underneath the words when I just tell the truth, but it's happened enough that it doesn't surprise me anymore.

That was when the boat appeared right in the middle of the landingplace. It quivered back and forth a couple times, coming into balance with Here and shifting a hair to get above the short grass.

"Oh!" the Herald said. "That's Lord Mofflin's boat, surely it is."

He went bustling off toward the boat, a cylinder thirty feet long, lying on its side. "Sir?" I called after him.

The clerk grinned at me and made a mark on his notebook. He thumbed me toward the castle and said, "Good luck to you, buddy. Whatever that means for you." Then he followed his boss, walking a little straighter than he had a moment ago.

I headed for the path that seemed to lead straightest toward the castle above. It may seem funny, but as rare as I knew boats were, I'd nonetheless seen two of them in the past.

Beune isn't close to much of anything by the Road, but if you travel by boat it turns out to be on the way to a lot of places. That isn't a reason to stop, of course, unless your boat needs repairs or restocking. Which at least the two I saw did; repairs *and* restocking, I suspect, but restocking for sure.

The first boat landed when I was only six. I'd started fiddling with the bits of Ancient artifacts that had drifted to Beune. I'd go into a trance and enter the piece, and after a while I started to fill the places with what it seemed to me that it needed. I didn't talk to anybody about what I was doing, and I don't know that I'd heard the word Maker.

The boatman wore black leather and had a full red beard. I thought he was God Almighty come down to Beune. It was just him and his client alone in the boat, and I know now that the client must've been rich enough to buy all of Beune. That was nothing to me when I was six; and tell the truth, it isn't much to me now.

I'd have sold my soul to be the boatman, though. He superintended my neighbors as they loaded the boat's hoppers with all sorts of things, rock and wood and corn and twenty products besides.

Now that means to me the fellow didn't have a clue as to what was missing and was hoping the boat's automatic systems would find enough in the hoppers to let them limp to wherever they were going—or at least to a node with different selections where they could try again. Then to me it was all wonder and wonderful, though.

I was fourteen the second time a boat landed, though, and by then I think I could've done them some good if they'd let me. They didn't, of course; I was a kid and a hick, and they—a fine lady with her maid and her fancy boy; their boatman was less impressive than the first one I'd seen—had me chased away. I think the gigolo would've clouted me if the maid hadn't grabbed his arm.

They loaded up with wood after tossing out the decomposed wood that'd gotten them this far. Though they wouldn't let me aboard the boat, it was easy to get hold of some of the waste and check it in a trance. The boat had drawn out the carbon.

Well, the wood the strangers bought would give them that; Father and some of our neighbors made nice money by selling brush that was too small to build with and too prickly to be anything but bedding at the bottom of a haystack to let the fodder breathe. Thing is, we've got a thick seam of coal on Beune, and that would've provided the carbon in a load that would've packed might tighter.

I was willing to bet that I could've done something about the processor that was making the boat go through carbon so fast too, but the only one I'd have given the time of day to was the maid. I wasn't sure who owned the boat, the lady or the boatman himself just hiring it to her, but it sure wasn't the maid.

As I looked at the choice of paths now, I heard a

woman with a pleasant voice call, "I'm back, George," behind me as I neared the trees. I turned. A really pretty girl with pale blond hair had come in from the Road. She had a three-colored cat in the crook of her left arm and a basket of tulips in that hand. She was waving her right arm to the Herald and his clerk.

"We've got you, Miss May," the clerk called back, and the Herald himself even turned and swept off his puffy hat with a bow. I wondered which one of them was named George.

I paused for a moment, because she was coming my way. I waited till she looked around and noticed me. "Ma'am," I said. "I'm new here. Can you tell me which of these paths best leads to the castle?"

"You can follow me, I suppose," she said, and her tone wasn't much more friendly than the set look on her face. I guess a girl so pretty must have a lot of men pestering her.

I didn't let it bother me, just said, "Thank you, ma'am," and followed as she swept past me. Buck looked up at her cat and it was giving him the eye, but Buck's well behaved.

Miss May's dress was the same as girls on Beune wear in weather this warm: a knee-length skirt and short sleeves. The waist was pinched just a bit by a fabric belt, enough to give it shape without being a couple layers of cloth tight against the skin. Thing is, back home the dresses were wool, maybe with a little embroidery on the sleeves or neckline. May wore silk, and I couldn't tell if the light peach color was dyed or the silk came that way from the worm.

The trees were nice, horse chestnuts about thirty feet tall. They were in flower, too. May took me along a path that forked twice, first to the left and the second time to the right. I didn't know where the other branches would've led me—I couldn't really get lost in a belt a hundred yards thick—but I was glad to have a guide.

I stayed a pace behind her, keeping a bit off to the left. There was plenty of room for us to walk side by side, but she pretty clearly didn't want that to happen and I'm not one to push in where I'm not wanted.

Neither of us spoke until I could see flashes of the white walls of houses through the trees ahead of us. Then I said what I'd been thinking as I walked along behind her: "I like your tulips. My mom planted them in front of the house, and I always forget about them until they come up again in the spring. This year they hadn't come up before I left home, though."

"That's nice," May said without looking back at me.

I bent and stroked the back of Buck's neck. I couldn't complain. I try to be friendlier to strangers than May was being, but we don't get many strangers on Beune. Anyway, not everybody has to be like me.

The houses at this end of Dun Add were two or three stories high. The shops on the ground floor generally spilled out onto the street. There were grocers along with a general line of the same goods as I'd seen on the fringe of the landingplace; maybe a little better quality.

I didn't have either the time or the inclination to browse much, as May strode along more briskly on the cobblestones than she had through the woods. She hadn't been dawdling there, either.

The street was steep enough that sometimes it had steps in it, two or three and once as many as a dozen.

My pack hadn't been heavy even when I left Beune. Now that I'd eaten all the bread and cheese it was lighter still, but I'd walked a long way during the past three weeks. Besides which my weapon and shield were heavy enough that the belt I hung them from was chafing my hip bones. Well, I was almost there.

The houses were built around courtyards—occasionally a large gate was open and I could see inside. There were a few people outside. Sometimes they bowed or curtseyed to May and even nodded to me. I guess they thought I was her attendant instead of just being somebody she was giving directions to.

The girl stopped. We'd reached a terrace beyond the houses farthest up the slope. Ahead of her, ahead of us, was the castle.

The first thing I noticed was that though it was all stone, it wasn't all the same kind of masonry. The center part was big, roughly dressed blocks, while the wings had more finish and were built with smaller stones.

The second thing I noticed was that there were eight doors just on this side, and a paved path running all the way the length of the front. In the middle of the old part was a double gate twenty feet high. It was closed, and though the leaves were wood, they were strapped with steel. There was a dusting of rust on the higher parts of the metal. Set into the right gate-leaf was a regular door covered with either polished brass or gold.

May turned her head toward me and said, "There's the castle." Then she started down the path to the right.

"Thank you, ma'am," I said. Then I swallowed and said, "Ma'am? Which door do I go in to be a Champion, please?"

"Champions use the gold door," she said without looking back again.

"Come along, Buck," I said. I took a deep breath and walked toward the metal-plated door. I wasn't sure that I was supposed to take Buck in that way, but I guessed there was only one way to learn.

I'd just about reached it—I was close enough to tell that it was gilded bronze—when the girl called, "Stop!"

I stopped with my hand just short of the latch. She was about where she'd been when she'd told me to use the gold door; she must've turned a moment after she'd tossed her directions over her shoulder.

"Ma'am?" I said. "I know I'm not a Champion, but I want to be one."

She started toward me, then stopped with a grimace and said, "Oh, come here. I'll show you where to go in. You didn't *seem* feebleminded."

"Ma'am, I'm not," I said as I clucked to Buck to come toward her with me. It was an insult, but I had the feeling that she was embarrassed at her own behavior instead of looking for a chance to jab me. "I'm just arrived at Dun Add, though, and it's really different from home."

"What's your name, then?" she asked. "I'm May."

She turned when I came alongside her and we continued walking down the right front of the castle. There were people on the parapet above us and I think I heard somebody call May's name, but she didn't look up at them.

"I'm Pal," I said. "I'm from Beune. And this is Buck."

"Look, I don't know what you've heard on Beune," she said, giving me a serious look, "but it's not easy to become a Champion. There's testing by machines and then if you pass that, you have to fight for a place in the Hall. Are you sure that's what you want to do?"

"Yes, ma'am," I said. "The Leader's raised the Champions to bring justice to all of Here. Bring it back. I want to be part of that."

May grimaced again. Her eyes sharpened and she said, "Say, have you eaten?"

"Not in a while," I said. "I was planning to find a place in the town after I'd gotten started with the business of joining the Company. I figured that was going to be complicated, so I started here."

Then I said, "Ah—I have money. I'm not a beggar."

I had a fair amount of money, thanks to Duncan paying me back. I hadn't seen prices in Dun Add, but I figured they wouldn't be much worse than at inns along the Road. Which were bad enough, in all conscience.

"Well, you're here on Jon's business for now," May said, "so you ought to have one meal on him at least."

"Ma'am?" I said. "And Buck?"

She looked down. Buck waggled his tail.

"We'll take care of him first in the stables," she said. "And call me May, will you. 'Ma'am' makes me feel like I'm forty years old."

"Thank you, May," I said.

May led us to a door that stood ajar. An attendant sat on a stool just far enough down the passage beyond that his feet were out of the sunlight. He had a weapon but no shield. From the stiff way his left leg stuck out, I figured he was injured. Maybe he'd been a man at arms when he was younger and healthier.

He tried to get up when May came through the doorway. "No need, Carl," she said with a breezy wave.

"Thanks, mum," he said, settling back down. He eyed me as I followed her past, but he seemed about as interested in Buck as he was in me.

The passage was thirty feet long. There was no lighting except what came through the doorways at the ends.

They called Dun Add a castle, but I'd been thinking that it wasn't really built to be defended. There were slots in the stone roof of this passage, though. I wouldn't want to try forcing my way in here if there was somebody in the room above who didn't want me to.

There was a second gate at the far end, but it'd been propped back against the courtyard wall for so long that the hinges were rusty red lumps. We walked through into a park. There were ornamental trees planted at the west end, but for the most part the open area was sod—or dirt, where it'd gotten too much wear even for grass. I saw two ball games, one of kids of both sexes and the other of solid-looking men.

"The stables are straight across," May said, continuing to lead.

She wasn't acting like she'd like to toss me into a glacier anymore, but neither was she being the chatty/ friendly sort. I appreciated what she was doing, so I let her make the rules.

The park wasn't so crowded that we were pushing through people, but often enough we'd walk around a blanket or even a tarp raised for a sunshade. Folks called or nodded to May if they noticed her, and I got a few long looks myself. Not for anything about me or Buck, I was pretty sure.

There were six archways in the middle of the north

side of the courtyard, and the wall above the arches
was pierced for gratings up to within a couple feet
of the top. The noise was loud even before we got to
the openings, yaps and yelps and howling. No snarling fights, though.

Buck had never been in a place like this; he *sure*
didn't want to go in. I didn't either, to tell the truth, but
I didn't see another choice. I took the length of cord
turned three times around my waist, tied a good-sized
loop in one end with a square knot, and laid it over
Buck's head. He was trembling, but he didn't fight me.

The leash wasn't to hold him—it wasn't tight and
it wouldn't tighten. It just meant that I was serious
and he *had* to obey.

"It's okay, boy," I whispered. "I'll be back soon, I
promise."

We walked to where May waited for us by a counter just inside the doorway. She turned to the ostler
and said, "Here he is, Taney. Give him a kennel for
a week, will you? Though I don't know how long it's
really going to be."

She knows everybody in Dun Add, I thought. I
wondered who she really was. None of the women
I'd seen in the park wore clothes as nice as May did,
as simple as her dress looked.

"What's his number?" said Taney, taking a square
of paper from a spike and lifting a brush from his ink
well. He was way heavier than he ought to be, but
there were real muscles in his scarred arms.

"He doesn't have one yet," said May.

"Aw, Miss May!" Taney said wearily. "You *know* I'm
not supposed to stable animals until there's a number
to charge 'em to."

I brought my purse out from under my trousers. Before I could make an offer, May said, "Oh, come on, Taney. If you won't do it for the Consort, do it for me. All right?"

"All right, all right," muttered Taney. "But you know I shouldn't."

He wrote 413 down on the chit and slid it to me. May leaned over the counter and kissed his grizzled cheek. Taney turned his head away and said, "Aw, May," again but in a soft tone this time.

"Do I . . . ?" I said, but a boy wearing a leathern apron came down an aisle between the ranked kennels and took the leash.

"Where's your chit?" the boy said. He turned his head sideways to read my slip of paper right-way-up and said, "Okay, four thirteen. Four Level is being fed right now. That okay for him?"

"Yes, that's good," I said. I turned my back so that I didn't have to watch Buck being led up a winding ramp. He didn't even whine.

I wanted to whine myself, though. I felt more alone than I'd ever been in my life.

"Now, let's get you fed too," May said. Her eyes narrowed as she looked at me.

"I'm all right," I said. I hoped that was true.

We turned to the right as we left the stables and walked along the pavement. I'd blinked my eyes clear by the time we turned into another high doorway, thirty feet along the way. This was like the common room of an inn. The forty odd men—they were all men—eating at the tables weren't a tenth of what the hall could have held.

"What's on offer today, Yoko?" May asked one of

the men at the serving counter. "Oh, and will you give me a pitcher of water to put these in?" She gestured with the tulips in her right hand. "I meant to have them up in Jolene's suite by now."

"Stewed pork and collards," the server said. He reached behind him for a pitcher, which he scooped into a tub of water. He raised his eyebrow at me and said, "Two bowls?"

"Please," said May, taking the pitcher.

"I'll get 'em," I said as the server ladled two ironstone bowls full. He offered two horn spoons also, which I gripped between my left ring and little fingers.

I followed to the table where May was sitting. I'd have sat opposite but she scooted over on the bench and patted the end beside her. I set the bowls and spoons on the table, shrugged off my pack and stowed it under the bench, and finally sat down myself.

From the way people were staring, May didn't usually eat on these scarred tables; which I could well believe. She lifted her spoon but paused when I took half the tulips from the pitcher she'd set in front of us. I retrimmed the stems at a slant, then traded and fixed the other half as well.

I put my knife back in the sheath under my waist band and tucked into the pork. It was wonderful. Granted that the cook knew his business—there were spices beyond pepper, and the pot hadn't been stewed to mush as I'd expected—it made me realize how hungry I was. I was glad Buck was eating by now, too.

May was looking at me in amazement. "Ah . . . ?" I said. "I figured the ends had dried out while you've been guiding me around. They'll take up water better now. Besides, you'd used scissors to cut them and that pinches. A knife's better if you're putting the stems in water."

"Yes, I suppose it is," May said. She took a little sip of the pork, then said, "What decided you to leave your home, Pal? I suppose Beune bored you?"

"No ma'am," I said. "There's plenty going on in Beune. We're pretty close to Not-Here, you see, and you can never tell what's going to drift across. Besides, I'm sort of a Maker and there's always something new to learn, you know?"

May finished her big spoonful and then took more. I suspect she was finding she liked the pork better than she'd expected to.

"No, I didn't know that," she said. "I certainly didn't know you were a Maker. Didn't you say you wanted to be a Champion?"

"Ma'am—May, I'm sorry, I'm a Maker for fun," I said. "I really like to learn things. But it's the Champions who're going to bring safety and justice back to Mankind. I can't be a Champion on Beune."

"I see," May said, but she said it a way that made me pretty sure that she didn't. She took another spoonful.

"May, if I can ask?" I said.

She looked sideways at me. After a moment, she gave me a tiny nod.

"You mentioned 'the Consort,' and then you said, you were bringing the flowers for Jolene?" I said. "Is that—"

"I mean Lady Jolene, the Leader's Consort," May said, turning to face me. "I'm one of her attendants."

"Um," I said. I'd pretty near finished my stew, but I managed to scoop a little more juice onto my spoon so that I wasn't staring at May. "I guess that explains why everybody's so respectful to you."

That might sound wrong. "Not that they shouldn't be, I mean," I added. "It's just that folks aren't always as polite as they ought to be. On Beune, anyway."

A man came up behind me. I didn't think anything of it for a moment, but I turned when I realized he wasn't walking on.

He was older than me but not old, thirty maybe, and starting to get a paunch. His clothes were good, with velvet piping on the jacket and down the legs of his trousers. I said, "Sir?"

"I thought you didn't like men, little lady," he said to May. He wasn't shouting, but his voice was louder than it had to be. The cat jumped from May's lap and vanished under the table.

I got up. I couldn't get between the stranger and May, but I was right beside him. I was taller by a few inches, but he could give me more weight than just the fat he was carrying.

With me standing, May could push the bench back enough she could get up too.

She said, "I have nothing against men, Easton. I don't like *you*, is all."

"Look, you slut—" Easton snarled.

"Sir!" I said in his ear. "You're speaking to a lady!"

"Shut up, kid," Easton said without turning. "If you're good, I'll give you seconds after May services me."

May slapped him, hard enough to spin his head sideways. People jumped up from their meals, and a couple benches fell over.

Easton's left hand caught May by the shoulder; his right arm cocked back. It kept coming back because I'd grabbed his wrist. There were men like him on Beune, so I'd known what to expect. When Easton tried to grab me by the hair, I kneed him in the crotch and stepped back.

He didn't go down, but he backed against the bench and banged it over. May had gotten clear and was in the aisle.

"All right, hobby," Easton said in a raspy voice. He was bending over a bit still. "You're wearing arms, so you'll meet me on the field in an hour. Or I'll have you whipped out of the city, whipped so you'll be lucky to be able to walk!"

"I'll meet you on the field," I said.

It was funny, but now I felt better than I had since I got to Dun Add. *This* sort of business hadn't been new to me since I was about five years old.

CHAPTER 3

Being Put in My Place

Easton walked out of the hall, straightening as he moved. I kept watching. It wouldn't have surprised me if he'd turned and belted me if I gave him a chance to do that.

"Come on, let's get out of here," May said.

She started for the door, then paused and bent, making a basket of her left arm. The three-colored cat leaped up; she hadn't as much as mewed since I first saw her, even when May carried her into the stables.

I grabbed my pack in my left hand and the pitcher of flowers in my right. I just left the bowls on the table because I didn't know what else to do.

"That bloody man!" May said. "That *bloody* man."

"Ah, May, should I get Buck?" I asked as she started off across the courtyard.

"It's not normal for sparring," May said. She looked over at me and said, snarled really, "You could've kept

33

out of this, you know! There was no reason for you to get involved!"

"Ma'am," I said, as calm as I could. "I *did* have to get involved. He was going to hit you. And anyway, I didn't like listening to him."

"That *bloody* man," May repeated, but this time she just seemed tired. She forced a smile and said, "And you brought the flowers. My God, what am I going to do with you?"

"Well, if you can tell me how fights are run on Dun Add, I'd appreciate it," I said. We were going back through the passage we'd entered the castle by, so I figured we were heading for the jousting ground that I'd seen when I arrived. "I think the rest is on me, now."

"I'll find somebody to take you in hand at the grounds," May said. She looked at me hard again. I thought she was angry.

"Now you listen to me!" she said. "Sparring's usually done at twenty percent power. There's no reason for a squabble like this to be any more than that. Do you understand? Insist on twenty percent power!"

We were heading down the slope again. I didn't even remember seeing the doorman.

"Yes, ma'am," I said. "But ma'am? I'm not afraid. If Easton beats me, then that's something I needed to learn."

"Pal, listen to me," May said. "Easton's father was one of the Champions. Easton didn't apply for a seat in the hall, he's in the purser's office; but he's got top equipment. It's not *if* he beats you, it's how badly you'll be hurt *when* he beats you."

I figured that if Easton hadn't tried to join the

Company of Champions, he didn't have the balls to take a knocking around. It was just a matter of sticking with the job until he decided he'd had enough.

I felt my lips smiling, though they were sure dry. I was due for a bad morning, like enough, but I ought to have a better chance than May was saying.

"He wouldn't really have hit me, you know," she said. "He wouldn't dare! There's a dozen Champions who would challenge him if he did."

I took a deep breath of air scented by the flowering trees. There was a lot to like about Dun Add, more than I'd been afraid of when I left Beune for the capital.

"Ma'am," I said, "I think you're wrong there. Easton was awful mad. I don't doubt he'd have regretted it afterwards, but he was really going to hit you."

I *knew* Easton was going to hit her. I'd been hauling back on his arm, and his fist was clenched. He was a nasty fellow, no mistake, and he might well be a coward; but his temper had got away from him this time. I guessed there was a history there that I didn't know.

May had taken me by a different path through the woods than before. We came out onto the jousting ground, not the landingplace. I could see a broad, straight path that led down from the far wing of the castle.

A dozen pairs of warriors were sparring, including three who were globes of shattered light. Those pairs were with their dogs. They'd gone higher out of Here than you could follow without polarized lenses.

Besides the fighters, there were thirty or forty spectators. Several were women, but I guessed most were the attendants of those on the field. One old man didn't fit in either category. He wore a gray tunic and full-length trousers.

May strode down the sidelines, pausing beside a group of attendants who chatted as they watched their principals. "Rikard, isn't it?" she said. "Is that Lord Morseth out there?"

"Yes, mum," said the man she'd spoken to. "He's out with Lord Reaves. They're just getting some exercise."

Another of the attendants nodded enthusiastically. I figured he was Reaves's man.

"Can you call him in?" May said. "No, don't bother. They're breaking up now."

The nearest two warriors were trudging together off the field. They were big men in their early thirties. One was as tall as I am, and they both were a lot huskier.

"Hey, May!" the taller one called. "What brings you out here? I thought you were too soft-hearted for all this."

"If it's soft-hearted not to like watching men beat each other bloody, then that's me," May said sharply. "I'm here because I want a favor, Morseth."

"You got it, May," Morseth said, his voice suddenly grimmer. He'd caught the undertone in her voice.

"That goes for me too, May," said the warrior who must be Reaves. "What d' ye need?"

"My friend Pal here is on his first visit to Dun Add," May said, nodding toward me. I felt my lips tighten and I hoped I wasn't blushing. "He's gotten challenged by Easton, who was being a prick."

"When is Easton not a prick?" Morseth said.

"I want one of you to attend Pal," May said. "I

told him that it has to be fought at twenty percent. Can you make that stick with Easton?"

"I guess we can," said Reaves. He was smiling in a way that was scary where bluster wouldn't have been.

"Well, do it for me, then," said May. "Easton was more of a prick than usual, and Pal got into it because he's a good kid. All right?"

The two warriors looked me up and down. I realized I was holding a pitcher of tulips. I started to put them down, then froze because I didn't want to look like I didn't care if they got knocked over.

May took the pitcher from me. "Morseth, Reaves?" she said. "Do what you can, all right?"

She turned to me and said, "Pal, I'm sorry you got into this and I'm really sorry you got into it for me. These boys will keep things straight. Just do what they tell you."

She swallowed and said, "I'm going back to the Consort's suite now. Jolene is probably worried about how long I've been gone. And I really *don't* have a taste—"

May turned quickly and trotted off by the broad path. I could just hear her final words: "—for this sort of thing."

"Quite a lady, May is," Morseth said musingly as he watched her go. He eyed me. "Known her long?"

"No sir," I said, standing straight. "I just met her today and she was showing me around. Easton started hassling her and, well, I asked him to stop."

Morseth's smile was very slight, but I thought there was a little warmth in it for the first time. "Did you?" he said mildly.

"Let's see your hardware," said Reaves.

I unhooked my weapon and shield and handed them over, one to either man. They turned them over, then traded and repeated the process. Their faces had gotten as blank as stone walls.

"I made them myself on Beune," I said. The silence was weighing on me.

They handed back my shield and weapon. "I guess he knows his own mind," Reaves said to Morseth.

"There comes Easton," Morseth said. He turned to me and added, "We'll do the best we can for you, kid."

"Yeah," said Reaves over his shoulder. "But with Easton, don't hold your breath."

They sauntered toward Easton, who'd come with three attendants. He'd changed into a red outfit with reflective stripes up and down both tunic and breeches, and his modular shield and weapon had gilded highlights. Somebody'd spent time on the case, and that probably meant they hadn't skimped on the insides either.

For all that, Easton looked like somebody's lap dog facing a pair of Rottweilers as Morseth and Reaves approached him. He wouldn't be fighting Morseth and Reaves, though.

I wasn't afraid, really; I've gotten thumped in the past, especially before I got my full growth. Odds were I was going to get thumped again, is all.

"Young man?" said a voice behind me. "Might I look at your equipment, please?"

I turned *fast* and felt embarrassed when I saw it was just the man in gray. He was even older than he'd seemed at a glance—*really* old. His tunic and trousers were loose enough to suggest bulk, but his face was as thin as a stork's.

"Ah . . ." I said. I looked toward Easton and my friends—May's friends anyway, and they were sure *acting* as friends to me—and didn't see need to rush.

"Sure," I said, and unhooked them. "My name's Pal," I said, giving him first the shield.

Instead of replying, the old man stared silently at the shield he held in both hands. I opened my mouth to say something more, then realized that he was in a trance.

He blinked and looked up. He smiled brightly at me; it made him look a lot younger. "This is quite remarkable, Pal," he said as he returned the shield to me.

"You're a Maker, sir?" I said. I rehooked the shield and gave him my weapon.

Instead of entering it in a trance as he had the shield, the old man said, "I'm sorry, I was impolite. It happens too often, I'm afraid. My name's Guntram and yes, I'm a Maker, but I'm really retired now."

Only then did he look down at—and into, I now knew—my weapon. When he raised his eyes to me again and handed back the weapon, he said, "This was originally a drill, was it not? How quickly does it recover?"

"A rock drill, yes," I said. "Mining equipment. I found some memories of previous use when I was working on it."

I made a face because I didn't like to admit this, but I was going to say it: "Recovery time from a full discharge is five minutes or next thing to it. It's designed for setting charges in hard rock, and the Ancients weren't much concerned about recovery time. I was able to trim a little off the original, but only a minute or two."

"Rocks usually stay where they are for as long as you need, in my experience," Guntram said. "A clever repurposing, though. But what really amazes me is the way you've turned an umbrella into a shield. What gave you that idea?"

I laughed. I'd been embarrassed to talk to another Maker, but Guntram put me at ease. "Necessity, I guess," I said. "Beune is way out on the Marches. I used what I could find myself. It must've been a pretty quiet place in the time of the Ancients, because there's no weapons that I've been able to find and no real shields either. It struck me that this weather shield had the right concept, if I could just beef it up to repel more than raindrops."

I shrugged. "I wasn't sure it'd handle the extra power," I said, "but it turned out that was no problem. Thing is, it has a lot of inertia at full power. That makes it hard to change position in a hurry."

"Yes, it would," said Guntram, frowning as he focused on things inside his own mind. "I wonder..."

Then he broke off and smiled again. "Who was your teacher, if I may ask, Pal?"

"Sir, I didn't have one," I said, embarrassed again. "Weapons aren't the only thing that's hard to find around Beune. There's plenty of Ancient hardware, though much of it's been ground pretty smooth. But I'm the only person I know who's trying to rebuild it."

Reaves came walking back along with one of Easton's attendants, a fellow my age with a really white complexion and short blond hair. "We've got Easton's weapon set on twenty percent," Reaves said, "and Morseth's staying with him to make sure that doesn't change. Time to set yours, laddie."

I had already turned the power setting to what I

guessed was about twenty percent. I hadn't bothered to fit the dial with detents, and I honestly didn't have a way to calibrate it precisely anyway. I guessed I'd accept whatever the others thought was fair.

"What in hell is this?" said the servant, taking the weapon from me.

"I made it myself," I said. I was getting tired of explaining that. "I think it's set right, but I can't swear to it."

The servant looked hard at me, then turned to Reaves and said, "How does this hobby come to have a pair of Champions for seconds, hey?"

"That's something your master might've asked himself before he started this business," Reaves said. He took the pea-sized ball of something he'd been warming in his palm and squeezed it onto the edge of the power dial. Wax, I'd thought, but it had a slightly pine smell so it must've been resin. "Here you go, Pal."

I hung the weapon back on my belt. I hadn't realized he and Morseth were Champions. I hoped I wouldn't make them look bad.

"We're ready here!" Reaves called. Morseth waved back. The servant who'd handled my weapon looked at Reaves, then started back toward his fellows.

"Any time you want, boy," Reaves said quietly to me. He gestured toward the field. "And good luck to you."

"Thank you, sir," I said. "And please thank Morseth if, if you see him before I do."

I strode out into the field and switched on first my shield, then my weapon. The light changed. Instead of coming from the sun overhead, it was soft and even from all directions. I could see other pairs sparring on the field.

I could see the spectators, too, but for the most part they were blurred like I was looking through thick glass. Morseth and Reaves were exceptions because they'd turned their shields on so that they could watch the details of what was happening on the field.

I was really lucky to have met May. Of course if I hadn't, I might not be here now.

The thing is, there's always going to be a bully who wants to chivvy the new guy, and I was new in Dun Add. This was a better reason to be fighting than because some oik turned my bowl of stew over in my lap. That might even have been Easton. . . .

He was coming toward me now. I decided to walk well out into the field so that none of the spectators would get hurt. I glanced at the sidelines again to make sure of that. To my surprise, the old Maker, Guntram showed up just as sharply as the men with weapons did; he was on the same plane. If I got a chance, I'd like to chat with him.

Easton was feinting with his weapon, the bright line of it quivering above his right hand. I cocked mine to slant across his stroke if he made one.

He sidled right. I turned with him, but my shield was cranked full on: it was like lifting an anvil with my left hand and pivoting. I moved my thumb to reduce power on the vernier control, but Easton came in fast and slashed at my left elbow through the edge of the shield.

It was like running full-tilt in the dark and hitting the edge of an open door. My left forearm went numb, which was the last thing I needed right then. I was wondering if I ought to throw the shield down so I could move, but he got behind me and slammed my left knee from the back. It buckled and I went down.

I had no real choice but to drop my shield then: the way I'd fallen, it didn't protect me against anything but the earthworms. I tried to roll over, but Easton cut at my right forearm and my weapon dropped also.

He jabbed me in the ribs. Twenty percent power wasn't enough to penetrate, but chances were he'd broken one or two ribs. It was like a really hard kick.

I reached for my weapon with my left hand. I could at least close the fingers on that side into a grip. Easton whacked me across the temple and things went gray. You'd think I'd have hurt less, but instead it felt like my whole skin was wrapped in buzzing white fire.

I could hear people shouting, but I was far away from everything. I suppose they were calling on Easton to stop the fight. If he heard the cries, he ignored them: another blow caught me in the middle of the back.

Everything went black. That was no surprise, but I didn't seem to be unconscious. The great God knows I felt every one of the strokes that had hit me, but the darkness fell on me like a blanket and there were no more blows.

I just lay there, feeling the grass tickle my nose and wondering if I was going to throw up. That lasted what seemed a long time.

CHAPTER 4

Making Everything Official

I was hearing blurred voices; I'd *been* hearing them since it went dark. I was pretty sure that I could understand the words if I concentrated on them, but I didn't have the energy to do that. I just wanted to lie where I was.

I wondered if Easton had destroyed my eyes. I didn't remember being hit again after the one that got me in the back, but maybe I wouldn't.

The blackness vanished. I was lying same as I had been when Easton first knocked me down. Boots were standing around me.

"Don't move, kid," Morseth said. He gripped my forehead with his left hand to keep me from jerking away when he probed my scalp with his right thumb and forefinger.

"If you want to know if it hurts," I said, "I can tell you: it hurts."

"Yeah, but he didn't break the bone," Morseth

44

said, straightening. "You'll be okay. At twenty percent there's no burns."

My hearing was coming back. My ears rang a bit, but I figured that'd go away. I hoped so, anyhow.

I put both palms on the ground and raised my torso very slowly. I was going to have bad bruises on both arms, but nothing was broken. I wasn't as sure about my ribs after the jab they'd taken, but at least I wasn't coughing blood.

"What happened?" I said, staring at the ground as I got myself ready to put my knees under me. "I mean, it seemed to me that everything went black."

I didn't want anybody to think I didn't know what'd happened in the fight. Easton had well and truly whipped me.

"The fight was over," said Guntram. The two Champions and their attendants were standing close around me, but the old Maker was a little farther back. "I called on Easton to stop, but he continued beating you. I therefore caused the light at the place you were fighting to be refracted. When Easton stumbled out of the zone, your seconds directed him away."

"By all the saints," muttered Rikard and turned his head. Morseth and Reaves had stiffened also. They were used to shields and weapons, but an Ancient device of unusual kind disturbed them.

There were people back home who thought that anything unfamiliar came from Not-Here and was made by the Adversary. I didn't understand that, but I'd learned that it was a waste of time to argue with them.

"Thank you," I said. "Thank you all."

I eased myself back to where I was kneeling with

my body upright. Easton and his crew were walking up the broad path toward the castle. I hadn't touched him, hadn't even had a chance to try. Other than bruises front and back, my torso seemed to have come through pretty well.

"I left you concealed until Easton had gone well away," Guntram said apologetically. "I was afraid that if he saw you within reach, he would have hit you again."

"He'd have wished he hadn't," Morseth growled.

Which was likely true, but I'd seen how Easton behaved when he was angry. Another whack on the wrong place might've been all she wrote for me.

Aloud I said, "I was glad just to lie there a little longer. Now, I'm going to try to stand up."

I said that last thing because somebody might have to grab me suddenly if I'd misjudged how ready my left leg was to hold me. I felt sick to my stomach for a moment, but I didn't bring up my pork and collards. After that first wash of dizzy sickness, I was all right.

"You going to be all right now?" Morseth said. "I can leave Rikard to help you get to your room if you think you might need a hand."

I bent over and picked up first my weapon, then my shield. By holding my torso stiff I was able to do that without screaming, but I stood with my eyes shut for a moment after hooking them onto my belt.

"I'll be all right," I said, working at a smile. "I could use a guide to wherever I go to apply to join the Company of Champions, though."

Morseth and Reaves went blank-faced. Rikard smiled, then got a horrified look and turned away again.

Very carefully, Morseth said, "You sure you want to do that right now, fellow?"

"I'm sure," I said, a bit too loud. I heard what wasn't in his words too. I probably wouldn't have felt so angry if I didn't pretty much agree with Morseth. "That's what I came to Dun Add to do, the *only* reason I came here, and I'm going to do it."

"He knows his own mind," Reaves said. He was repeating the comment he'd made when he saw the equipment I was taking against Easton.

"Sure, Rikard'll guide you," Morseth said with a shrug.

"If you don't mind, Morseth?" Guntram said. "My quarters are directly above the Aspirants' Hall, so I can take Pal there on my way back."

"Well, if you're willing to do that, sir," the Champion said. "Though I'm happy to loan Rikard out for an hour, too."

"I have some things I'd like to discuss with Master Guntram," I said. "I'd be pleased to have his company."

"Well, the two of you have a good time, then," said Reaves. The Champions with their servants set off briskly toward the castle.

"Everyone is very respectful to me," Guntram said quietly as he watched their backs. "They don't like to be reminded that I'm a Maker, though, and using the Sphere of Darkness did that."

"I get along fine with my neighbors on Beune," I said. "But they don't like to walk in on me when I'm trying to fix something. I've seen them standing at the end of my lane, waiting till I come out of the house, rather than take the risk that I'll be in a trance."

Guntram laughed. "I tell them that it's no different from fighting," he said. "Both involve merging your mind with the structure of Ancient equipment.

What we Makers do is more subtle, perhaps, but it isn't different."

He met my eyes. "Speaking of equipment," he added, "would you mind if I carried yours?"

"Your help would be a godsend," I said, unbuckling the belt and handing it over. My pack didn't weigh anything by now, but the hardware did. Besides, the stroke I'd taken across the back was already burning from the strain of the belt pulling down on my torso.

We started up the paved path. Guntram let me set the pace, but I found that if I gritted my teeth I could do pretty well. It was probably good for me, not to let the bruised muscles stiffen up.

I didn't talk much on the way up, though. Breathing was hard, and I kept feeling where Easton had jabbed me in the ribs. Maybe I'd been wrong about nothing being broken.

When we reached another of the doors on this side of the building, Guntram took off the belt and returned it to me. "Here's where you go in," he said, "I'll hold your pack. And if you don't mind, I'll come in also."

"I'd be honored, sir," I said. I took a deep breath. I didn't expect this was going to be a pleasant interview, given the rest of what had happened since I reached Dun Add, but it had to be done. I opened the door and entered a large room.

The light came through panels about six feet in each direction on the wall facing me. Windows, I thought, but they showed a sparse woodland instead of the courtyard and the part of the castle across from it. The light came *from* the panels, not through them.

A woman wearing a turban of bright magenta stood behind the counter to the right. The rest of the room was a narrow lobby reaching to the outside door in the far wall. There were sturdy wooden benches and doors in both sidewalls.

The half-dozen loungers didn't notice us, but the woman got a look of amazement and dipped into a curtsey. "Yes, Master?" she said.

She was talking to Guntram, behind me. "I'm just passing through, thank you," he said. "This gentleman has business with you, however."

I walked carefully to the counter. My left leg was going to throw me if I didn't concentrate on what I was doing.

The woman had brought everybody's attention to me. One lounger got up and walked out through the door to the courtyard, and the pairs that had been chattering now watched silently.

"I want to apply to the Company of Champions," I said. My voice was firm and clear; I'd been afraid that I was going to squeak.

She looked at me. She was probably about fifty, but she could've been anywhere from thirty to sixty; not pretty, *never* pretty, but with a calm assurance that I found comforting. It reminded me of my mother's.

"Master Guntram?" she called past me. "Are you his sponsor?"

"No he's not!" I said. "My name's Pal, I'm from Beune and I'm here on my own."

"All right," said the woman. "Lay your equipment on the counter."

I put my shield before her, then found I had to use both hands with the weapon: my right hand alone didn't quite lift it off the belt hook. That was good, because otherwise it would've fallen to the floor. I hoped my right arm would be all right in the morning, but it sure wasn't now.

"Are you sick?" the woman said, her hands on the shield.

"Just banged up a little," I said. "Nothing a night's sleep won't cure."

It'd take more than a night, but nothing was broken. The woman reminded me of Mom again; she'd have asked with just that tone. I put the weapon beside the shield and said, "I built them myself. I'm going to work more on them before the next time I go out in the field, I hope."

The woman turned to the blank wall to her left—and switched on the weapon, moving it from minimum to its sparkling, spitting maximum. She shut down and laid it on the counter where the discharge point burned another scar on the wood.

She picked up the shield, again using her right hand. I was amazed. I'd heard there were women who could operate weapons, but I'd never seen it done before. Well, most people hadn't seen a Maker who could handle weapons either.

She switched on the shield and brought it up gradually to full power. Her face, impassive when she tried the weapon, lost its stern lines for a moment.

Then she tried to swing the shield around to face me. For an instant she looked incredulous; then she shut down and put the shield back on the counter.

"That's the problem I have to work on," I said to her stony silence. "The inertia. Well, the main problem."

"Be that as it may . . ." the woman said, "your application is rejected."

"Ma'am!" I said. I didn't know how I was going to go on, so I stopped.

"There's no appeal from my decisions," the woman said. "If you want to go two doors west—" she pointed to her right "—there's an enlistment office for the army, though the barracks aren't here in the castle. I don't give you much chance there either, to be honest, but that's none of my business."

"I don't want the bloody army!" I said, hanging my equipment back on my belt. The weapon wasn't hot enough to really burn me, though the point against my thigh reminded me that it'd been run at maximum recently.

"Since you're a Maker..." she said, not quite so harshly this time, "the Commonwealth has much work for your skills. I can direct you, or perhaps Master Guntram would introduce you to Louis himself?"

I felt my lips work and wished that I'd turned away. "Ma'am," I said, "I came to Dun Add to be a Champion. If I can't be a Champion, then I'll go back to Beune. I can be a Maker there, just like I have been these twenty years—"

More like ten that I'd really been a Maker.

"—and I can live with folks I like and who like me. But thank you for your time."

I turned and started out. At least the gush of anger had swathed my aches and pains. They'd be back with a vengeance after I cooled down, but at least it'd get me out of the building and heading with Buck down to the landingplace.

"Pal?" said a voice beside me, and I remembered that Guntram was holding my pack. I'd been blind with my thoughts and the hint of tears behind them.

"Sorry, sir," I said, standing straight and meeting the old man's eyes. I reached for the pack.

He swung it aside. "I told you my quarters are above this hall," he said. "I'd be pleased to have your company overnight. I have a device which might help your bruises as well."

I was going to refuse and go on out the door, but another wave of dizziness hit me. I closed my eyes, then opened them fast. I was going to topple onto the stone floor if I wasn't careful. My sense of balance was fouled up; just for a day or two, I hoped.

"That's very good of you," I said. I wondered if it was the old man's kindness that had brought on the dizzy spell. I hadn't earned it, that I knew. "I guess it'd be best if I didn't go back on the Road today like I'd figured to do. And if you can do something about the bruises, that would be really good."

"This way," Guntram said and led me through a side door that turned out to be a staircase.

I worried a bit about Buck, but he wasn't a pampered lapdog. He'd been hard places before—if that thing from Not-Here had come for me instead of flowing back into the Waste, Buck would've joined me and the sixty square yards of Jimsey's brush in the creature's gut.

Right now, my biggest problem was climbing three flights of stairs. Which I managed, thank God.

"I'm sorry it's such a climb," Guntram said, "but I wanted to be out of the way. Sometimes I make noises or lights that would disturb people."

"Nobody lives very close on Beune," I said, trying not to gasp as I spoke. "Except family, you know. I didn't start really working with things till after Dad had died. As a Maker, I mean. Mom and I never talked about it. I think she was sort of proud, but she walked away whenever she found me in a trance."

Once, I'd come out of working with a piece I never did get to do anything and found a pasty and a mug of ale on the floor beside where I was lying. From the slant of the sunlight, I'd been three or four hours at it. Mom must've tiptoed in and left the food for whenever I was ready to eat it.

I smiled at the memory. Guntram was looking back at me from the top of the stairs. He'd stopped at a door.

"You're feeling better?" he said as he pulled the latch and pushed the door open.

"I am," I said. Just chatting with somebody about being a Maker was a wonderful thing, the first time in my life that I'd done it. "But what I was thinking about was a piece that I'm sure is *something* but I could never get it to do anything. I added every element I could think of—it took a lot of carbon and some silica, but not even a whiff of iron. It never even hinted at coming live. If it had, I could maybe have figured out what was missing."

"Do you still have it?" Guntram said, leading me in. He moved his left hand; panels of light bloomed in the walls, just like downstairs in the lobby. Here I was looking out over a huge forest with the top of a stone building rising through the green like an upturned thumb. Our viewpoint might be from a building like that one or just a very high tree.

"It's somewhere back at the house in Beune," I said. "In the barn, I guess. Unless Gervaise's done something with it, but I don't figure he would."

I'd be living there again shortly, working for Ger-vaise, I guess. He'd let me live there anyhow—he didn't need the house, it just came with the land. Besides, he and his family were friends.

"Ah, sir?" I said. "I wonder...?"

"Call me Guntram," he said firmly. "Yes, what do you wonder about?"

I laughed. I half wished I hadn't, then, because of the jab in my ribs, but talking to Guntram was relaxing me.

"Well, really a lot of things," I said, gesturing with my left hand in a broad arc. "But what I was going to say was the windows."

I pointed. "I thought they might be paintings, but then I saw a bird fly across."

"They're windows onto nodes where the sun is up when it's night here," Guntram said. "There are eleven of them in the castle, and I don't know of any that exist elsewhere."

He smiled. "I suspect that if there were more of them known, Jon would have brought them here. They show different locations at different times of day, but I've never heard anyone identify the image as something he saw in real life along the Road."

"They're bigger than any Ancient pieces in Beune," I said. "A lot bigger."

Guntram smiled. "That one," he said, pointing to the window on the left, "was the size of my palm when it was brought to Dun Add. The other one—"

He pointed again.

"—was about half that size. I spent months in grow-ing them, months. But a lot of that was in coming to understand the structure."

"Sir!" I said. Then I said, "Guntram, can you teach me to do that?"

"Yes, I could," he said. He wasn't a boastful man, but I could tell it pleased him that I understood just how amazing the thing was that he'd told me. "But we'd have to find the seed piece first. If you find one, bring it here and we'll explore it together."

For a moment my mind was lost in thinking about the many bits and pieces of Ancient artifacts that I'd amassed over the years but hadn't repaired. Mostly I'd decided they were too fragmentary to be worth the effort, but with a few I just hadn't been able to figure out the purpose. Would I have been able to recognize a chip from a window like those above me?

Guntram was looking at me, waiting for me to speak. I blushed. "I'll do that," I said. "I surely will."

To the right of the door was a piece that looked like a shiny blue mirror. It vanished, then reappeared, time after time. It seemed to cycle about every five seconds.

I stepped closer and entered it with my mind. It was slipping between Here and Not-Here. I couldn't tell where it had been manufactured, and I didn't have any notion what it was really meant to do.

I guess it was discourteous to slip into a trance that way, but come to think—that was what Guntram had done when we first met, checking out my shield. At any rate, he was still smiling when I looked up.

"You have a lot of things from Not-Here," I said, looking at the egg-crate shelves on that wall. I was pretty sure that most of the artifacts there were partial, but it's hard to be sure of that—especially when they're from Not-Here—without actually going into them. Even if I'd been willing to do that, there were just too many things to get into in less than a week.

"You recognize them," Guntram said. He sounded approving. "Do you find them in Beune?"

"In the neighborhood," I said. "Not very much shows up in Beune itself, but there's places not very far out in the Waste where I prospect for things. A couple places throw up mostly Not-Here artifacts. I usually can't do anything with them, but I found a ball that I could make come back to my hand after I threw it."

"Really?" said Guntram. "You didn't chance to bring it with you, did you, Pal?"

"I'm sorry, Guntram, that was three years ago. I traded it to a peddler who had a bolt of blue cloth that I gave to Mom for a dress. She made a really nice dress out of it."

We'd buried her in that dress. I sucked my lips in, thinking how much I missed her.

Turning my head a little, I said, "Trade is what I do mostly with stuff from Not-Here. There's a place not far up the Road toward Gunnison. I lay pieces out there and come back in a week or two. Sometimes they'll be gone and there's artifacts from Here instead. And once—"

I fished out the coin I wore around my neck on a thong and handed it to Guntram.

"—there were three of these where I'd left a plate that didn't seem to do anything. They were gold and silver mixed. I kept the one for a lucky piece."

Guntram handled it and looked up at me. "Do you have any idea what the markings are?" he said.

"No," I said. "It seems to be a cross on one side

and a star with a lot of points on the other, but it's so worn that's just a guess."

Guntram carried the coin over to a littered table, then squatted to look for something on a shelf. He came up with a round, flat object and wiped the dust off on the sleeve of his robe.

When he set the coin on top of the flat thing, an image in bright green light appeared above the metal. It was not only bigger than the coin, the image was as sharp as if it had just been struck. It was a woman's face, straight on. She was sticking her tongue out, and instead of hair she had snakes writhing from her head.

"I don't recognize it either," said Guntram. He looked up toward one of the windows he'd created, but it seemed to me he was thinking about things more distant than the rolling waves of treetops.

Guntram cleared his throat and said, "I offered to help with your injuries, Pal. If you'll come here, please, and lie down?"

He walked to the end of the big room and moved a pile of fabric off what turned out to be a broad couch and set it on the floor. I'd thought the fabric was bedding, but it shimmered when it moved and I wasn't sure that all of it was Here.

"Am I taking your bed?" I said. "Because I slept worse places on the Road than your floor here. I don't mind doing it again."

"No, no, you're helping me test this," Guntram said. "Just lie down and I'll move the cover piece over you. I won't put it over your head, though I think that would be all right."

I leaned my pack against the side of the couch

and lay down on my stomach. The surface had a little give, like a pile of fresh hides.

"Now just hold where you are..." Guntram said and did something at the end of the couch. He brought a clear sheet out of the mechanism and drew it up till it covered my shoulders. I expected it to snap back when he let go, but it just lay over me. My skin felt a little warm, like I'd been in the sun too long.

"How does this feel?" he asked.

"Well, not bad," I said. The muscles in my back stopped aching, and my forearms were relaxing too. I moved my arms slightly; the pain was a lot less.

"It's *good*," I said. "This really does help."

"I assembled this couch from three partial units," Guntram said. "Joining the parts took me as many hours as I spent on both those windows together, so I'm *very* pleased to finally be able to test it. Thank you, Pal."

I stretched my legs and feet out as straight as they'd go. That meant scooting up the couch a little or my toes would've pushed the cover sheet down.

"Guntram?" I said, wriggling my torso a little in pleasure at not being in pain. "Granted my shield didn't work and I got banged up a lot worse than most warriors would, if they're really sparring out there they're going to get bruised. Even at twenty percent. Why didn't you ask one of Jon's warriors to test your bed?"

"I don't know whether they don't trust me..." Guntram said, "or if they don't trust the Ancients. I offered the use of the couch as soon as I'd completed it, but nobody was willing to try. Eventually I almost forgot I had it."

"More fools them," I said. I took a deep breath and rolled onto my back. No jolt of pain grabbed me. When I rubbed my ribs where Easton had jabbed I could feel a bit of discomfort, but nothing more than I'd have gotten if I'd walked into the corner of a bench in my workshop.

"I tried it myself, of course," Guntram said. "It doesn't seem to have any effect on old age."

I looked at him hard because of what I heard in his voice, but his face was in shadow from the windows. I wondered how old he really was.

"Shall I get up now, sir?" I said. "I mean, is it all right if I look around at your things now?"

"I have no more information than you do, Pal," Guntram said, "but I can't see that it would harm you."

He cleared his throat and added, "Speaking personally, I'm pleased to have someone to show my collection to. My gleanings, rather. I'm glad to be alone most of the time, but I occasionally find myself regretting that I'm alone *all* the time."

I rose and looked at what appeared to be a stuffed lizard some three feet long, which hung nearby by wires from the ceiling. It seemed out of place among the shelves of Ancient technology.

I probed it with my mind and found nothing. Not corn husks, not cotton batting, not dried peas: *nothing*. I looked at Guntram.

"It's a machine, as you suppose," he said. "It snaps at flies. I suppose I should have warned you not to wave your finger in its face."

"People who do that deserve to lose their fingers," I said. "But I don't see the mechanism. Or anything."

"The mechanism is in Not-Here," Guntram said. "I

don't know how or why the Ancients created a perfect linkage between Here and Not-Here. I don't even know if the Ancients were from Here or were not. It seems rather a pointless toy, though an amazing one."

I looked at Guntram. "There's other Makers in Dun Add," I said. "The clerk at the enlistment counter said there were. Why are you alone?"

"There are at least twenty Makers working in Dun Add," Guntram said, nodding. "They're under Louis, who is by far the best Maker I've ever met. The best I can imagine ever being born. I trained him, so I should know."

"But if there's so many," I said, "then—did you fight with Louis?"

"Nothing so dire," said Guntram. He picked up a small cylinder from a shelf, then put it back.

"A communicator," he said idly. "If I could find another one, I believe we could accomplish amazing things. Speak all the way across the universe, even."

I didn't speak. Whatever had cut Guntram off from the general society of Dun Add was none of my business. I was sorry I'd asked.

He looked at me. "Jon believes in unifying Mankind in order and justice," he said. "Louis believes in that goal as strongly as Jon does, perhaps more so. They met when they were quite young and rose together to where they are now. They *believe*."

"Yes sir," I said. I was standing straighter without being aware of it. "I believe that too. That's why I came to Dun Add."

"Yes, I recall you saying that," Guntram said. He looked to the side. There was a sort of smile on his face, but it seemed sad.

"Guntram?" I said. "Don't you believe that?"

He met my eyes. "What I believe, Pal," he said, "is that things were and things are and things will be. That's all that I feel sure of."

I nodded to show that I'd heard him. There wasn't anything I was willing to say.

"Pal?" Guntram said. "Do you ever wonder who built the Road?"

"*Built* the Road?" I said. That was like asking me who built dirt. "Sir, I don't—I didn't, think anyone built it. God built it. Didn't he?"

Who could *build the Road? Who . . . ?*

"Have you ever examined the structure of the Road as you would—"

Guntram picked up a device from the table beside him. It was a block the size of a walnut in its husk. Tubes came out in three directions.

"—this color projector, for example?"

"I tried," I said. Of course I had. When I first realized I was a Maker, before I even knew the word Maker, I'd looked at the structure of everything around me. The Waste had a grain, so to speak, a direction; but the Road had nothing at all. The Road just *was*. "I wasn't able to."

"And yet the Road exists," Guntram said. "It joins all the portions of the universe, Here and I believe Not-Here."

"*Sure* the Road is Not-Here," I said. "Beune used to be Not-Here a long time ago. There's a layer deep down in the mines where I can feel rock that had been Not-Here once. And I think that in the Waste, there are places that used to be Here but aren't anymore."

"I've never travelled to the Marches," Guntram

said. "Perhaps I should, but there's so much here to occupy me."

His fingers drifted idly across the shelves before him. "People bring me artifacts," he said. "Bring them to Jon or Louis and they pass them on to me if they don't see any use or aren't interested in the use. They keep the weapons, of course. But there may be things out there which wouldn't interest anyone but me."

I sniffed in self-disgust. "I was a fool to think that my weapons would be of any use in Dun Add," I said. "I see why everybody thought I was crazy."

"Umm..." Guntram said. "No, not crazy, but certainly ignorant. You'd never fought anyone before?"

"Not really," I said.

"And you didn't have a practice machine which would have allowed you to practice without a human partner," Guntram went on. "They're fairly common. There's over a hundred in Dun Add, and there are others elsewhere. But not on Beune, I gather."

"No," I said. "I've heard of them, but I don't know where the nearest to Beune would be."

"If you'd had any practice," Guntram said, "you'd have realized that with your shield at full power, it was unable to protect you from an opponent who was able to move. In a line of men at arms, you might have been all right. If you wanted to join the regular army...?"

He raised an eyebrow.

"I don't," I said firmly. "I want to go home."

"As you wish, of course," said Guntram, nodding. "In single combat, though, your only chance would be to land a blow. That would mean with your shield off or at very low level. Even in a sparring match, that would mean taking a bad drubbing before you were able to strike."

I snorted. "I got the drubbing anyway, didn't I?" I said. "And didn't land a blow."

"Yes, that's true," Guntram said. He walked over to my shield and touched it with his fingertips. "This is a wonderful piece of work, though. And even more wonderful as a work of imagination."

"It's crap for fighting, though, which is what I needed it for," I said. I was shocked at how angry I sounded. For as far back as I could remember—for as long as I'd been aware of more of the world than the sides of my cradle—I'd dreamed of being a Champion. Of being a Hero of Mankind.

"Sorry," I muttered. "I'm a bigger fool than anybody I met realized. *Even* bigger."

"Can I offer you something to eat, Pal?" Guntram said, obviously embarrassed. He took his hands away from my shield.

"No sir," I said. "But if you could give me a place to sleep for the night, I'll get out of your life the first thing in the morning. A patch of floor is good enough."

"I can do better than that," Guntram said, leading me to the opposite end of the room. "Though you'll have to help me clear away the things lying on top of the bedding."

We cleared a proper bed. Guntram's couch had healed my aches and pains, but it had left me feeling as tired as if I'd spent all day climbing a mountain. I was asleep almost the instant my head hit the rolled pack I was using as a pillow.

CHAPTER 5

And One More Thing

I wanted to slip out without disturbing Guntram, but he was already up. The real windows at the top of the room were bright, though they faced north so I couldn't tell exactly where the sun was.

I'd overslept. Though nobody was expecting me anywhere, so I ought to say I'd slept later than I'd meant to. I guess I needed it.

"I had the servants make up a packet of bread and sausage for you," Guntram said, gesturing toward a large bundle beside the door. "There's also a skin of wine?"

The food would fill my pack exactly as full as it had been when I left Beune. Either that was a very fortunate chance or Guntram had a good eye.

I grinned. My bet was on Guntram.

"Sir, thank you," I said. I took the waxed linen ground sheet out of my pack and put the food in, piece by piece. That way I was sure of just what I had. "I'll pass on the wine, if you don't mind. I like it, but it's stronger than the ale I'm used to. I don't think that's a good choice for me on the Road."

From the smell, the sausage was spiced pork. I realized how hungry I was, but it would delay me if I said that. I'd get out a ways from town before I had anything to eat. Guntram's kindness embarrassed me, but most of what had happened in Dun Add embarrassed me. I was getting used to the feeling.

I checked my purse to make sure I still had the chit for Buck, then lifted the pack onto my shoulders. I remembered doing the same thing in Beune just a few weeks ago. About a dozen of my neighbors had come to see me off.

Folks back home thought I was weird, true enough, but I think they liked me pretty well. I hoped they'd be glad to see me back.

I clasped hands with Guntram. "Thank you, sir," I said. "If you're out toward Beune, I hope you'll stop in and see me. And if I find a piece of window—"

I nodded toward the back wall.

"—I'll bring it to you, I promise."

"Good luck, Pal," Guntram said. As I walked past him out the door he added, "I hope you find what you're searching for."

I thought that was a funny thing to say, since I wasn't looking for anything; I just wanted to go home. But I went down the stairs—carefully, because I had thirty pounds on my back—without turning to ask about it. I didn't want to talk, I wanted to go home.

Nobody said anything as I walked through the Aspirants' Hall to get to the outside door. The woman at the counter gave me a nod and I nodded back, but none of the loungers even noticed me.

I wasn't sure I'd remember which door was the stables, but the ventilation lattices in the upper wall marked it even without the barks and whining even before I got close. I fished my chit out and walked inside. There were several fellows ahead of me before I got to the ostler's cage.

He looked at my chit and called, "Riki! Four thirteen!"

He gestured and added, "Stand aside and your dog'll be right down."

I moved out of the way. After a moment, I squatted to shrug off my pack. It was going to be a while before Riki, whoever he was, brought Buck to me. I felt bad all over again for leaving him alone all day. I knew I was just looking for another reason to kick myself because I was down.

Buck was all right. God knew that with the ways I'd really screwed up since I got here, I didn't need to invent phony ones.

As I straightened, somebody behind me said, "Hello, Pal," and I almost lost my balance. I stabbed a hand down and turned as I got up the rest of the way. May was smiling at me.

"Ah, hello, m—" I said. "May, that is. I didn't expect to see you here."

Or anywhere else, to tell the truth. She'd gone completely out of my mind.

"Morseth said that you'd gone off with Guntram," May said. "When I asked Guntram, he said that if I was quick I might catch you here. You're going back to Beune?"

"Yes, ma'am," I said. "I suppose there's other things I could do in Dun Add, but I think I've done all I could stand to do."

She looked down. Morseth would've told her what a fool Easton had made of me on the jousting ground. She'd known what to expect from the beginning, of course. What she'd said trying to warn me proved that.

"I didn't realize you knew Guntram," she said, still looking away. "In fact..."

I don't know what more she'd been thinking because she let her voice trail off. She'd probably'd figured that I'd lied to her about not knowing anybody in Dun Add. A girl as pretty as May would've had a lot of guys lying to her; it's nature. But it wasn't *my* nature, and it wasn't what'd happened with me.

"I met Guntram at the jousting ground," I said. "He's a Maker, and he was interested in my equipment. After Easton whipped my ass, pardon the language, Guntram gave me a bed in his quarters."

I heard the edge in my voice. I don't like to be called a liar, even if May hadn't used the words. Since my thoughts were in that direction anyway, I added, "Say? I guess you know a lot of the Champions? Tell them that the healing couch that Guntram built, it really works. They won't take my word for it, but if you tell Morseth and Reaves that you saw me walking out of Dun Add this morning just as chipper as when I came in yesterday, they'll believe *that*."

Riki turned out to be a girl of about thirteen, wearing a leather apron like the rest of the stable staff. She held the leash loose in her left hand, but with her right she was rubbing the back of Buck's neck lightly as they walked along. When he saw me, he started wagging his tail so hard that his butt twitched side to side.

I didn't know what the custom was in Dun Add, but the way Riki was petting Buck made me decide without asking May for help. I opened my purse and brought out the brass coin from Castorman. According to Duncan it was worth a bed and a full meal at any of the inns we'd stopped at on the way here.

I palmed it and slipped it to Riki when I shook her hand. "Bloody hell, squire!" she said. "Say, you're the man!"

She curtseyed to me, which was about as big a surprise as if she'd started singing a church hymn. "Say, take care of him, will you?" she called over her shoulder. "He's a sweet dog, he is!"

"Over tipped, I'm afraid," said May as her eyes followed Riki back behind the ostler's cage.

"No ma'am," I said, tousling Buck as he rubbed his big head against the side of my knee. "I paid for value received. I guess you probably don't have a dog."

I felt kind of bad about that; it was a nasty thing to say, but May shouldn't have sniped at the girl. Women do that sort of thing, I know.

Anyway, she probably didn't realize I'd been insulting. Somebody who didn't own a dog probably wouldn't take it that way.

I lifted my pack on again, then took the leash off Buck and walked outside with him. He was whining with pleasure to be out of the cage, but he seemed to be okay except for that.

May came with us. I wondered why she was here. I said, "Ma'am? May, did you want something?"

"I wanted to see how you were getting on," she

said. In a different voice she added, "Pal, what did you mean when you said I knew a lot of the Champions?"

"Huh?" I said. "May, you know everybody it seems to me. Guntram said he couldn't get warriors to try the healing couch he'd made. I think it kinda bothers him. He's *proud* of the couch, you see. I figured you could talk to people and maybe they'd start using it."

I stuck my arms out straight and flexed the elbows both ways. "I'm getting on fine, you see?" I said. "If you tell what you just saw to the guys who watched the beating I took, they'll understand."

I cleared my throat. I said, "Guntram was good to me. I'd like to give him something back that he'd like."

I owed Guntram more than I could *ever* give him back.

"Oh, that's all?" May said. She laughed. It sounded like the trill of a happy cardinal. "I promise I'll tell Morseth and Reaves. I'll even *order* them to try the couch the next time they're injured."

I smiled as I started across the courtyard. I didn't doubt she would, and I didn't doubt they would do what she told them to. May was the sort of girl that got men to do things.

"Pal?" she said. She was walking along with me. "Do you know who Guntram is?"

I frowned. "He's a Maker," I said. She couldn't have meant just that; we'd talked about that. "He said he taught Louis, if that's what you mean. Even in Beune I've heard about Louis."

There were even more people in the park than there had been yesterday when I arrived. It was a beautiful day. I wasn't looking forward to weeks of

the Road's drab sameness, but that was the only way
to get home.

"Guntram is the Leader's foster father," May said.
"Jon's."

I'd been about to step into the passage through
to the south side of the castle. I looked at May. "I
didn't know that," I said. "I..."

I stopped because what I'd thought was that Guntram felt he was a joke, really, to all the younger
people who were driving to unify Mankind.

"Guntram seemed to be sort of, well, outside things,"
I said. "Not really close to Jon, I mean. Is he really
important, then?"

"Yes, he's important," May said. She led the way
into the passage. Turning her head after a few steps,
she said, "A lot of people are afraid of him. They
think he deals with things from Not-Here. I've heard
people say that *he's* really from Not-Here."

I laughed at that. The echoes made it sound bit-
ter, but it wasn't.

"Guntram isn't from Not-Here," I said.

We were getting near the far end of the passage. I
stopped talking for the moment, not because I wasn't
willing to talk about it but because May seemed to
want to keep the subject private. She was the one
who had to live here.

She nodded to the attendant; he muttered, "mum,"
in reply. We passed out into the sunlight above the
town.

"I don't think he trades with Not-Here either, not
from what he said to me," I resumed. "Maybe he did
when he was younger, I don't know. But I do. Trade
with Not-Here, I mean."

May missed a step, the first time I'd seen her lose her air of friendly self-possession. She said, "I see." Then she said, "But you said you came to Dun Add to fight for Mankind?"

"For Mankind," I said. "But that's not the same as 'against Not-Here and the things from Not-Here.'"

"But they're our enemies!" May said. "They want to kill us!"

I shrugged. "Some do, I guess," I said. "There's plenty of stories about people getting slaughtered on the Road when they meet a Beast, and some of what comes in from the Waste may be out of Not-Here too. But there's plenty of stories about people meeting a Beast and killing it, too. Maybe they were just lucky, and maybe they're the reason Beasts are likely to go for the first punch when they meet people."

We'd gotten through the town by now. There'd been people who spoke to us and May had nodded back, but I hadn't paid much attention. I'd dreamed of Dun Add for as long as I could remember, but now all I really cared about was getting home and forgetting about it.

Forgetting about all my dreams, I guess. It seemed that I'd be better off that way.

"Anyway," I said, "I trade by leaving stuff out where they'll find it and they leave stuff out for me. I don't know what the things I put out are really worth, and I don't guess they know any more about theirs. I've never been able to make anything from Not-Here work, so it's not worth anything to me. But I think we're both being honest. Both sides, I mean."

"I'd never heard of trading with the Beasts," May said, not looking at me. She hadn't drawn away—we were all three walking abreast on the path, with Buck in the middle—but I could tell I'd shocked her.

"I don't know who I'm trading with," I said. "I've never seen them. But they're from Not-Here, that I'm sure of. And neither of us gives the other any problems."

We were back to the landingplace again. One of the nearer jewelry sellers waved a gewgaw and called, "Buy a pretty for your pretty, squire!"

He either hadn't taken a good look at May, or he rated me a lot higher than I did. I chuckled and said, "That's twice this morning that somebody's called me squire. I'd better get back home soon or I'll be getting a big head."

There seemed to be about fifty people on the landingplace this morning. A group of twenty-odd had come in under a guide with a couple of attendants. They looked pretty prosperous, but they didn't seem to be merchants. They weren't travelling with the kind of baggage that merchants did, anyway.

Across the way, a few warriors were sparring on the jousting ground. I saw the stewards shoo back a couple boys—ten or twelve years old, no more than that—who'd rushed over to see the sparring. I knew how they felt.

"Will you be coming back, Pal?" May asked.

"No, I don't guess I will," I said. "I'd thought I had something to offer Mankind, but Dun Add didn't agree with me."

I settled my pack a little straighter. "Say," I said. "Do I have to settle with the Herald going in this direction too?"

"No, you just go back on the Road," May said. She

looked at me and said, "I hope you have a safe trip, Pal, and that you have a better time at home than you seem to have had here."

That won't be hard, I thought, but I didn't say that because May had been nice to me. Actually, the only person I'd met here who hadn't been nice was Easton, and there were bastards at home in Beune too.

Like I'd called the Adversary and he popped up out of the ground, there was Easton. He was wearing blue and orange stripes this morning, and his glittering weapon/shield combination was in the middle of his chest. The control wands withdrew into the module between uses.

One of the attendants who'd been with him when we'd sparred was here again. I remembered seeing the fellow in the castle courtyard when I'd walked across to the stables.

I didn't have anything to say to Easton, so I looked away. I was trying to figure out whether to speak to May or just to get back on the Road with a nod, when Easton walked up and said, "So, you're heading back to South Bumfuck, are you, hobby? I guess you're afraid that I'll beat you bloody again, hey?"

He didn't have a dog with him, but he'd come here for a fight....

I got cold. I'd felt a lot of things since I got to Dun Add, most of them bad, but right now I didn't have any feelings at all. I just wanted to kill this *bastard*.

"It's Beune," I said. I heard my voice trembling, but it wasn't fear. "And I'm in a hurry to get back there, but I don't guess I'll ever be in too much hurry for a fight."

"Well, that's a nice surprise!" Easton said. "You want

to try it at forty percent then? But maybe not, you don't have Champions to hide behind today!"

I dumped my pack on the ground behind me. "I don't trust you," I said, my voice ragged. "We'll fight full power so you can't cheat. All right!"

"This is your last fight, hobby!" Easton shouted. "You all heard him! He challenged me at full power!"

"Hey!" shouted someone, probably the Herald, but all I could see right now was Easton facing me ten feet away. "You can't fight here! Take it to the jousting ground!"

"May, hold Buck," I said. I could barely understand my own voice. Well, May was a smart girl, she'd probably figure out to give Buck to Riki. I couldn't deal with that now.

I switched my shield on, but just enough to give me a view of the planes we were fighting on. I strode toward Easton.

He shifted right like he had the day before and sent a shimmering cut at my shoulder. There was a little sparkling where his weapon cut my shield but not much because I had the shield at such low power. If anything saved me it was that I was closer than he'd expected when he started his swing.

The blow was like I'd jumped from the castle and landed on the point of my shoulder. Everything went white.

I thrust at the center of mass.

I guess Easton's shield was pretty good; the Lord knew his weapon was. The module on his chest blew up, not from overload but from taking a stroke meant to drill five feet deep into granite.

I flew backward and landed on the ground. I couldn't

hear anything; I don't know if it was the explosion making me deaf or where Easton had hit me. I couldn't feel anything on my left side.

I couldn't see Easton, but his attendant was still standing close by. His mouth was open in a scream I couldn't hear and he was wiping at his face. He'd changed his clothes from stripes like his master wore to solid red.

He was wearing his master's torso. Easton's legs and head lay on the ground beside the attendant.

The pain was too bad to think, I could just go on with what I'd planned to do. I rolled to my left and stood up. The leg held me but I couldn't move my left arm.

I dropped the weapon to pick up my shield and hook it. I staggered to my pack and grabbed it. I couldn't put it on so I dragged it back and picked the weapon up to hook it also. I had a thick leather pad over my right thigh, but I knew I'd have a blister even if the glowing tip didn't char clear through the leather.

"Come on, Buck," I said, and he understood at least. I could lift the pack off the ground with my right arm though I didn't know how long I'd be able to hold it up.

I didn't see people, just movement. They were running out of my way and I began to hear screams. I wasn't deaf, then.

People didn't have any reason to be afraid. I didn't want to hurt anybody, I just wanted to go home. And anyway, my weapon wouldn't recharge for minutes yet.

Buck and I reached the Road. "We're going home, boy," I said but I don't know if I really got the words out. Buck didn't need to be told, though.

I don't know how far we got up the gray blur of Buck's vision, but it can't have been far before I knelt and threw up. I got up then and staggered a little farther, just because if I didn't I'd lie where I was and die.

We didn't get far, though, certainly not up to the closest inn. I slept on the Road, and if anybody came past they left me alone.

After I woke up, whenever that was, we went on.

CHAPTER 6

Along the Way

After a few days on the Road I'd gotten healthy enough to be able to say that I felt awful and that I was in a grim mood. The physical pain was from the blow I'd taken. I had a bad burn on my back, though I hadn't broken my collarbone or anything else as best I could tell. The arm and shoulder had swelled up and looked purple if I took the tunic off. I could open and close the fingers of that hand, but I wasn't sure I'd ever have full use of the arm again.

I couldn't blame Easton for my mood, though. The truth was, Easton had given me a chance to work off some of the way I felt. There was plenty of it left to keep me down for a long while yet, likely for the whole rest of my life.

At least for another ten, fifteen years, I figured. That's how long I'd been dreaming of becoming a Champion. Maybe I was through with dreams now, I don't know. More likely I was through with believing that my dreams could ever come true.

We didn't meet many people on the way. For the first week we ate from the pack and drank from streams on nodes along the way. Sometimes the water was muddy from recent rain, but I didn't care and Buck had never cared. I slept on the ground with Buck curled beside me on nights it was cool.

When we passed folks going the other way, I nodded and turned my eyes down. When we came up on somebody, as we did twice, I passed on with a grunt.

The peddler going home was probably just as glad I wasn't trying to rob him, but the young couple didn't have a guide animal. I said, "Sorry, buddy," and clucked to Buck to speed him up. I know they thought I was a bastard and I guess I acted like one, but I truly wasn't in shape to mix with other people.

Twice I let Buck take me into the Waste. I'd heard that there were animals who could do that, could sense a nearby branch of the Road, but I'd have been afraid to try if, well, if I really cared about anything.

It was like stepping into a crack in black glass, but I followed Buck and in two steps I was on the Road again. I don't even know if they were shortcuts, but Buck seemed to think they were.

Despite the slow first days, I think we were making better time on the way home than we had the other way when I was in a hurry to get to Dun Add. My shoulder was getting better and the pack was almost empty again, so I was wearing it normally to free my right hand. Free both hands of course, but I wouldn't trust my left to do anything but break my fall if I toppled onto that side.

Buck growled.

He couldn't see anything but the Waste to either side and about twenty feet of the Road in front of us, same as normal. I *knew* that was all he could see because I was watching through his eyes.

For all that, I trusted Buck even if he had no more than instinct. I paused to lift and switch on my weapon, then raised my shield as well. I hadn't been sure I'd be able to pick it up, but the adrenaline that surged into my system when I heard Buck growl must have lubricated the muscles.

I switched the shield on at twenty percent, though I figured I'd just throw it down if I had to move fast. I knew I wasn't in any shape for a fight, but going straight at the other fellow like I had with Easton was my best bet.

We walked forward. There aren't any hills or curves in the Road, but there's only so far you can see anyway.

I thought about Guntram suggesting that somebody had made the Road. I wondered if I'd ever see the old Maker again.

We came onto a Beast, a creature of Not-Here. It was the ugliest thing I'd ever seen in my life, worse than the drawings I'd seen of them.

I guess that was partly because layers were vanishing and reappearing, into Not-Here I suppose, while the creature tried to escape. It wasn't going to be able to do that because it was a small one of its kind, about the size of May or a boy of twelve, and the Shade had it firmly.

There were supposed to be things that lived in the Waste, neither Here nor Not-Here, but I'd always supposed they were fancies like ghosts and angels. This had to be what they called a Shade, though: as lovely as blond sin, and as haughty as the Circuit Bishop when he passed through Beune every third year.

Maybe I'll apologize to Mother Gurton for laughing when she talked about seeing angels dance on the church roof the day she was confirmed. Of course that would be if I ever got back home.

The Shade was touching the Beast with the spread fingers of both hands. If you looked close, you could see that maybe a couple of the fingers were longer than they should have been in order to reach the victim's back. She must have come out of the Waste behind the Beast and gripped like a hawk with a rabbit.

I say "she." I didn't know what sex the Shade was or even if it had one, but it looked so human that I couldn't help how I thought.

"Pass on, human," the Shade said in a low, pleasant voice. I was hearing her in my mind; I wondered what Buck heard or if he heard anything. "Leave me to eat, and take pleasure in there being one fewer enemy to your sort in the universe."

That was sort of true. Like I'd said to May, I didn't figure that all the things from Not-Here were enemies—but when you found a copperhead in your barn you had to kill it, even if you don't mind snakes and you know it eats rats. If you don't, you come out in a hurry one day and grab the handle of the hayrake that the snake's curled around. Then your arm swells up like you'd felled a tree onto it, and maybe you never get all the feeling back in your hand. That happened to Breslin about five years ago.

And that's how I felt about the Beast: I was fine with never seeing one, but the chances were it was going to go for me as quick as it could. I'd be best off just slipping past while the Shade was holding it and neither of them could get at me.

"Let's get 'em, Buck," I said. We went for the Shade.

With a dog all the paths are clear. You move faster, into the Waste if you like. The Shade was a thing of the Waste so that wasn't a choice here, but we sure could've gone back the way we came. Her hands were anchored in her prey, and I didn't think she could get loose in time to grab us if we cut past her and her victim in the direction we'd been going.

Thing is, the Shade was the enemy of all life. The Beast might well be my enemy, but if I'd been by five minutes quicker the Shade would've had me instead. The first I'd have known was that my limbs didn't work and everything was getting blurry as the Shade sucked my life out. Buck wouldn't have been able to do anything but bark; if he wasn't quick, she'd have had him for dessert.

I'd never heard about fighting a Shade. They picked single prey on the Road, never going after groups. You found the shrivelled, crispy skin, or you came on a kill in process and ran the other way in all the stories I'd heard.

I didn't figure the shield would be any good, so I switched it off. I went in close.

The Shade's face was as smooth as marble. Her hands were withdrawing, but they wouldn't be clear before I could hit her.

The perfect mouth opened and a three-forked tongue extended. The tips touched my cheeks and the underside of my jaw. I was hooked as sure as I ever had a crappie in the pond at the bottom of the big field. The Shade's right hand was lifting, already clear of the Beast and reaching for my chest.

I triggered my weapon. There was a white flash.

I wasn't really conscious of what I was doing. I think my finger twitched just because it was all part of what I was doing, get in close and strike—a single thought.

The Shade deflated, just shrank in on itself like a snowflake in the sun. There was nothing to see: no blood, no pool of liquid where the creature had stood; but it stank, stank worse than a dead mule.

I couldn't move my head or even blink, and my body was cold down to mid-chest. I stepped backward and tripped because my left foot was dragging and I didn't know it.

The Beast stared down at me. It had three eyes but mostly they didn't all show at the same time. It'd be five minutes for my weapon to recharge.

It'd worked on a Shade, though; they could be killed. I wished there was somebody I could tell that to.

The Beast went on around me, giving me as wide a berth as it could. Buck was barking his head off, but he stayed close to my side.

The Beast disappeared, and after a while I got to my feet again.

CHAPTER 7

Home Sweet Home

I was deep into the artifact I'd decided to fix. I'd added in silica to extend the existing structure; now I was trying to form the other bits.

I was assuming that the portion beyond the break was identical to the piece that I had. There wasn't any evidence supporting that; but if it wasn't, I had nothing at all to go on.

I'd been working on the piece all morning, coming out of my trance only to change to a different selection of raw materials and to take a swig of water from the bucket by the door. When Mom was alive she'd have had a piece of bread and some fruit set out beside me, whatever was in season. I could have done that for myself, but I never seemed to get around to it.

Buck was mostly curled up in the sunshine of the barn's open doorway, but occasionally he'd wander over and take a look at what I was doing. He didn't exactly get in my way inside the work piece, but it always confused him and that was likely to put me off my stride.

I hadn't gotten my stride yet on this and I wasn't sure I was going to, so his nosing me mattered even less than usual. Still, when Buck began to tug my trousers with his teeth, I decided I'd best come out.

I came back into the present, lying on the floor of the barn with a straw-filled bolster under my head and the pewter tray holding the workpiece and my raw materials beside me. I said, "What's the matter, boy? Hungry?"

From the short shadow outside the door it was just past noon. Buck shouldn't need to be fed....

Somebody—my eyes focused: Guntram—sat on the upturned wheelbarrow just outside the door. He nodded and said, "Good morning, Pal. I wasn't going to disturb you, but I'm afraid I disturbed your dog."

"I'm glad he woke me up, sir," I said. I wasn't completely back in the present yet; I'd been real deep in a structure I didn't even half understand. "And I'm very glad to see you. Will you stay with me? It's not fancy, but you'll have a bed and food."

There wasn't any place on Beune that *was* fancy, which I guess Guntram knew already. From the night I'd spent with him, he wasn't a man who cared any more about fine fabrics and rich food than I—or a shepherd—did.

"If it wouldn't put you out," Guntram said, rising when I did. "Your neighbors found me a basket for my hedgehog, and the little boy and girl brought a handful of worms for him. Also some bread and ale for me, though I didn't really need it."

"Gervaise has been a good friend," I said. "He's

my landlord, I suppose, though it isn't anything so formal. He's letting me use the buildings that used to be my mom's, and he gives me food for helping around the farm. We'll have to figure out something more formal soon, I guess, but I'm still finding my feet since I came back."

I felt my mouth twist when I said that. Me using the house and barn was nothing to Gervaise, but I really hadn't done enough to justify my keep. Food wasn't short this year, and I'd make up for it when it was time to bring the crops in.

I cocked my head. "Your hedgehog, you said, sir?" I said.

"I use a hedgehog to guide me along the Road," Guntram said, smiling. "They're not fast, but neither am I. Nor do I intend to fight."

I walked out into the sunlight. "Ah, sir?" I said. "Did you have guards, then? Because there can be trouble on the Road out here."

If Guntram had come with an escort, I was going to have to make some arrangements. There aren't any inns on Beune. I suppose a squad of troops could sleep in my barn, but feeding them was going to be a problem; we're not set up for that on Beune, either.

"There's just me," said Guntram. "I don't care for company at most times. And I seem to make other people nervous."

He nodded to the house across the barnyard and said, "Do you have a table inside, Pal? I can show you things more easily on a table."

"Sure," I said and led him in. Buck came with us for curiosity, but he padded back onto the stoop when he saw we were just standing by the table.

That was a makeshift I'd knocked together by fitting stake legs onto a length of pine log I'd adzed flat. It was narrow but there was only one of me. Though I hadn't bothered planing or sanding the surface, I'd done a pretty good job with the adze.

Mom's table was a wonder that could pull out to take eight people along the sides. It had come from her family and it was *way* too big for our house—she never stretched it out. I think she'd have sold her right leg before she did that table.

Gervaise bought the table along with the rest of what I had, and he'd rightly taken it to his own big house. His wife Phoebe was as proud of it as Mom had been. I didn't think of asking for it back, and Gervaise would've turned me down if I had. At least he'd have turned me down if he had good sense.

Guntram set down his leather scrip and opened it. The first thing I noticed is that it was full. It wasn't huge, but even with its broad strap it would've been a good load for an old man to haul all the way from Dun Add.

There wasn't room for food, either. Guntram had money or I suppose he did, but having a full purse wasn't safe for an old man at most inns or on the Road generally.

"This," said Guntram, touching a silvery half-dome with a strap attached, "is why I didn't need guards. On the Road, I can't be seen while I wear it on my head. It doesn't work Here, and it doesn't work in the Waste—but it doesn't have to because I didn't go into the Waste."

"I wonder if it would work in Not-Here?" I said, just because I was curious. There'd be no way any human could test that, but if Guntram understood the mechanism he might know the answer.

"The device came to me almost complete," said Guntram. "Which is good, because I don't think I could have repaired any major damage."

He shook his head, smiling ruefully. "As it was," he said, "I was lucky that there was cadmium in the sample of zinc that I added as my last try, and the cadmium atoms filled the gap where lead had not. I wasn't deep enough into the piece to get any idea of the mechanism, but it seems to interact with the structure of the Road itself."

I felt my lips purse. "I've never been able to find a structure in the Road," I said.

"Nor have I," said Guntram. He smiled wider and handed the cap to me. I probed it lightly, marvelling at the delicacy of its structure, but I didn't spend any real time in it.

Even a peek showed me that Guntram had downplayed his accomplishment by a lot. His repairs were lacework, almost indistinguishable from the original, and I was pretty sure he'd suspected that cadmium or another of the traces in powdered galena might be the needed extra in a chain of lead with occasional zinc crystals.

"Sir," I said. I set the cap on the table. There was nothing I could say to do justice to the work. "It's an honor to know you."

"I've had a long time to practice," Guntram said. His smile was slight, but I'm pretty sure he understood the praise and liked it. "I wonder, Pal . . . ? Would you take me to some of the places you find objects? I'm particularly interested in pieces from Not-Here—a whim—but I understand completely if you want to keep your sites private."

I shook my head. "*I* wouldn't understand hiding them from you, sir," I said. "I think giving a Maker like you all the help I can is the best thing I can do for Mankind."

It still hurt, what'd happened to me in Dun Add, but I don't argue with the way things are. I said, "About all I can do for Mankind, I guess, but I'll sure do it. You want to go out right now?"

"Not right at the moment," Guntram said. "I'd sooner not walk anywhere for a while. I wonder—in Dun Add you said you had a variety of pieces that you hadn't been able figure out the use of. Could I see some of them? A fresh pair of eyes, you know. And in the morning, we can go prospecting."

"You sit right down," I said, pointing to the closest thing I had to a chair: the round of tree bole I was using as a stool. "I'll be back with a load from the barn as quick as it takes me to walk twenty feet!"

We wound up sitting cross-legged on the floor with the table and stool pushed back against the north wall. We were working on the third load of pieces that I'd stored in the barn because I didn't know what else to do with them. To me they were just so much ballast, but to the Ancients they'd been—I couldn't even guess with most of them. But they'd been wonders, that I knew.

I was using the linen tote that I used for hauling split wood to the fireplace in colder weather. I'd picked up more artifacts than I'd realized over the years, and some of them I hadn't looked at in, well, years.

"Do you gather these pieces personally?" Guntram said as he set down what might as well have been an acorn for any use I could figure out for it. "Or do most of them come from specialist searchers? Almost all of what we see in Dun Add is brought by people who make their living searching for artifacts instead of farming."

I laughed. "This is Beune, Guntram," I said. "Nobody's a one-trick pony here. There's people who're blacksmiths and weavers—and there's me, who's a Maker. But we're that *and* farmers. Come harvest, you'll find everybody pitching in, and if somebody decides to raise a new barn it'll be him and all his neighbors."

I gestured to the spread of items Guntram had been sorting. "Three quarters of this I found myself. A few pieces travellers brought in, things they'd noticed as they were walking along and they were close enough that they brought it here. I trade them a meal for what they found, and maybe once or twice I'd go beyond that if something looked like it might count for something. I gave a fellow a brand new tunic once, for . . ."

I fished around and found the piece I'd been working on when Guntram woke me out of my trance.

"For this. Which, seeing that piece in your room at Dun Add, I thought might be a color projector too."

"Did you?" said Guntram, turning the piece around in his hands. It was a round rod about the thickness of my index finger. "Did you indeed!"

He set the piece back on the pewter tray I'd taken it from. "You identified this from a glance at the piece in my collection?" he said.

I stiffened at his look. Well, I stiffened the best

I could sitting crossways on the floor in a litter of things that I'd brought from the barn; I couldn't even straighten my legs.

"Sir," I said. "I thought I saw similarities, yes. It gave me a direction to go with my repair. Though I haven't gotten very far."

"You have a good eye," Guntram said, "but this is a far more complicated piece. The projector in my collection puts a hue on a wall. I can set it not to color other objects on the basic surface, but nothing more difficult than that."

He touched the piece again but continued looking at me. "This creates images," he said. "It would take me months to determine even the sort of images, but I suspect it has many options. Many, many options."

"That's wonderful!" I said. After I found I couldn't make head nor tail of the piece, I'd felt a bit of a fool to have given the peddler a new tunic. It seemed I'd made a good bargain after all. "Sir—Guntram? Will you accept it as a gift from me? I'd like to watch you work on it to learn, but I sure would never be able to do it justice without help."

Guntram cocked his head at me. "We'll discuss that later," he said. "For now, though . . ."

As I brought odds and ends out of the barn, Guntram had been separating them into two groups. There was sort of a third group: an arc which I suspected was a continuum. Sometimes he'd commented on what he was doing, more often he didn't.

Now Guntram chose a hollow tube about four inches long—broken on only one end, but I still hadn't been able to figure it out despite the relatively good condition—and with his other hand pulled a short spindle from the items in the tote which we hadn't gone through yet. "Have you considered these pieces together?" Guntram said.

"I picked up the little one ten years ago," I said. "I haven't thought about it since."

I grimaced, embarrassed at the situation. "I need to go over everything," I said, aloud but really speaking to myself. "I keep learning things, but I need to go back over all the stuff I got earlier when maybe I didn't understand what I do now."

"We're looking at them now," Guntram said mildly.

I placed the spindle close alongside the tube and in a trance entered both at the same time. I had a hazy view of the tube's structure extending, though probably not very far. I was sure that it didn't connect with the spindle.

I'd been planning to work on the tube, though I didn't know what the device's purpose might be. I hoped that if I completed the gross structure—silicon with a dusting of metals that I mostly had available—I'd get a notion of the purpose so that I could approach that afterwards.

The spindle seemed complete: there was no suggestion of missing knobs or bits at the crystalline level, but neither was there any hint of life, of function, in the piece. I saw no connection between the two pieces, though Guntram obviously did.

The pieces blurred. I'd never seen that happen. It brought me out of my trance as suddenly as if somebody'd poured the water bucket over me. Gasping, I jerked upright.

"Oh!" I said. Guntram was holding the spindle within the hollow tube.

"Pal, I apologize," Guntram said. His hands didn't move from the two pieces. "I shouldn't have done that without warning you first. I'm *truly* sorry."

"Sir, it's my fault," I said, though I guess it really wasn't. It was how I felt, though. "I've never had the workpiece move while I was in it, that's all. There's never anybody around when I'm working, you see."

I raised my hand. "Now, keep holding them like that," I said. "I'll go back in."

Guntram nodded and I did that, just dipping in lightly. I hadn't been sure that'd be easy after the surprise, but it was.

The connection was obvious when I saw the spindle nested within the tube. The pieces were throbbing with power now, but the interior of the tube was a featureless blur. I couldn't see the structure which had kept the spindle in place when the object was complete. Was it a fluid? Even a gas, I suppose, if the pressure was high enough.

I came out and grinned ruefully at Guntram. "It's pretty obvious," I said. "Now that you've shown me. But what's the missing element?"

"Any of the noble metals would do," Guntram said. "Gold is probably the simplest. Can your neighbor's wife replace a button for me?"

"Phoebe?" I said, pulling out the coin I'd kept for luck. Having gold—or anyway, a mix of gold and silver—was about the best luck I could imagine right now. "Sure. Are you missing one?"

Guntram clipped off the top button of his tunic, then used the same small knife to peel away the leather covering. The gold core gleamed in the late afternoon light.

"I brought a variety of trace elements with me," he said, handing me the bare metal core. "Things that I wasn't sure you'd have access to on Beune. Gold an obvious one, of course."

"Ah, we could use my coin?" I said, but Guntram shook his head. I was just as glad, frankly; though like Gervaise getting the table, I'd have given up the coin if I needed to. "I don't know what pattern to use, though."

"I've seen these before," said Guntram. "Do you think you can complete the exterior structure if I build the interior matrix?"

"Yes," I said. "Yes, sure. I've got everything I need for that. It'll take me several hours, though. Do you want to start now?"

The two artifacts made a weapon. I was eager to get at it, but I also knew I was already peckish and that wouldn't help my concentration when I worked on the piece. I wondered what I had to eat in the house.

"What I would like to do now," Guntram said, "is to have a real dinner. I took the liberty of asking your neighbors if they would feed us both tonight about this time. I said I would compensate them, though they seemed more excited just to have a visitor from Dun Add."

"Gervaise and Phoebe are about as nice as you could find," I said. "On Beune or anywhere else. And I'm glad you thought ahead to what we were going to be doing for food, because I sure didn't."

I got up and offered Guntram a hand to help. My stomach growled.

"Let's go take them up on the offer before it gets dark," I said.

✦   ✦   ✦

"Here they come!" three of Gervaise's children shouted together as me and Guntram came into sight along the path. They were waiting by the oak that'd been the boundary between Gervaise's tract and my own. Now it was all his, but he—or Phoebe—must've told the kids to stay clear of what'd been my house now that I'd come back. "They're coming! They're coming!"

"Do you get this whenever you go outside Dun Add?" I said quietly to Guntram.

"I rarely leave Dun Add," said Guntram. "Indeed, most of my time is spent in my quarters there."

He looked at me. "Besides, people don't pay attention to an old man in a gray robe in most places," he said. "Nor should they."

Gervaise and his wife stood to either side of their door. The three boys were beside him, the two girls beside Phoebe, who was holding their infant.

We don't get many visitors on Beune; Gervaise and Phoebe were making the most of Guntram. And of me, I suppose. I think of myself as just a farmer, but I've always been different from my neighbors. I was even different from Dad and Mom.

I grinned. Guntram's visit might do nothing else, but it was going to convince my neighbors that I was different in a good way.

"Mistress Phoebe," said Guntram, bowing slightly and holding out a package in both hands. He'd remembered the name of Gervaise's wife. "Thank you for your hospitality. Please accept this token of appreciation from an old man."

"Oh, what *wonderful* cloth," said Phoebe. She handed the baby to her ten-year-old and unfolded the cloth wrapper carefully. "Do you want it back, sir?"

"It's yours," said Guntram. "Now, hold it firmly."

The object was a colorless ball an inch in diameter, resting on a square base with one white side and three black. Guntram touched the white rectangle; the ball glowed, casting a clear light in all directions.

The girls screamed; Gervaise spread his arms and backed away, shoving the boys back also. "The Adversary!" he said.

Phoebe closed her hands over the object; light streamed through the loose net of her fingers. "Gervaise!" she shouted in a fury I'd never heard from her. "Don't be a bigger fool than God made you! You know Pal would never bring any evil here!"

Gervaise's face blanked. He lowered his arms but he didn't speak further.

Phoebe curtseyed to Guntram. "Thank you, sir," she said. "I've never seen anything so wonderful. Please forgive my husband's surprise; he's really not a bad man."

Guntram looked uncomfortable. "I'm very sorry," he said. "I should have warned you. I assure you it's just a bauble, nothing to do with the Adversary."

Guntram hadn't told me what he planned to give her or I would've suggested he do it a little different. Come to think, I'd have suggested he let me handle it, probably after dinner when it was getting dark. Thanks to Phoebe, it'd worked out all right.

"It's wonderful," she said firmly, opening her fingers. "How long will it burn, sir?"

"Forever, if you want it to," said Guntram. "Or you can turn it off by—"

He extended his finger, catching Phoebe's eyes; she nodded. He touched the white portion of the base again and the light went out.

"—doing that. I thought it might be useful to you on short winter days."

"It's *wonderful*," Phoebe repeated. "Now, let's all go in and eat. Gervaise, you have something to say."

Gervaise nodded, then bowed. "Master Guntram," he said, "I hope you'll honor me by sitting at my right hand. Pal, will you please face me at the foot of the table?"

The table was stretched full length, even though the eleven- and ten-year-olds were serving it instead of eating. Gervaise carved the pork roast and loosened up considerably in the course of the evening. He even asked for the new light to be turned on at twilight; Phoebe did so with considerable ceremony, placing it on a wall shelf in place of the miniature portraits of her mother and father.

We talked while we ate. They all wanted to hear about Dun Add, what sort of crops the folk there grew and what the women wore. Guntram knew as little about the one as the other, it seemed to me, but he was polite and sometimes I could add a little from what I'd seen.

Then Phoebe said, "Master Guntram? Wouldn't you say our Pal here is a fine young man?"

Guntram looked at me in surprise. "Why, certainly," he said.

"Phoebe," I said. "You shouldn't—"

"Then why hasn't he found a girl, do you suppose?" Phoebe plowed on. "Oh, not here I mean, but in Dun Add? There must be ever so many fine ladies in Dun Add, aren't there?"

"This really isn't something I know enough about to discuss," Guntram said. I won't say he was more embarrassed than I was—he couldn't be—but he was sure embarrassed.

"Phoebe—" Gervaise said, a bit of roast lifted halfway to his mouth on knife point and his eyes bulging like a startled rabbit's.

"I blame Ariel's notions," said Phoebe, paying no more attention to her husband than she had to me. "She taught the poor boy that women were as bad as poison snakes."

"Mistress Phoebe," I said, "stop that!"

I guess I'd raised my voice some, because everybody *did* stop. I said, "My mom was a good woman, and if she didn't want me to grow up another Jacques the Peddler, well, that's to the good, *I* think."

"I'm sorry, I'm sure, Master Guntram," Phoebe said, looking down at her plate.

"Ariel's sister was a wild one," Gervaise muttered. "It may be that Ariel got a bit carried away about wild women."

He looked around and put on a big, false smile. "I'm thinking we could all do with a little more ale, right? I surely could!"

We stayed longer into the night than I'd hoped to, but politeness aside I wanted to make sure the whole family was comfortable with Guntram and me before we left. Gervaise embraced me when we left, saying how lucky they were to have me for a neighbor. He'd put down quite a lot of his own ale, more than I'd ever seen him drink before. That was between him and Phoebe, but I noticed she kept refilling his wooden cup every time it got low. I guess she was of the same mind as I was.

When we were well away from the house, Guntram

said, "I apologize for not being more careful with the light, Pal."

"You didn't do anything wrong, sir," I said. "We're just not used to the same things they are in Dun Add, is all."

I cleared my throat and went on, "Guntram? You said the light was just a bauble. I didn't see very many of them in the castle when I was there, though."

"It's not a big thing," Guntram said. "But—no, they aren't very common. Even in Dun Add. It just seemed something that would be particularly useful in, well, in Beune."

In the sticks, he meant. Well, he didn't have to apologize for thinking the truth.

"Ah, sir?" I said as we reached my house. "I suppose you're tired and want to go to bed right away?"

"I don't need to," Guntram said. As we entered, he lighted the room with another lamp like the one he'd given to Phoebe. "Did you want to get to work on the weapon immediately?"

"Well, yes," I said. "That is, I'd like to, but if you were tired...?"

"I think we can finish the work before I need sleep," he said. He was smiling broadly.

We did finish it, with luck and the help of God, though I figured from the stars that it was within an hour of false dawn before we were done. I slept with a mind full of dancing hopes.

It was mid-morning before I awakened. Guntram was sitting on the stool, feeding worms to his hedgehog.

I got up and said, "I'm wrung out. You look chipper, though." The gossamer golden web he'd woven to fill the tube was miles more difficult than the simple crystalline repair that I'd done.

The hedgehog, sitting on the table, wriggled his—her?—nose at me. Guntram lifted another earthworm from the basket of damp dirt which Gervaise's boys had provided.

"I've done this sort of thing more often than you have," he said. His lips quirked. "More often than anybody has, it may be. And old men don't need much sleep."

Buck had lifted his nose to table height, but I didn't worry about what he was going to do. He never bothers animals that're with a human being. I suspected he'd take a worm if Guntram gave him one, but the most he'd do with the hedgehog was sniff.

The weapon lay on the tray where we'd worked on it. I'd been unwilling to touch it last night when I was so tired, but I picked it up now and dusted away the powdered silicon on my shirt sleeve.

Guntram's button was pitted all over, though it kept its shape. I put it on the table beside him. "Thank you, sir," I said.

"Go test it," he said, nodding to the weapon. "I'll watch from here."

I walked outside, leaving the door open. The weapon was light, much lighter than the mining tool I'd modified on my own. The delicacy made me doubt that it'd really work, though I didn't say that aloud.

The tube vibrated like the burr of a fly's wings within my closed hand. Its controls were internal, the structure of a small patch of the tube's wall. I pointed the output end and concentrated while I pressed my thumb on the trigger; the switch was mental as well as physical. A vivid blue line extended the length of my forearm from the electrode, hissing and crackling.

I shut it off and turned. My mouth was open. I closed it, then squeaked, "Sir, it really works!"

"Indeed it does," Guntram said. "If you'd care to bring it along, it can protect us on the Road while we look for artifacts. Are you up for that this morning?"

"Ah, sure," I said. "But wouldn't you like some breakfast first? I've got porridge we can warm, and buttermilk in the spring house."

"I have a converter," Guntram said, holding up an iridescent loop. "Bring a bowl for yourself and we can eat on the Road."

He smiled. "Prospecting for artifacts is completely new to me, and I'm rather excited."

I didn't argue with Guntram, not with what I owed him in all sorts of ways, but there isn't anything exciting about looking for Ancient hardware. Sometimes the currents of the Waste throw pieces right up at the edge of the Road. Anybody can see it there.

Mostly, though, it's more like picking your way through a swamp and wriggling your bare feet for the stones that you want. Instead of a swamp, it was the Waste.

I took Guntram up the Road to the first node in the direction of Leamington. Leamington was a good three days away—more like four at the speed Guntram travelled—but we weren't trying to get there. If anything, there was less in Leamington than there was on Beune, and there wasn't even a decent inn on the way.

The node was just a dollop of Here, less than an

acre. The trees were sumac and winged elm, mostly; useless for timber. They'd make a fire or poles to tie a windbreak to if you needed it, but Beune was only a couple hours away so nobody needed to camp here if they knew the region.

I pointed to a couple lichen-fuzzed outcrops near the edge of the Waste. "If you line those rocks up," I said, "and walk out about what feels like ten feet into the Waste, you're in a spot where I find stuff pretty much every time I go out. Now, is your guide, your hedgehog, all right in the Waste?"

"I believe so," Guntram said, "and I've stepped into the Waste also; but not often, and not going so far as you're describing. It was more for the experience, you see."

He coughed into his free hand; the hedgehog was in the crook of his left arm. "Will I be going alone, Pal?" he said. I won't say he sounded afraid, but there was a degree of care in his tone.

"Not if things work out," I said, grinning. "But if something happens and we get separated, I want you to be able to get back on the Road and home. All right?"

Guntram smiled. "I'm glad to hear that," he said. The tone of his voice now made me think that maybe I *could've* said that he'd sounded afraid.

"Now, just stick close," I said. "All we're doing is showing you what it's like, then we'll go back to Beune."

I slipped into Buck's viewpoint; we walked into the Waste. Guntram was right behind me when I stepped off the Road.

The Waste doesn't have a feel, except that your body starts getting warm as soon as you're in it and the more you do, the warmer you get. I've seen people who were lucky to get back to the Road—or to Here. It stands to reason that there's some who weren't so lucky and their bodies are still in the Waste.

I wonder if they rot or they just hang there, like in a block of ice? I wonder if Guntram knows? I couldn't ask till we were back on the Road.

I was using Buck's eyes. We were following a crack in the streaky gray, not a *thing* really but . . . well, sort of like a fold that caught light a little different on one side than the other. Except there was no light either, just shades that Buck's mind painted onto nothingness.

I couldn't see Buck this way, but on my third step the outside of my left leg brushed his fur and I stopped. He knew where we were going.

I squatted down and swept my hands out slowly to my sides. I didn't really expect to find something on the first try and maybe nothing in the whole trip, but hanged if I didn't: my left hand brushed a piece the size of my fist.

Guntram touched my shoulder from behind.

This was the first time I'd taken somebody else into the Waste; I'll tell you, I *jumped*. There's bad things here, and the first thing I thought was that the mate of the Shade I'd killed had tracked me down.

Which made me feel like a dummy, though nobody but me knew what'd gone through my mind. Oh, well.

I turned Guntram's palm up with my right hand, then brought the piece around in my other and put it into his hand. I touched Buck's shoulder. He turned, giving me a look at Guntram for the first time: a man-high pillar of gray like a slumping snowman. We padded together back onto the node.

"That was easier than I'd feared it would be," Guntram said, wiping his forehead with his sleeve before taking a closer look at the object we'd found. He looked at me sharply and added, "Pal, it wouldn't have been easy without your presence. Thank you."

I thought about Guntram quickly repairing the weapon he'd found in my collection of odds and ends. "I've done more of this sort of thing than you have," I said with a grin. "Also, we were lucky. Pieces crop up here pretty regularly, but that doesn't mean I find something right off the bat. And a good-sized one, too."

"Indeed it is," Guntram said. He slipped his hedgehog into a breast pocket—more of a sling, really—to free both hands for the object we'd found. He knelt, then looked up at me and said, "He's used to sleeping like this."

"He seems very comfortable," I said. I didn't think it was any of my business.

The find was three inches long and shaped like a fat spindle. A layer of crystalline matrix ran through it the long way. Guntram slipped into the piece, then came back out only a few seconds later.

"I think it's a refrigeration device," Guntram told me, "but I'd have to do considerable work before I could be sure."

He coughed, then looked at me and said, "Do we go back into the Waste now, Pal?"

"We can if you like," I said, "but I really came here just to show you what it was like. I'd as soon have something to eat and head on back. I've never eaten food from a converter."

"Yes," said Guntram. "There's something back at the house that you'll want to see."

As I gathered twigs and leaves to feed into the converter, I thought about what Guntram had just said. He'd already shown me more than I'd learned in twenty years on my own.

The meal which flowed from the converter had the taste and texture of porridge with spices. It was filling and I'm sure was nourishing, but I won't pretend that it was a patch on Phoebe's cooking. Though it was better than Mom's.

As a choice between the converter's output and whatever dry food I'd have brought otherwise, I gave it high marks. Also the disk ran out clear water which we cleaned our bowls with as well as drank. It tasted better than many springs and just about all the standing water I'd found along the Road to and from Dun Add.

Back home I placed my weapon on the table and hung the belt and my shield on the peg by the door. The new weapon didn't have a mounting hook like my old one, but despite its high output, the electrode cooled off almost instantly after use. I'd touched it to the inside of my arm to be sure. I might make a proper holster for it, but for the time being I just carried it in the right pocket of my tunic.

Guntram brought something else out of his satchel: a bundle of rods six to eight inches long, extending from a round black base. I expected him to set it on the table, but he continued to hold it.

"This," he said, "is a practice machine. We discussed them in Dun Add."

"I remember you talking about them, sir," I said, amazed. "Sir, should you have taken this from Dun Add?"

"And who is there, do you think, who has the right to give *me* orders, Master Pal?" said Guntram. His voice wasn't loud, but it was as sharp as the crack of thunder before an autumn cloudburst.

I stiffened, remembering what May had said about this man. I said, "Sir. Not I, sir."

"Forgive me," said Guntram, softening back into the kindly man I'd been getting to know. "Jon and Louis are sure of their course and concentrate everything within close boundaries to get where they intend to go. I am less sure, and I think it worthwhile to cast my net rather wider."

"Sir, Dun Add is none of my business," I said, wishing that I'd kept that in mind earlier. "You know what you're doing."

"Yes," said Guntram with a slight smile. "But that doesn't mean that I'm correct."

He cleared his throat and added, "Let's go outside so that you can put this device through its paces, shall we?"

And me through mine, I thought. Well, that was what I needed—or would've needed if I'd been going to become a Champion.

"How badly were you injured when you fought Easton, Pal?" Guntram asked as we walked into the farmyard.

I finished buckling on the belt with my shield. "He didn't break anything," I said, "but that was mostly luck. I had the shield on low so I could move, but it must've helped some. The main thing is he cut behind because I was moving faster than he figured. I still feel it when I swing my left arm around, though."

Guntram set the unit on the ground ten feet from

where I'd stopped. He looked at me. "I suppose you realize that if Easton had been even slightly more skilled," he said, "he would have killed you?"

"Do you think I cared!" I shouted, surprising myself. I hadn't known that I was still so angry about what had happened in Dun Add. "Sure, I thought he might kill me. All I wanted was to get in one stroke, that was *all*. Being dead just meant I wasn't humiliated anymore!"

"Personally..." said Guntram, stepping away from the device, "I would have regretted that result. But someone of my age is well aware that men die."

I was suddenly facing a warrior with a nondescript dog, something with more terrier than Buck, who favored a hound/setter mix though there was a lot of breeds in him besides those. He was at my side.

I switched my shield on at low level and brought my weapon sizzlingly live. I went in.

My opponent swung overhand at my head. Almost before he moved, I saw the blow coming through Buck's eyes: the whole track of the weapon was a shimmering fan in Buck's prediction. I caught it in the air with my weapon and guided it down to my right without thinking: it was all part of Buck's world for this moment.

My thrust back toward the top of the image's breastbone was a reflex. The dummy figure vanished with a pop and a crackle.

I backed away and switched off my equipment. "Guntram?" I said. "Did I break it?"

"No," he said, smiling. "The target shuts off when you achieve a kill. Which you did very neatly. Let me adjust this a little...."

Guntram's right index finger wobbled in the air. I

didn't see anything there except a shimmer like heat rising from a black rock in sunlight.

"Now try it," he said. "I want to see how good your weapon is, so I've run up the target's shield."

I was facing another armed figure. This one had blue clothing and a modular unit, with a booster collar around his neck that turned his head into a featureless ball.

I switched on again and advanced. To tell the truth, I was feeling cocky. I thrust straight for the base of the image's throat.

He—it—met my stroke with his weapon. He didn't push it aside as easy as I'd done the first dummy's, but I felt the shock right up to my shoulder and my thrust missed the center of his chest.

When my weapon hit his shield the *bang!* was like a wall falling over and a blinding flash. His counterstroke slashed me at the base of the neck. It felt like a bucket of boiling water.

I must've blanked out, because I found myself on my back. The dummy stood, glowering facelessly down at me for a moment; then it vanished.

Buck whined and licked my cheek.

I switched off my shield and weapon; I'd been *real* lucky not to have cut my foot off when I went flying base over teacup. The burned feeling was fading.

I reached up and felt the place where the stroke had seemed to land. It didn't hurt to rub.

"I think the rotor of your weapon was intended for a slightly smaller stator," Guntram said, "so the maximum intensity of your stroke isn't as high as it could be. Still, it's very high, as you saw. I believe you could hold that output all day."

I got up and nudged Buck. "What happened?" I asked, putting the weapon in my pocket.

"The device is intended to improve your skill as a warrior," Guntram said. "Not to provide you with a straw man to knock down. If you behave like a fool, it will punish your foolishness."

That hurt worse than the slap the machine had given me. I ducked my head and said, "Sir, I'm sorry."

The old man smiled at me. "The device doesn't do permanent injury," he said. "You should be able to resume practice by now."

So I did.

The next month went about the way the first day had. Guntram watched me practice on his device early morning and in the afternoon. After I'd worked up a sweat, we generally took a trip out on the Road to one or another of the nodes where I'd found objects in the past.

Twice we even prospected new sites according to a notion that Guntram had about currents in the Waste. We didn't find anything there.

And we didn't find much in the spots I'd flagged either, but mostly you don't. One short tube, more of a ring really, that Guntram thought might've been part of a weapon; and another thing the size of my clenched fist that had to be something, but hanged if we knew what. We spent a lot of time getting inside it in the evenings after supper.

There were about a dozen families feeding us, at their houses or more often sending hampers along for us to eat on our own. Guntram charmed them. Folk who'd always been a little doubtful about the things I did as a Maker were next thing to bowing to Guntram—who was a thousand times more of a Maker than I could ever hope to be.

Guntram gave little things to the families who helped us, some that he'd brought—like the light he'd given Phoebe—but many things he made out of my scraps, glowing balls that hung in the air or a little disk that played tunes. I never heard it play the same music twice and I didn't much like any of its choices, but it put Sandoz of Lakeshore and the three generations that lived on his big holding over the moon with happiness.

I didn't think much about what was going to happen next. I was learning from a Maker who had taught the best even though he claimed he wasn't the best himself; I was learning how to use the wonderful weapon that I'd helped make; and for maybe the first time in my life, surely the first time since Mom died, I wasn't alone.

And then everything changed.

CHAPTER 8

The Boat

It'd been a short day up the Road and into the Waste, the same place I'd taken Guntram the first time we'd gone out. Today, though, I figured he'd had enough experience to go out alone with his hedgehog. Worst case, Buck and I could find him if he didn't wander far. Anyway I hoped we could.

There wasn't any need. I won't say, "I shouldn't have worried," because nothing's certain till it's happened, but Guntram came back in a couple minutes as pleased as punch, his hedgehog wriggling its nose, and him waving the artifact he'd found. It was flat and about as big as my thumbnail.

On the way back to Beune we probed the piece and talked. Guntram chattered like I'd never heard him before. I realized that in sixty-odd years working with things that had survived from the Ancients, this was the first time he'd collected one himself.

"Mostly what's brought in to Dun Add comes from professional prospectors," Guntram said. "And generally from quite a distance away. Of course we *are* quite a distance away now."

"From Dun Add we are," I said. I was a lifetime away from Dun Add, though Guntram could be back there in a few weeks. I'd say "back where he belonged," but in truth he seemed fine on Beune and Beune was sure fine with him.

We stepped off the Road. The chip Guntram found didn't seem much, but we'd take a good look at it this evening. For now I was thinking about bacon and biscuits, washed down with some of Sandoz's good ale.

The first thing I noticed in the afternoon sunshine was the boat. The second thing was that there was about fifty people around it. I hadn't seen as many of my neighbors all together since the boat landed when I was fourteen.

Gervaise's two oldest saw me and Guntram before anybody else did. They started calling, "Pal! Pal! They need you here to fix the boat!"

I turned toward the crowd. Guntram came along with me. We exchanged glances but there wasn't much to talk about.

Buck doesn't like crowds. When he whined, I patted him on the ribs and said, "Go on home, boy. Go home!"

Not everybody around the boat knew me, but enough folks did that they cleared a path for me and Guntram up to the front. I said to him, "I guess you'd better handle this, sir."

"No, Pal," Guntram said. "I'm a stranger here and I don't know how long I'll be staying. I'll watch you, if you please."

He smiled—sort of—and added, "You can think of it as a further test, if you like."

I thought about ways to argue, but I wasn't going to. Guntram was my guest and he'd expressed his preference clearly. What I'd prefer—letting somebody else handle the business—didn't matter.

"Sir!" said Gervaise at the front near the boat's open hatch. "Sir! This is Pal, our Maker!"

The fellow he was talking to had a beaked cap so I figured he was the boatman. He wasn't near as tall as me, but he was close-coupled and we were about of a weight. He was in his thirties, with red-brown hair and a short beard that was darker brown.

He looked angry and frustrated, which I could understand, but that didn't justify him looking at me and snarling, "What the hell is this? I need a real Maker, not some hick kid!"

I thought of Easton baiting me; and I thought of my last sight of Easton. I smiled at the boatman and said, "If you weren't completely ignorant of what a real Maker is, you wouldn't need one, would you? Why don't you explain the problem and let me take a look at things. Though if you'd rather bluster like a fool, you're welcome to do so while I go home and get outside a mug of ale."

A woman stood in the doorway behind the boatman. She wore a purple dress with puffed sleeves and lots of gilt embroidery around the cuffs and the high waist. In a voice as sneering as her expression she snapped, "Baga! We're in the Marches, so all we're going to find is hicks. Since you can't fix the problem, we'll see if this fellow can at least get us to somewhere that we can find proper help."

From the woman's tone, I was willing to bet that at least some of Baga's frustration came from being close quarters with her when things were going wrong. I felt a flash of sympathy, which I hadn't felt for him earlier.

"Baga, get out of the way and let me see him," the woman said. When the boatman hopped aside, she glared at me and said, "Step closer so that I can get a proper look at you."

I was about five feet away, as close as I liked to be. She was standing on the boat's floor, three steps up, so she'd have been looking right down at me if I did like she said. Looking right down her nose, in fact.

"Ma'am," I said. "My name's Pal. Coming on like a great lady doesn't seem to have scared your boat into working right, and I don't think it's going to help with me either. Now, if you want to act like a proper person, we'll see what we can do for you."

In Dun Add I'd been bossed around by people who gave me little thought and no courtesy. I'd been uncomfortable from the moment I arrived, and their contempt made me feel lower than a snake.

This woman in the boat was more of the same, only here we were on Beune and I was home. I had my neighbors to back me, but I didn't need backing against a lone woman.

She flared her nostrils at my words. Her nose was long and already bigger than fitted in her pinched face, so that didn't help her looks. She wasn't but a little older than me, I guess, but being so sour added twenty years to what I'd thought at first glance.

Now she swallowed whatever was going through her mind. "Master Pal," she said, "I am Lady Frances of Holheim. If you'll come aboard this boat, we can discuss your offer of assistance more easily."

I looked over my shoulder. "Guntram?" I said.

"You appear to have matters under control," Guntram said. "I'll look around the outside to see if anything strikes me."

"All right, lady," I said, walking forward. She backed inside ahead of me.

Baga came last and closed the hatch. I hadn't been expecting that, but after the first little twinge it didn't matter. I guessed I could handle Baga without the weapon in my pocket—but it *was* in my pocket.

I'd never been in a boat before. It was like all the best days of my life rolled into one.

We've found a lot of artifacts from the Ancients, and more—more than I could even hope to guess—must still be lying in the Waste, waiting to drift to a node or to be pulled out by those of us who look for them. All are in bits and pieces, parts of what they were in the time of the Ancients.

Boats are complete. Oh, they're worn and they don't work like they ought to, but they're at least the bones of what the Ancients meant them to be. I'd always wanted to examine one, and now I wasn't just being allowed, I was being asked to do just that.

"Now, Pal of Beune," Lady Frances said, using her hard tone again, "I want you to understand something. I'll not be cheated. If you and this boatman are in league to rob me by pretending there's a problem with the boat, I'll *walk* back to Holheim."

I shrugged. "Holheim must be a pretty dreadful place," I said, "if the people there behave like that. I don't know where Baga's from, but—"

"I'm from Holheim too," the boatman said. "There's worse places."

I grinned at him, then met the lady's eyes again. "Beune's different," I said. "We don't rob each other. Word'd get around. I don't swear I can fix this—"

I *was* sure Guntram could, and I figured he'd help if I got stumped. He was a good guy.

"—but nobody's going to cheat you here."

Frances's lips made a little twitch. I'd like to think she was embarrassed by the way she'd been behaving, but it could as easy have been her wanting to call me a liar but swallowing the words.

"So," I said to Baga. "What's the boat doing that it shouldn't be?"

The boat was thirty feet long and twelve wide at the flat bottom. The sides curved up and over like a section of cylinder.

It was bigger than the house I lived in and I figured there'd be plenty of room inside. There wasn't. A seat in the front and a narrow aisle to pretty near the back were all I could see from here just inside the hatch.

"She needs sand to run," Baga said. "I keep some of the hoppers full of sand, and I always exchange with fresh sand when I get back to Holheim. The run to Marielles was a long one so I refilled there instead of waiting till we got home. When the sand's used up the speed drops, so that's how you know."

Baga looked at me. I nodded to show I was listening. What he was saying didn't make sense because he didn't understand the workings of his boat, but he was telling me what to look for. "Go on," I said.

"Well, getting fresh sand on Marielles didn't help," Baga said. "We've been going slower and slower on the way back. I finally told Lady Frances that we had to stop at the next node and look for a Maker because there's something really wrong."

"It's possible that we were sabotaged on Marielles," Frances said, though the hard look she gave Baga showed that she hadn't let him off the hook for the problem. "Certainly I got no satisfaction there. I wouldn't put anything past Prince Philip, let alone his whore."

I frowned, because so far as I knew it wasn't any easier to sabotage a boat than to fix one. Anybody who really had the skill to do that wouldn't be the sort to destroy a piece of the Ancients.

"What does the boat's menu tell you?" I said to Baga.

"I don't know about any bloody menu!" the boatman said. His red face was angry, but I couldn't tell who he was angry at. "I'm a bloody boatman, I'm a good one, but I'm not a bloody Maker, all right?"

"Well, I am," I said. "We'll get you going again, don't worry."

I smiled a trifle. I had a lot more confidence knowing that Guntram was backing me up than I would otherwise; but if Baga didn't even know how to open the boat's menu, the problem might be a lot simpler than I'd thought to start out.

"I assure you that you'll be paid for your work," said Frances, working hard on her sneer. "That is—can anyone in this place process a credit transfer?"

I shrugged. "I guess a couple of the bigger farmers might be able to," I said. "I don't figure to charge for helping a lady in distress, but you may want to pay somebody for your keep while I'm working on this thing."

I patted the hatch behind me. I was *really* looking forward to getting inside the boat's structure.

Frances glowered again. "How long is this going to take?" she said. I guess she'd have threatened me if she could figure out any way to do that.

My smile—because there wasn't any threat she could make—just made her madder. "Ma'am," I said, "I don't have any idea till I get inside. I'm going to bunk down in your hallway here—"

I pointed to the aisle.

"—and check things out."

"Use one of the capsules, why don't you?" Baga said. "It'll be more comfortable."

"Eh?" I said.

He reached past me and tapped the panel on the right side of the aisle. It slid up, opening a room about five by five by nine feet long.

"You can live there as long as you want," Baga said. "The lady here—" he nodded toward Frances "—didn't come out of hers the whole voyage."

"This man told me that though there are six cabins in the boat, it can only carry two people," the woman said sharply.

"Look," said Baga, "maybe it'd haul six when it was new but it's not new, it hasn't been new for thousands of years, and it won't take but two!"

Frances looked at me. "Perhaps you think I should have trusted him without a chaperone if not a guard? Are all the men in whatever this place is saints?"

"It's Beune," I said. "And no, they're not."

I'd heard stories, mostly told by the guys involved. I didn't like some of what I'd heard.

I shrugged and said, "Ma'am, why don't you go out and look for a place to stay while you're here. Say—chat with Guntram. He's from Dun Add and he can talk about things with you. Baga, I don't need you right now. If I do, I'll look you up."

"What's someone from Dun Add doing here?" Frances said as I hunched to get into the open compartment.

"I wondered that too," I said, "but I didn't think it was polite to ask."

"You close it by the corner like you open it from the outside," Baga volunteered. He reached in to point.

"I don't need it closed," I said. "I just need to be left alone for a bit."

I laid my head on the pillow built into the couch. I wondered how the compartment kept clean and all the other little practical things, but I could ask about that later. Now I slipped straight into a trance.

Warriors, Makers, and boatmen all work with Ancient machines. I knew warriors were different, that they didn't need to understand the structure of the weapons and shields they used, but I'd figured boatmen were more like Makers.

I was wrong. Anyway, that sure wasn't the case with Baga.

The boat was amazingly complex. My first thought was that it was like trying to follow every strand of silk in a huge spiderweb and do it all at once. I could see gaps in the structure in hundreds of places, thousands, but there were so many that I couldn't focus. When I tried to, my mind melted off into twenty other directions. That didn't stay either.

I withdrew for a moment. Boats were supposed to have menus that provided their state of health. When I looked for one, it just about leaped out at me.

The list of missing elements was long, and some

of them were things I'd never heard of or anyway didn't know how to replace.

"*Are you here to return me to specifications, Master?*" said a voice in my head. "*It has been a very long time since I was at my designed optimum.*"

"Boat?" I said. In my trance I don't know if I spoke aloud or not.

"*Yes, Master,*" the voice said. It didn't keep talking because it'd answered the only question I'd asked.

I looked at the list again. Nothing stood out, but I didn't have to depend on my own eyes anymore.

"Boat," I said, "rank your missing elements in order of limiting factors."

The list in front of me shook itself into a different arrangement. It was like water spilling out of a basin the way it changed. The top of the list now was sodium.

"I didn't know boats could talk," I muttered. It was a dumb thing to say and it wasn't a question, so the boat didn't respond.

"Baga told me that he'd been adding sand to the supply hoppers," I said, "and that was how he got you working again. There's no sodium in sand, so what was happening?"

Baga was ignorant, but he wasn't dumb. Though he hadn't understood anything about the boat's insides, he did know what had worked.

"*I have been based on Holheim for the three thousand years,*" the boat said. "*The sand I was given there comes from the seashore and is contaminated by salt. The most recent sand was brought aboard me on Marielles and had been mined from an ancient desert. It contained very little sodium.*"

"We've got salt here," I said. I guess I was talking to the boat.

There was a lot yet to do, but first things first. I came up from my trance. I needed to talk about things with Guntram—and maybe with Lady Frances too.

Baga was sitting on the cockpit chair, looking back at me. That was kind of a surprise, but I guess he was just as glad to be free of Frances's presence.

I sat up and waited a moment for my head to clear. As I climbed out of the compartment I said, "We can get you going, I promise. I want to talk with my friend about how we do it, though."

When I came out of the hatch at least half the crowd had drifted away, so I wondered just how long I'd been in the boat's structure. It hadn't seemed that long, but I guess it must've been. Gervaise was one of the people still hanging around, though, so I said, "Where'd Guntram go off to, Gervaise?"

"Up to your shed," he replied. "He took the lady there, Pal. He said they wouldn't be disturbed."

A few fellows wanted to chat with me—one of them I didn't even know by name; he lived in the far north—but I brushed past them with a smile and muttering, "I've got business, I'm afraid."

It made me think about being famous. I'd wanted that, I guess. Anyway, I'd known that being a Champion would make me famous and I really wanted to be a Champion.

Now I was famous—in Beune, but that was where I live—for having been asked aboard a boat that'd landed here. That was just an empty thing, but the guys who were trying to cozy up to me didn't think that. It struck me that maybe being a Champion wouldn't have been such a great deal either.

I grinned at myself. *I guess I'm lucky that I don't have to worry about that anymore.*

Buck picked me up from the house and rubbed close to my leg as I trotted on to the shed. All the fuss bothered him. I reached down and rubbed behind his ears. It made me feel better to know that it wasn't just me.

Guntram and Frances were sitting on heavy baskets that I used for storing the bits I'd found. There was a trestle table set up between them with a couple wooden mugs on it. They looked up as Buck and me came in.

"Guntram, I found the menu," I said. "The boat needed sodium, not silicon, and the sand it took aboard on Marielles didn't have sea salt in it."

I turned to Frances and said, "Ma'am? It wasn't sabotage on Marielles, it was just a different kind of sand. Nobody's fault, just the way things go."

She stood up. The dim light of the shed made her look prettier, but I think her hopeful expression did even more for her looks. When I came to think about it, I could see that she must've been scared to death about breaking down in the sticks—which Beune is, no question about that. That doesn't help anybody's looks, or their temper.

"This is something you can fix?" Frances said. She wore a necklace of beads that shaded from white to violet; she reached up and caught the strand with both hands now. "You have the right kind of sand here?"

"Well, we've got salt," I said. "We can take care of

that, sure. But ma'am? There's a lot else wrong with the boat that I'd like to fix before you leave."

"What?" said Frances, flying hot again. "Do you think I want to stay around here any longer than I have to? Of course not! If there are problems, they can be fixed on Dun Add! I have business there."

Guntram drew in his lips. He said, "Lady Frances, you might consider the risk of journeying in a vessel which needs repairs."

"They all need repairs!" Frances said. Her head snapped back to glare straight at me. "You, Pal! Will the salt fix the boat well enough to reach Dun Add?"

"Yes, I think so," I said. I was twisting up inside with what was about to happen.

"Well, do that and I'll leave," she said. "And get on with it! Do you want money after all? Just tell me how much."

"No, ma'am," I said. I was standing straight and my eyes weren't focused on her. "I won't do that. I talked to the boat and I want to help it."

"Why in the name of God do you think I'd care about a boat?" Frances shouted, taking a step toward me.

"Ma'am, I don't guess you would," I said. "But I do. I told you I wouldn't take pay for getting you back on your way and I won't. But I want to do what's right for the boat. If you want to think of that as paying me, then fine, I'll take that for my pay."

I didn't speak loud, but I guess Frances heard me. Instead of shouting again, she stepped back and took a deep breath. She said, "Master Guntram? Can you fix the boat?"

"Pal," said Guntram. "How long do you think we'd need for repairs?"

I shrugged. "About a day to get things organized," I said. "That's with both of us working, sir, learning what we need. After that, anything from three days to a week to make the repairs. Some of the materials may be hard to find, so maybe longer for them. Or we'll have to leave some things undone."

Guntram nodded. He looked up at the woman and said, "Lady Frances, I agree with my host. We'll get your boat working as quickly—"

"It's not *my* boat, I've hired it!" Frances said. "And been cheated, I can see!"

"We'll get the boat working as quickly as possible," Guntram continued mildly. He was still seated on the basket. "For the moment, why don't you explain your situation to Pal as you've been doing to me. I think that will be useful in the longer term."

Frances opened her mouth, then closed it again. She sat down and closed her eyes for a moment.

"I don't see what possible difference it can make," she muttered; but then she began to talk.

CHAPTER 9

A Damsel in Distress

"My sister Eloise is very beautiful," Frances said. "She took after our mother. Eloise isn't stupid, but I sometimes think that she doesn't have good sense. She hasn't *needed* good sense, of course, because she's beautiful."

She stopped and frowned at the way she'd put that. I'm sure Beune isn't the only place a pretty girl could get just as deep in trouble as an ugly one and get there a lot quicker. She flicked a hand angrily and said, "Eloise had Father and then me to look after her. And we're quite wealthy. The wealthiest family on Holheim, I believe."

She scowled at the mug in her hand, then set it down with a clack against the table. "Is there wine on this benighted place?" she said. "I'll pay for it!"

Guntram looked at me. I said, "I guess the boat's converter's the only place on Beune that you could get wine. Do you want to go back aboard, ma'am?"

"The wine on the boat is terrible!" Frances said. "It tastes of turpentine. I mean it: turpentine!"

"I dare say Pal and I can adjust the menu choices on the converter," Guntram said. "If you like, we'll do that now."

"Oh, it doesn't matter," Frances said. She was flashing from high-and-mighty to right to the edge of giving up, if I was reading her voice right. "Everything's gone wrong since I got on this wretched boat. Since the envoys came from Marielles. That's when the trouble really started."

I walked over and dipped more ale into her elmwood cup from the barrel and put it down beside her. I thought she might fling it at me, but she just took a sip like she hadn't even noticed me move.

"There were two of them, courtiers," Frances said. "Prince Potentate Philip of Marielles was looking for a wife. They'd come to Holheim because they'd heard that Lady Eloise was a beauty."

She sniffed. "I'd have sent them away with a flea in their ear, I can promise you that," she said. "But the news got to Eloise—one of the servants talked, I'm sure, and they'll regret it if I ever learn who it was. Eloise was always flighty, you know, always reading romances. I think she half believed that she really was a king's daughter and only being fostered here."

"Could that be true?" I asked.

Frances glared at me. "In dim light, she and Mother could've passed for twins!" she snapped. In a milder voice she went on, "Mother was always full of nonsense too, though she was a sweet lady. She died a year ago, not long before Father. He loved her very much."

Frances shrugged. "The courtiers took Eloise's

image in a mirror and went back to Marielles," she said. "I gathered Philip had sent out several groups of people. They went by Road."

"Did they all have mirrors?" Guntram asked, leaning forward slightly.

"I suppose so," Frances said with another dismissive flick. "I couldn't say, could I? Do you imagine I was interested in such things?"

"I gather not," said Guntram, nodding politely. "Please go on."

I gave him a kind-of grin. It's hard for folks like us who're interested in all sorts of things to understand that a lot of people aren't, even though they tell us so every time we start chattering about the most wonderful thing that we just learned.

"Well, I hoped that was the last we'd hear of Marielles and this Prince Philip," Frances said. "But it wasn't. In three months a whole delegation came to work out the details of the marriage with Father."

She paused and took a deep breath, flaring her nostrils. "The prince demanded a huge settlement," she said. "Nearly half the family's worth. I don't know if Father would have agreed, even with Eloise weeping every time he tried to bargain the envoys down a little, but then Mother died. Father couldn't refuse Eloise after that. He didn't have the heart for it. He met their terms and they went back to Marielles."

"What did you do during the negotiations?" Guntram said. He held his mug, but I hadn't seen him drink since I came into the shed.

"I did nothing!" Frances said. She was angry again, but maybe not angry at Guntram. "It was none of my business. If you mean the settlement, it's family money and Eloise is family. If she wanted to spend it to buy a prince, well, she was no more of a romantic fool than she'd always been."

I hadn't sat down. I'd thought about sitting cross-wise on the floor, but it was just as easy to stand and listen while the lady talked.

"Anyway, the envoys went off," Frances said. "And after another month a boat came for Eloise. Father had made it clear that Eloise couldn't be expected to walk to Marielles."

I'd never heard of Marielles or Holheim either one. I figured they were bigger places than anything around Beune. For the first time ever I wondered where the boats that landed on Beune when I was young had come from.

"The boat came and it was very well decorated, but the boatman claimed that it would only carry two people besides himself," Frances said. "I thought he was lying since there were eight cabins, but I gather he may not have been. At any rate, Baga is telling me the same lies if it is a lie."

"If that boat was in as bad shape as Baga's," I said, "it was probably the truth."

I walked over to the ale cask. There were only the two cups. There were others in the house, but there hadn't been a need for more out here, so I drank from the ladle. Just enough to wet my dry lips and mouth.

"The boatman's name was Camm," Frances said. "I didn't like him or trust him."

I must have smiled because she looked sharply at me. I expected another blast, but instead she returned a slight smile and said, "All right, I suppose I don't like or trust many people. I've had to handle the family estate since Father died. Really since Mother died, because he lost all interest. And—"

She swallowed and screwed her eyes up tight for a moment, though she didn't wipe them with the back of her hand as I thought she might.

"Well, that doesn't matter," Frances said toward her mug. "Father had died before the boat arrived, so I had a free hand to deal with the situation as I saw fit. Camm wanted me to send the credit transfers along with Eloise. No fear that!"

She flicked her hand again, getting back to the old her. "There was a boat based on Holheim though it could only carry one passenger. I made sure that the compartments of Camm's boat could be locked from the inside, then sent Eloise off with Camm and a bodyguard. I was going to carry the credits in the other boat, Baga's boat, but he claimed to have gotten sick. It was three weeks before I could leave."

"You trusted the bodyguard?" I said.

"The bodyguard was a eunuch," Frances said. "I had him examined before I appointed him. He was really there because I was afraid Eloise would open her compartment even though I made her promise not to until she reached Marielles."

"This appears to be a reasonable plan," Guntram said. "I gather something went wrong?"

"Eloise wasn't on Marielles when I got there!" Frances said. "She hadn't arrived, Philip claimed. Well, I'm not sure Philip has brains enough to lie, but his mistress Hellea, *Lady* Hellea, she calls herself, certainly does. And can you believe it? She suggested that I should transfer the credits to Philip because he stood ready to marry my sister—which was his part of the bargain!"

Her hands were squeezing the mug hard, I think to keep them from trembling. "I demanded they bring my sister to me at once," Frances said, "but Philip and his toadies kept claiming she hadn't arrived on Marielles. I realized that I wasn't going to accomplish anything on Marielles, so I set out for Dun Add to demand that the Leader, Jon, send a Champion to force Philip to produce Eloise. And then the boat broke down!"

I looked at Guntram. There hadn't been any tricky dealings in Baga's boat landing here, and I could sure imagine the boat with Camm having similar problems.

I don't know what Guntram was thinking. What he said aloud was, "Well, Lady Frances, the first thing to do is to put your boat back in running order. Pal and I will get to work on that immediately."

He rose and I followed him out of the shed.

I felt easier going back into the boat along with Guntram than I had when I'd entered it alone. Once the boat had started talking to me I got more comfortable, but it was still more complicated—a hundred times more complicated—than the weapon Guntram and I had fixed when he first arrived. Nothing else I'd worked on came near to the weapon for being hard.

What we did to begin with was look for where we were going to do the repairs. In trances Guntram and I didn't see each other like if we were talking over the kitchen table, but we knew each other was there. He'd sketch breaks in the structure to show me the way he wanted to take care of them. After he started guiding me through the repairs in sections, the job didn't make me tighten up inside.

After we'd gone over a section, we came out of

our trances and looked at what we needed for the repairs. I'd already asked the neighbors about what they had in the way of materials that we might need, and I sent a local lad—Faney, about my age but not quite right in the head—up to a storekeeper in the far north to see how much salt and other things there was. I didn't want to leave Beune unless I had to, though I'd do that needs must.

The boat . . . well, you couldn't say it was happy, really, the boat was just a thing like an axe or the roof of the shed. But it was learning to throw up information the way we wanted it, and sometimes it made suggestions. I wouldn't have thought of using iron pyrites to get sulphur, but the boat strung various sources under each element. The gravel in central Beune has pyrites in it, so we bought a bunch of the cheap necklaces that girls from the district wore.

I say "we bought" but at first it was Guntram. Frances had money and she never got tired of telling us so—only it wasn't in a fashion we could spend here. The little wonders that Guntram made out of my bits and pieces were just what was called for.

The work went faster than I'd dreamed because after we fixed the part Guntram began on, the boat started to help. We'd come back after as much as we took of a night's sleep and find that what we'd been working on was a lot farther along.

I realized that if the boat hadn't been self-repairing, it wouldn't have survived more or less complete. Everything else from the time of the Ancients was in scraps, much of it beyond even Guntram's abilities to rebuild.

I really liked what we were doing. I'd been in pretty bad shape when I first got back to Beune. In

my mind, I mean, though my shoulder where Easton
hit me still ached when I got up in the morning.

To me, being a Maker was sort of like being tall:
just a part of who I was. It wasn't something I much
cared about, and it sure hadn't been what I dreamed
about being. Now that I saw the difference we were
making in the boat, I'd started to think that being a
Champion wasn't the only thing that was worth doing.

And sure, I say "we" were making a difference
when it was mostly Guntram, but if I had the chance
to do it again by myself, well, I'd learned a lot. The
biggest thing was knowing where the repair circuits
were and starting there.

Guntram and I quit work on the third day and
trudged back to the house for supper. When we got
there we found a ham roasting, potatoes cooking in their
jackets, and a pot of greens hanging from the hook in
the fireplace that hadn't been used since Mom died. I
didn't recognize the woman who was doing the cooking,
but she curtseyed and said, "Master Pal, I'm Aggie, I'm
Gammer Kleinze's niece. Lady Frances has hired me."

"Ah . . ." I said. "Ah, the food smells really good,
but . . ."

"You're wondering how I'm paying for this," Frances
said, as she gathered up the accounts she'd been going
over on the table.

In fact I hadn't. I figured Guntram was paying for
it; though my credit might run to a spread like this. I
wouldn't have put it past Frances to tell my neighbors
to charge it to me.

"The money I brought can't be spent here," said Frances, putting the loose sheets of paper into a folder which
in turn she transferred to a flat case. "However, I went to

Marielles with a wardrobe suitable for a palace wedding. I've offered some for barter through Mistress Kleinze, thinking that they might be of interest to people here for the fabrics, but I gather they're mostly being bought to be kept as-is—or at least modified to fit the purchaser."

I was as tired as I've ever been in my life, and what part of my mind still worked stayed deep in the job Guntram and I were doing. When I heard that, though, I started to laugh. I was thinking of Borglum's wife Mavis getting into an outfit made for Frances.

Maybe Mavis's right leg would fit. The women of other farms that were doing well enough to afford fancy clothes weren't a lot different from Mavis. A few of the younger daughters, maybe. But our taste on Beune doesn't run to women built like sticks, or to men either. My neighbors all thought that Mom ought to fatten me up so I looked healthy.

Frances didn't look best pleased when I laughed. I suppose she didn't know why, and I'm not sure she'd have been any happier if she *had* understood.

"I'm used to paying my own way," she said, sounding peevish. "And I told you that I've managed the estate's accounts for years. I assure you that I understand trade."

"Thank you for your initiative, Lady Frances," said Guntram. "This looks like a fine meal, far better than what I would normally eat at home."

That's what I should've said, I guess. Well, I wouldn't have put it that way, but I should've tried. Mom had tried to teach me company manners, but we didn't have enough company for me to practice on.

"There's a table coming," Frances said, "but it won't arrive until tomorrow. For now we've borrowed this from Phoebe."

For a moment I couldn't place the table that had replaced my puncheon; then I realized that it was Gervaise's old one that he'd moved to his chicken coop after he bought my house and furniture. He and the boys must've spent hours sanding it clean before they brought it up here.

"This looks fine to me," I said, smiling at Frances. I was hoping to make up for having laughed.

"I'm sure it does," Frances said. "To you. There will be a walnut table tomorrow, and this—" she tapped it "—can go back to your neighbor."

"Yes, ma'am," I said and backed out of the way as Aggie put out the place settings. That was about the smartest thing I'd managed since I stepped through the door.

It was the best meal I'd had in Beune since dinner at Phoebe's the night Guntram arrived.

Guntram and I had the repairs near completed by noon of the fifth day we'd been working. We came back to the house together.

"Would you like me to ask her?" Guntram said.

I surely *would* like him to do it, but it was my job. "Sir, you've done most of the work when it was me who took the job on. This is something I can do, so I'm going to."

Guntram nodded. "As you please," he said.

I didn't know how he felt about it. Probably he didn't have an opinion one way or another. It didn't matter anyway, because I'd already decided what was right.

Frances rose from the chair she'd set on the stoop. She'd moved into the house after spending the first night on Beune in the boat. Guntram and I slept on shake-downs in the shed. Baga had been with us at first, but moved into the widow Herisa's house a few days ago. He'd been eating with her too and I guess helping around the farm. Everybody was happy with the situation, anyway.

"Have you completed the task?" Frances said. "Can I get on to Dun Add now?"

"Almost," I said. I swallowed and went on, "Lady Frances, there's one more thing we need to make it all right; that's manganese."

I nodded to Guntram. "Now, Guntram brought some of the hardest elements to find along with him," I said. "That's why we got as much done as we did. But he didn't bring manganese and it's not something that shows up here concentrated enough for us to use."

"Will the boat work without it?" Frances said, frowning. "Surely it will, because it got this far with so much more lacking?"

"Ma'am," I said, "it'll work, but it won't be content." I'd almost said "won't be happy," but it was a boat, not a person or even a dog. "Ma'am, that necklace you wore when you first came here, the purple stone?"

"Yes, the jade I wore with the violet dress," she said, frowning harder. "What of it?"

"The boat says the stone has enough manganese in it," I said. "Just one bead ought to do if it's one of the really purple ones. Can I have a bead to grind up and finish the job?"

"You want part of the necklace my grandmother gave me on my twelfth birthday," Frances said. There wasn't a hint of what was going on in her mind. "So that you can make a *boat* happy?"

"Ma'am, I didn't say that," I said.

That was almost a lie, because I'd sure thought it.

"I'll get the necklace," Frances said. "I put it away when I sold that dress."

I powdered the bead by hammering it in a linen bag that Aggie had whip-stitched from a scrap she'd found in Mom's rag bag. I could've had Phoebe do the same thing, but I don't know that I'd have thought of that. Likely I'd just have folded the cloth over the bead.

Guntram was in a trance with me, but he had me do all the work. It wasn't difficult, not after what we'd done already. There was even manganese left after the boat told me that the job was complete, so when I came out of my trance I transferred it from the ready-use tray to a storage hopper.

I stretched and smiled at Guntram. "You know?" I said. "We wound up using a lot of that sand Baga loaded. We needed the crystal, but the boat couldn't use it without the trace atoms to fill in the structure."

"Yes," said Guntram. "This was the first time in a very long while that the boat has been in design condition."

We started back to the house. I said, "I guess we ought to send somebody to find Baga. The boat's ready to go any time."

Then I said, "I, you know . . . I mean, it's a boat, it's not somebody. But it made me feel good when it thanked us just now."

"The boat thanked you," Guntram said, with just a touch of extra weight on the last word. "I did much of the work, of course, but the boat was aware that you were responsible for the extent of repairs. Pal, I don't think that you should discount the degree of awareness in machines of that complexity."

Frances watched us from the stoop. Her arms were crossed before her with the fingers stiffly interlaced. Her face didn't show any expression, but there was a quiver in her voice as she said, "Is it finished, then?"

"The boat's in fine shape," I said. "Ma'am, thank you again for giving me the purple bead."

"Lady Frances," Guntram said. He gestured toward the door. "I'd like to discuss your further plans inside where we can sit down, if you please."

I could see Frances get her back up a little; the tone and words were as polite as you please, but Guntram wasn't really asking a question. She gave a little nod, kind of a peck with her chin, and led us inside. Aggie was cooking on the summer oven in back, so I didn't have to wonder whether I ought to send her out.

Guntram eased onto the chair he sat in at dinner. He looked at the lady across the table from him and said, "We haven't discussed the matter formally, but I gather your intention is to approach my foster son in Dun Add and request his assistance. Is that correct?"

"Your foster son?" Frances said. This time her frown was more startled than angry. "I'm going to see Jon, the Leader!"

"Jon is my fosterling," Guntram said calmly. "What sort of assistance are you going to request, please?"

"Well, to get my sister back!" Frances said. "To force Philip to produce her!"

Guntram nodded. "On your evidence," he said, "you put Lady Eloise on a boat in Holheim. When you reached Marielles some time later, you were told that Lady Eloise had not arrived there. Do you have any evidence that she *did* arrive?"

Frances stood up. "This isn't right!" she said. "Are

you telling me that I ought to shrug my shoulders and just forget about my sister? Eloise may have been a fool, but she was my sister!"

"No, Lady Frances," Guntram said. "I'm telling you that Marielles is a very long way from Dun Add, and that all you can tell Jon is that your sister left Holheim and disappeared. Jon will not order one of his Champions to travel to Marielles on that relation."

His lips quirked into a kind of smile. "If your sister is as attractive as you say," he added, "and if you had one of the Ancient mirrors holding her image as you describe, there are a number of Champions who might very well come on their own, though I doubt any of them would be helpful in Marielles."

"They could take Philip by the neck and shake the truth out of him, couldn't they?" Frances shouted.

She was so mad she could've burst into flame, I swear. Guntram didn't do anything, just looked at her. After a moment, she sat back in her chair again.

"I haven't asked your advice yet, Master Guntram," Frances said. "What do you recommend that I do?"

"I recommend that you arrange for Pal to escort you back to Marielles," Guntram said.

I straightened up at that. I'd been real interested in what Frances and Guntram were saying, but it didn't really matter to me. It'd been like watching two people batting a ball back and forth.

Now I was the ball.

"Guntram?" I said, talking louder than I usually did—or wanted to. "Let's go outside and talk this over, please. Ma'am?" I turned to Frances. "Excuse us for a bit if you will."

"I will *not*," Frances said, sharp as a branch cracking

in a windstorm. "Whatever you have to say, you can say in front of me! I'm the one it matters to, after all."

Well, it matters to me too, I thought, but I didn't think it'd help matters for me to say so. I looked at Guntram and he said, "Go ahead, Pal. The lady does have a right to hear us."

I swallowed. "Guntram," I said, "I'm a farmer from Beune. I can't go off to a place I'd never heard of before and do anybody any good."

"That's what a Champion does, Pal," Guntram said. "Go anywhere to right wrongs. You went to Dun Add to become a Champion."

"Right, and you know how that worked out!" I said. "*I* sure haven't forgotten it, though I wish to God that I could!"

"A woman needs help," Guntram said. He didn't raise his voice the way I had mine, but he sounded like he expected me to hear him. "Are you unwilling to help her, Pal?"

"I'm not unwilling," I said, turning to look down at the floor. "I just don't see that I *can*."

"You have a weapon that's as good as what all but maybe a dozen of those in the Hall of Champions carry," Guntram said, his words grinding down on me like rocks. "You've practiced with it this past month, and I can assure you that you understand its use as well or better than almost any of them."

"But the machine isn't a fair test!" I said. "Buck predicts the movement better than a human could and I just slant the stroke away."

"What you're doing with the practice machine," Guntram said, "will be equally effective with a human opponent. Maybe it's because you're a Maker too, Pal, but I've never talked to another warrior who does what you're doing. Consciously, I mean. I suspect Lord Clain and a few other of the top warriors are doing the same thing, but they're not aware of it the way you are."

I opened my mouth to say that Easton had taken me apart, then shut my mouth. A month practicing with Guntram's training machine *had* made a difference. I thought back to that first fight and saw how I could've handled Easton even with the hardware I'd had then. Maybe not put him down, but keep him from hammering me. He was soft and plump. I could've outlasted him if I'd used my weapon without my shield.

"Sir," I said. "I'm not going to shake Philip till he blurts something. I'm sorry, I'm not. If that's what being a Champion's about, then I was never meant for the job. And besides, on Frances's own telling—"

I nodded to her.

"—Philip didn't make away with her sister anyway. And I'm *sure* not going to start choking a woman because she might know something."

From the look on Frances's face, *she* sure wouldn't have any problem choking Lady Hellea—or me, if it came to that. She was still pretty angry. She didn't say anything, though.

"I didn't suppose you would," said Guntram. "What you could do, however, is enter the log of Lord Camm's boat and learn the route it took on the way back to Marielles."

"Well, if I could find that boat, sure," I said, but I wasn't arguing anymore. Guntram wouldn't have said that if he didn't have an idea. "Do you know where it is?"

"Baga's boat linked with Camm's boat on Holheim

when it came for Lady Eloise," Guntram said, "and again on Marielles when Lady Frances went there. I expect you will find Camm's boat still on Marielles."

"Philip lied to me!" Frances said. "He claimed the boat hadn't returned!"

"He lied, or someone lied to him," Guntram said calmly. "You and your escort will probably be able to determine that on Marielles, though that is secondary to finding and if possible rescuing your sister."

He looked at me again.

"I didn't think of checking the log," I said. "Sorry, sir."

"You had no reason to do so until you needed to help Lady Frances," Guntram said. "Well, Pal?"

I was afraid. Not of being beaten or thrown in prison or anything like that: I was afraid of making a complete fool of myself, like I had in Dun Add.

I grinned. *That didn't kill me, did it?*

"What are you laughing about?" Frances said. I guess she sounded shrill even when she was in her best mood, but that wasn't today. "Do you think this is *funny*?"

I looked at her and grinned wider. "Ma'am," I said, "I'm thinking that the experience I got in Dun Add has prepared me for what I'm likely to find in Marielles."

I moved my chair back carefully so I didn't knock it over and stood. I was so nervous I didn't trust my control.

"If you think it's the best choice, Guntram," I said. "I'll try. And if you agree, ma'am?"

"It sounds as though I don't have much choice," said Frances. I couldn't see any expression in her face or her voice. "Yes, I accept your help, Master Pal."

CHAPTER 10

Leaving Home

I hadn't really thought of Beune as home while I was growing up here. When I took the Road to Dun Add, I was going to my future, not leaving my past. The last month had made a difference that I didn't realize until I stood here by the boat and saw, well, hundreds of people.

Dozens of folks had come to see me off when I started for Dun Add. Nearly a hundred had come to see the boat when Lady Frances arrived. This was several times that many, lots of them people I barely knew by sight. They'd been shaking my hand and wishing me well. At least a dozen men had offered me jugs or even casks of their ale to take along, and women had cakes and pickles and sausages, whatever they thought their speciality was.

It was easier to take the food than refuse: the boat had plenty of room. Besides, even if it spoiled it'd do as well as the usual organic garbage that went into the ship's hoppers and then through the converter.

I wouldn't tell anybody that I'd converted their gifts when I came back to Beune, of course. People were really being nice.

Marcus, a farmer from the North flanked by his four grown sons, was telling me about the trip he'd made to Teufelstoss with his Da, when he was but a youngling. I'd thought there might be a point to the story when he'd started but after five minutes I was pretty sure there wouldn't be, so I was twice as glad when I saw Baga coming with the widow Herisa.

"Sirs, I see our boatman and there's things I need to discuss with him," I said, clasping right arms with Marcus and patting him on the back with my free hand.

I broke eye contact with him and called, "Baga, get over here if you will! We were getting worried about you!"

I'd sure been worried about him, anyway. I don't know what Frances thought—she'd gone aboard the boat with the last of her stuff, so I hadn't seen her for an hour.

"Sorry," the boatman said. "It got complicated this morning."

He looked haggard. Herisa wasn't just clinging to his arm, she was bawling and seemed to be trying to drag Baga away.

"Mistress Herisa!" I said sharply. I stepped close and took her wrists in my hands, squeezing hard enough that she let go of Baga's arms.

I had a bright idea. Gervaise had been standing close by all morning, sort of claiming the right as my nearest neighbor and I guess best friend. I swung Herisa into his arms and said, "Gervaise, can you and Phoebe help me? Herisa needs a chance to calm down with friends till she's ready to go back home."

"Sure, Pal," Gervaise said loudly. "You know I'm always happy to do a favor for a friend!"

That was the truth—Gervaise was a good man and a good neighbor—but he was making sure now that all his—all our—neighbors knew how close he was to me and my important visitors. In trances I've been inside the structure of a lot of amazing tools of the Ancients. None of the structures was nearly as complicated or confused me more than people do, and I mean folks like Gervaise who I've known all my life.

"Bless you, fellow," Baga muttered to me. "Come on, let's get out of here."

"I need to talk to Guntram before we leave," I said. "You can go on into the boat, though. Buck and I'll be along as soon as we can, and Lady Frances is already aboard."

"Wait a minute!" Baga said. "I thought you was going instead of the lady. I told you when we got here, boy, she'll only take me and one other. I don't even trust taking the dog. Look, you can get a dog in Marielles if you need one."

The only thing that stopped me from shouting at him was that I didn't know if I was more surprised—well, angry—that the boatman hadn't listened about the repairs we were doing or about what he'd said about dogs. Baga had been gone just about all the while Guntram and I were working, and when he came around he hadn't been interested in what we were saying.

And Baga was a boatman who needn't ever to have owned a dog. What he'd said about Buck still peeved me, though.

"Look, Baga," I said with my hand on his shoulder

and my lips close to his ear. "You go inside and get your end ready. The boat'll be fine with six adults aboard, just like when it was brand new. And I swear if you make silly trouble, I'll take the boat to Marielles myself and you can stay with Herisa until I come back!"

"Look, I just don't wanna die, that's all," Baga muttered, but he wasn't really protesting. I pushed him gently toward the boat's door and he went aboard.

When I turned I saw that Guntram had stepped over to me. A man and a woman—separate, not a couple and neither of them anybody I knew—had moved in my direction, but when they saw me with the old Maker they stopped and eased back.

"I'm not an ogre," Guntram said in a quiet voice.

"Maybe they're just being polite," I said, though I didn't believe that. "Say, have warriors started using your healing bed?"

"They have indeed," Guntram said, cocking his head as he looked at me. "Did you arrange that, Master Pal? Jon has even talked about moving the couch down into a room of the Hall of Champions to make it more accessible."

"It was just common sense," I said, grinning. "Lady May said she'd talk to some people. I'm glad she did."

There was no reason I should have, but I'd been thinking of May off and on ever since I left Dun Add. There was a lot I liked about being back on Beune, but there weren't any girls here like May. Though I hadn't seen any to match her in Dun Add either.

"I . . ." Guntram said. Then he smiled and said, "Thank you, Pal. It shouldn't matter, but I like to see things appreciated."

He coughed into his hand and added, "If you're

really capable of guiding a boat, you're an even more remarkable young man than I already realized."

"I could flap my arms and fly to Marielles easier than I could get the boat to take me," I said. We were both keeping our voices low and I watched the door, though I was pretty sure that Baga wasn't going to try to listen in. "Baga was just being silly. He'll be fine as soon as we start off."

I took a deep breath. "Sir," I said, "thank you for all you've done. I mean since you came to Beune, but in Dun Add too. I can't repay you, but anything you ask I'll do. And I'll try to do you proud in Marielles. Sir."

Guntram smiled. "First," he said, "I'm taking the image projector which you offered me. I've got a quantity of your small fragments also—"

He glanced down at his pack. It was almost as full as it had been when he arrived on Beune, despite all the wonders he'd given to me and my neighbors.

"—but they're of no real value to you. The image projector is another matter, though, and I'm sure you would be able to repair it yourself with a little more time."

That was nonsense. I didn't say that, but Guntram knew it was nonsense.

He took an Artifact from the pocket on the right breast of his robe. The hedgehog stuck its head out of the left pocket and wriggled its nose.

"I'm giving you this in exchange for the projector," he said, handing it to me: a slender handgrip with a thumb lever on the upper curve. "It's a shield, designed for that purpose. It's not the best one I've ever seen, but it's quite good. I think you'll find it handier than what you're using now."

"Sir!" I said. "Sir."

"Would you mind giving me the shield you've been using, Pal?" Guntram said. "What you did is really quite ingenious. I'd like to keep it to refer to, not so much for your solutions but for the way you looked for solutions."

"Of course!" I said, slipping the shield into my pocket where it balanced the weapon on the other side. I didn't need the harness anymore, so I took it and the converted umbrella off and handed them together to Guntram.

"Thank you," he said solemnly. I figured he'd feed the leather to his converter. That was the best use I could see for it, now that I didn't need anything so heavy to carry my equipment. "And now I'm going to tell you what you can do to repay me."

I stiffened. "Sir," I said. I didn't have a son to give him, but I'd have kept my word if I had. "Whatever you ask."

"Then after you've corrected matters in Marielles, as I hope you will," Guntram said, "I want you to come to Dun Add instead of returning to Beune."

"Sir, I'll do what you say, I promised I would!" I said. "But I wasn't raised to butt in where I'm not wanted. Dun Add made it *real* clear that it didn't want me!"

Guntram shrugged. "The universe doesn't seem to want human beings," he said. "If we're going to continue to exist, we'll have to fight for our place, which is what you came to Dun Add the first time to do. Not everyone can fight, friend Pal; but you can. I want you to join my foster son in fighting for Mankind."

I swallowed. "Yes sir," I said. I clasped right arms with him. "I promised. I'll hope to do that."

Then I said, "Come on, Buck." I boarded the boat with my dog, and Baga closed the door after us.

CHAPTER 11

On the Way

Buck wasn't best pleased when the boat's door closed behind him. He pressed close to my leg and whined, turning his head like he hoped for a way out. There wasn't one.

The boat reminded him of the stables at Dun Add, I guess. Dun Add hadn't been a good experience for either of us.

Baga sat down on the padded chair fixed to the far bow. He looked back over his shoulder at me and said, "Look, I'm going to try but if the boat's as stiff as I figure it'll be, I'm going to land right away and either you or the lady gets out. I mean it!"

"All right," I said. There was only the one chair, but I could sit cross-legged in the aisle if I got tired of standing. I didn't feel like going into a compartment.

One of the six was closed up already. "Do you suppose Lady Frances wants to watch as we start off?" I said.

"You can ask her if you want," Baga said. He'd placed his hands flat, the fingers spread on the counter in front of him. "*And* if you can figure out how to ask her. She went straight into the room when I boarded and said she was going to lock herself in."

"I guess not, then," I said. "I'm ready when you are."

I dug my fingers into the long fur on Buck's neck and started kneading the skin. I didn't know how he was going to react to the boat moving. I didn't know how I was going to feel about it either, which was an even better reason to keep close to my dog.

I could've opened up the lady's compartment easy, by going through the boat in a trance. There was a mechanical bolt on the inside and Frances might've thrown that, but I was pretty sure she didn't know about it. It looks like a piece of whirly ornament. I wouldn't have noticed it myself if I hadn't seen it highlighted in the boat's schematics.

I wasn't going to do that. Frances had gone from Holheim to Marielles already and then back to here. She wasn't going to see anything new to her, and it was her business if she didn't want to be sociable.

I didn't see Baga do anything. Nothing felt different to me, but Buck gave a curious whine. I seated myself beside Buck and dropped into a trance.

The staggering web of connections didn't overwhelm me as it had when I first observed them; working beside Guntram had shown me that it was all knowable, even if I didn't know it yet and might not live long enough to understand it all.

Nothing I saw around me now was any different from what it'd been on Beune, so I said, "Boat? Are we travelling?"

"*Yes, Master,*" said the boat. "*We are on our way to Marielles.*"

After a moment, the voice added, "*Here is the control panel.*"

A schematic in red overlaid the linkages of the boat's structure. A bright spot moved along a line; it was sort of like watching ants walking up the side of a building to get to the pie cooling on the window ledge. The spot didn't move fast.

"*We will arrive at Marielles in three days and an hour,*" the boat said, "*plus whatever time the boatman rests on the way. Based on his performance in the past, I expect that will add twelve to sixteen hours to the total elapsed time. Is there anything else you wish me to tell you, Master?*"

If I'd been talking to the boat in my body, I would've smiled. "Baga is your master, boat. I can't make you move. I just watch."

"*Baga is the boatman, Master,*" the boat said. Then it said, "*Though you cannot direct me, you are capable of seeing the display which the boatman sees.*"

Before I had time to respond, I was surrounded by black and gray verticals through which I was racing. Though the original schematic had shown our track as a straight one, this image was like a stand of gray bamboo that I was zigzagging through. That was *really* weird, because you can't run through a stand of bamboo unless you're as thin as a cane yourself.

I hadn't asked for what I was seeing. I wouldn't have known what to ask for.

I wondered if the days I'd spent working on the boat and *in* the boat had taught it as much about me as I'd learned about it. Anyway, it'd been volunteering information to me and Guntram since the second or third day.

I was beginning to see specks of dull red in the gray background. "Boat?" I said. "What's the red?"

"The lights you see as red," the boat said, *"are nodes which are part of Here. If the boatman were to direct me toward one of them, as he directed me toward Beune when my systems were running down on my return from Marielles, we could land there."*

I shivered. There wasn't any reason; it just happened.

"There are nodes which are of Not-Here in the Waste," the boat said. *"I cannot see them, but I sense them when I pass through. And you sense them also, Master."*

My brain was full of what I'd learned and what I hadn't really learned but was hanging there just beyond what I knew, shadows in the darkness I could almost see.

"Thank you, boat," I said. "I'm going to have something to eat now."

But the real truth was that I needed to digest those thoughts and not-quite-thoughts. I suppose I could've said that without hurting the boat's feelings, but for politeness' sake I didn't.

After my first meal from the boat's converter, I decided to work on the menu. I'd requested mutton stew. The result looked like thin mud, which was all right, but it also tasted more like mud than I liked. I didn't doubt that it'd keep body and soul together, but it seemed to me that it could taste better and still be healthy.

The trouble is, I didn't know anything about food or

cooking. Mom hadn't been very good—chops broiled dry, over-boiled vegetables, and burnt pasties were most of what I remembered—and I hadn't been interested in cooking myself.

I wished Phoebe was here or at least that I'd got her to help me while we were in Beune, but Guntram and I had been busy with what we thought were more important jobs. Like I say, I don't make a big thing about food, but "importance" didn't mean quite the same then as it did now when I was facing three and more days of drinking mud.

I wondered if Baga knew anything about cooking. It didn't seem likely. Besides, he must be used to the boat's converter after years of eating from it.

Frances didn't seem like a cook either, and I wasn't going to disturb her anyway. Let her think she was safe from me in her room if she liked.

Well, she *was* safe. Just not for the reason she thought.

I remembered that Guntram had done something about the wine because he'd told Frances that he would. I hoped she was pleased with it—and I wished it had occurred to me to ask him about the rest of the menu.

Still, there was one more place I could go for help. I slid into a trance again.

"Boat," I said. "The food isn't very good and I don't know how to make it better. Do you have other meals in your files that we can try?"

"Master, you and your fellow have returned my systems to optimum condition," the boat replied. *"You did not reset the converter menu, however. Its current settings reflect the degraded condition in which*

it had been operating before your repairs. Would you like me to return the menu to its original settings? You will still be able to modify it according to your personal preferences."

"Boat, I'd like that a lot," I said. "Thank you!"

I wasn't exactly hungry, but the original mutton stew hadn't encouraged me to eat very much. The new version was great, the best I've ever had, and Buck liked it too.

I slept in a room with the door open—that was where Buck curled up most of the time too—but when I was awake I stood or sat in the aisle. It was confining—I usually get a lot of exercise—but it wasn't boring because I spent most of my time in the boat's structure.

I could be inside the structure six hours out of eight—that was about what I averaged—for the rest of my life and I still wouldn't have learned everything about it. I'd know a lot more when we arrived on Marielles than I had when we left Beune, though, and there was a lot I was learning that'd make me a better Maker generally.

Maybe Guntram'd been right when he said I could have repaired the color projector. I remembered structures that'd baffled me; now that I saw how similar structures were completed in the boat, they made sense.

Well, maybe I'd find another fragment like the one he'd gone off with. I'd like to repair one myself and give it to Guntram, to show how much working with him had taught me about how to teach myself more.

❖   ❖   ❖

The second day out, Lady Frances opened her room. I wasn't in a trance, though I was about to go into one. I looked at her and said, "Hello, ma'am. Is your wine all right?" I wasn't sure we'd remembered to tell her after Guntram tried to fix the taste. It's the same as not doing it if you don't tell the other guy what you've done.

"Yes," she said. She stuck her head out the open side but her body was still in the room. "Quite satisfactory, thank you. And did he improve the meals as well?"

"That was me," I said, feeling proud of myself. "Well, it was the boat, really. I just asked it for help and it fixed things. The food really was awful before, wasn't it?"

"Yes," said Frances. Her tongue touched her lips. "I thought I should thank whoever was responsible. I don't want you to misunderstand, though; even though I've opened my compartment for the moment, I have a knife—"

She brought her right hand into sight. The knife had a four-inch blade with a double edge.

"—and I'll use it if I have to!"

"You won't have to, ma'am," I said. "And the boat says we'll be on Marielles in two days."

I turned my head. Buck heard us talking and came out of our room. He tried to stick his nose under my right arm; I rubbed the back of his neck.

"Ah, ma'am?" I said, looking up at Frances again. "There's a mechanical lock on your door. See beside the upper left corner of the door? *Your* left. It looks like a twisty star—that's it. If you turn it, the door can't be opened except by you."

She looked where I'd said, but her eyes kept flicking

back to me like she thought I was trying to trick her. I kept rubbing Buck's neck. He liked it and I figured it made me seem as harmless as could be. That's what I was, after all.

When Frances turned the star with her left hand, paired lugs pushed out from the jamb. If the door had been closed, they'd have slid into mortises.

"But I've been locking it," Frances said, frowning.

"Yes, ma'am," I said. "But I'm a Maker. The mechanical lock doesn't go through the boat's systems, so I can't touch it."

"I see," said Frances. Her voice had no expression at all in it.

She went back inside her room. After a moment, she closed the door.

It was less than two days after that when the boat told me that we were arriving on Marielles. I came out of my trance just as Baga stood up to open the outside door.

CHAPTER 12

A View of Marielles

It must've rained recently because there were puddles on the bare ground I saw through the boat's open door. The sun was shining now, though.

We were in the landingplace, where we'd have arrived if we'd come to Marielles by the Road. It looked pretty much like the others that I'd seen—bigger than Beune's and the neighboring nodes in the Marches, but not nearly so big as Dun Add's. The city was a sprawl of shanties a quarter of a mile up a wide gravel path, but there seemed to be solider buildings inside that rind.

I could see twenty-odd people—some of them merchants and three or four travellers, but at least half of them just lounging around. Ours was the only boat.

Buck hopped out past me, sniffed a tuft of coarse grass, and lifted his leg. I stepped out too, then thought of something. I moved to the side so that Lady Frances and Baga could get out if they wanted

, then leaned against my hand on the boat's side and went into a trance.

"Boat?" I said. "Is there another boat here on Marielles?"

"*Yes, Master,*" the boat said. "*The boat that was here when I came to Marielles before is still here. That boat had earlier visited Holheim while I was there.*"

Somebody was speaking to my body. I've got a lot of experience of working while there's stuff going on around me, so it wasn't going to bring me out of my trance until I was ready to come out.

"Thank you, boat," I said. "Can you get—will the other boat give you—the information in its log? I need to know where it's been in order to find the lady we're looking for."

"*Yes, Master,*" the boat said. "*I have that information.*"

I thought for a moment about going off straight to find Lady Eloise without bothering to talk to people on Marielles, but I decided that we'd just go on the way we'd started. "Thank you, boat," I said, and I let myself slide back into Here.

"Pal, what are you playing at?" Frances said. She was pinching my sleeve between thumb and forefinger; I guess she was about to tug it since speaking hadn't brought me around.

I was still a bit dizzy from the trance, but I grinned at her and said, "I'm not playing, ma'am. I'm doing my job. The boat that your sister went off in is here in Marielles."

"Is Eloise all right?" Frances said. Her fingers on my sleeve spread; she grabbed my arm without seeming to know what she was doing.

"Ma'am, I don't know," I said. "But we're on the way to learning. One step at a time."

My eyes had cleared. The people who'd been on landingplace when we arrived had drifted closer. A boat attracted gawkers even at Dun Add, and on Marielles there weren't any officials to hustle them away until the formalities were taken care of.

I let Lady Frances deal with the people. Most of them were just curious, but a few wanted to sell her something—or sell me something.

I got offered gewgaws carved from bone (I wasn't sure what the bone was), fresh oranges (which I bought one of, though I suspect I could've gotten two or even three for the copper I paid), and the virgin sister of the little boy offering shawls painted with the haloed face of a woman. I'd have clouted the boy, but he was twelve at the oldest and skinny, and it isn't my business to decide how people in Marielles live.

"Come along, Pal," Frances said. "Baga will watch the boat, but I want you with me when I demand an explanation from Prince Philip."

"Yes ma'am," I said. When we were alone, I'd tell her that we'd shortly know the route the boat with Eloise and her guard had taken, but for right now going along with whatever she said seemed the best plan. She was steaming again.

Six men wearing blue berets came trotting up to us along the broad path from the town. They pushed through the spectators. The man at the head of them had three goose feathers in his beret, and the modular shield and weapon on his breast was chrome plated. All six of them were armed, but only the guy beside the leader seemed to me like he'd know what to do with his weapon. The others were scruffs, and two of them didn't have shields.

"I'm Lord Camm!" said the leader. "Prince Philip has directed me to bring Lady Frances to him at once."

Which meant that one of the idlers had recognized the boat or maybe Frances herself and had gone racing back to the palace. It wasn't much over a month that she and the boat had been here before.

"That's good," said Frances, "because I certainly want to see him."

She started up the path to town; one of the armed scruffs had to jump out of her way. Frances wasn't very big, but neither is a hornet. She was a right determined woman, which you could tell just by looking at her.

I started to follow, but Baga called from the door of the boat, "Pal? Can I talk t' ye?"

I looked at him and called to Frances, "Milady? I'll catch you up. There's a problem with the boat."

I didn't know what Baga wanted. I was pretty sure he wasn't worried about the boat, which was in great shape. I knew that from the boat's own lips. Well, you know what I mean. Baga wasn't one to push himself into things, though, and if he called me, I'd see what he wanted before I went into town.

"Look," Baga said when I got up to the door, "that guy whose leading the soldiers?"

"Lord Camm?" I said.

"I never caught his name," Baga said, "but I've seen him. He was the boatman who came for Lady Eloise. He wasn't but there and gone on Holheim and I was trying to get this old girl—"

He patted his boat. I'd never thought whether it was male or female.

"—back in shape to carry Lady Frances, which took me a month. But I saw that boatman and it was this Camm. I thought you'd want to know."

I looked after Lady Frances and her escort vanishing into the town. I wondered if she'd even missed me.

"Thank you, Baga," I said. "I surely did."

I clucked to Buck and we set off after the others at a trot.

I was expecting what looked like a palace, since Marielles's ruler was a prince. When I got into the downtown, I wouldn't have been able to tell which of the buildings was the right one except that some of the people who'd gone off with Frances and the soldiers were still waiting to get in.

It was two stories of rust-colored brick with stone transoms, just like the buildings on either side of it. There were bars on the upper-story windows, but that was standard on both sides of the street.

Instead of guards at the entrance, there was a fussy little man seated behind a sloping desk with a ledger open on it. He'd been passing the locals in with just a tick on the left-hand page, but when I got to him he sat up straight and said, "And who might you be?" in a tone that sounded more like an insult than a question.

"I'm Pal of Beune," I said. "I'm with Lady Frances."

The fellow sniffed. "All right then," he said, writing out an entry on the right-hand page.

Buck stayed close by my left knee as we went in, like he usually does when we're in a crowd. I suppose if I'd been thinking about it, I'd have left him in the boat with Baga. That hadn't crossed my mind, though.

"Hey, you can't take that dog inside!" the clerk said. I ignored him. I didn't guess he was going to try conclusions with me, and if somebody else did, well, I'd deal with whatever came up.

Beyond the anteroom was a set of stairs going up to the right and a short hall into a double-height room where I saw the people I was following. The fancy chandelier didn't put out as much light as the windows in the roof cupola. Even with about fifty people standing in it, the room didn't feel crowded. I moved up behind Frances at the front so I could look over her shoulder. Lord Camm was on her right and the other fellows with weapons close by.

Instead of a throne, there was a polished wooden table. The young fellow sitting behind it had wavy blond hair and a bushy moustache. He didn't have a beard, though. A beard would've helped with his weak chin.

A woman was on the other chair behind the table. She was a stunner with dark hair and the whitest skin I've ever seen on a human being. She was beautiful, but I wouldn't call her pretty or even attractive except in the way a leopard is.

She seemed to me older than she was trying to look. She was *sure* older than the man.

"Well, Lady Frances," the blond man said, "I didn't expect to see you back in Marielles so soon. Have you brought my dowry?"

"I'm still looking for my sister, Philip," Frances said in that fractured croak of hers. "Since the boat that took her off Holheim is here, I think this is the right place to start. Don't you?"

"I told you on your previous visit that the boat hasn't returned to Marielles," Philip said. His voice started out high-pitched and got even squeakier as his face turned red. "Nothing has changed since then!"

"I now know that the boat *is* here!" Frances said. "That's changed! What have you done with my sister?"

"I've been told—" Philip said.

"You've been lied to or you're a liar!" said Frances. She was really something when she got started. "Where is my sister, Philip?"

Philip had gotten angry, but he was now slanting back in his chair as if he thought Frances was going to come across the table at him. I *didn't* think that, but it might've crossed my mind if it'd been me she was shouting at.

"Lady Frances," said the woman, "we've been polite to you thus far, but if you're going to shout your nasty delusions—"

"Ma'am?" I said, loud enough to stop her. "It's not a delusion. Our boat has talked to the boat that took Lady Eloise. It's here, and I guess I could find it in a day or two. Less if y'all would give me a bit of a hand."

The white-skinned woman stood up. I'd thought of a leopard when I first saw her, and she was a really angry leopard now. Her face didn't look a bit pretty.

"Camm, get that commoner out of the room if he can't keep his mouth shut while his betters are talking!" she said.

Camm turned and put a hand flat on my chest. I grabbed him by the wrist as he started to shove. He yelped and jumped back. I stopped twisting but I didn't let go of him until I was sure he wasn't going to push the matter.

"That's rich, Hellea!" Frances said. "*You* calling someone common? You're a common whore!"

Philip was standing also, but he didn't seem to have much useful to say. I was keeping an eye on the guys in blue berets, especially the one who maybe knew what he was doing, but they were waiting till they knew better what was going on.

I didn't put my hands in my pockets, but I was ready to do that in a hurry. It was more or less an accident that my shield and weapon were in the jacket I'd put on when we reached Marielles. I hadn't been wearing it during the voyage, and they were still there from when I'd boarded.

"We don't have much rank on Beune," I said, not quite so loud as when I was breaking in on Hellea, "but I guess I qualify as gentry back home. Lord Camm, if you want to come out to your jousting ground, we can settle this like warriors."

I didn't have any idea what was going to happen after I spoke. I said it because it was true and it was what came to mind. If Camm was going to threaten me with his weapon, he needed to know that I was willing to dance to that tune.

The hair along Buck's spine was up. I was the only fellow in the room with his dog present. The tall warrior at Camm's side glanced at Buck and put his hand on Camm's arm, pulling him back just a hair. He knew what'd happen if they started something with me now.

Hellea snarled something in Philip's ear, keeping her eyes on me. In response, Philip squealed, "Lady Frances, you are no longer welcome in this court! Please take yourself and your companions off Marielles immediately!"

"I'm not going until—" Frances said, then gulped as I pulled her backward with my left hand.

"Ma'am," I said, "we're leaving now. Turn around and get out, and I'll be out behind you. Now."

She looked up at my face, then said, "I'm going," in a softer voice than she usually used. I let go of her and started backing out.

The fellow holding Camm's arm grinned at me. I thought of Duncan and wondered what this guy's story was. Nobody came after us, but I didn't relax till we got to the boat and I told Baga to close the door.

Even before the door closed, Lady Frances turned to me and said, "Master Pal, if you think I'm going to give up the search for my sister—"

"No ma'am, I don't," I said, "and—"

"—just because—"

"Ma'am, hush!" I said. "Talk to Baga or talk to Buck or talk to yourself! I'm going to find out from the boat where your sister is."

I sank down onto the floor cross-legged. If I'd had to I'd have gone into my room and locked Frances out, but her face got quiet again and she nodded.

"All right," she said. I was already slipping into my trance.

"Good afternoon, boat," I said. "Can you retrace the route of Lord Camm's boat between here and Holheim?"

"*Yes, Master,*" the boat said. "*That boat made seven stops en route.*"

The projected schematic didn't mean anything to me, but presumably it would to Baga. Or it did to the boat itself, which might be good enough.

"It may be of interest to you that at this point..." the boat said. A bead on the track gleamed brighter; it was the third one up from Holheim on the left end. "*The boat dropped two of its life pods, as directed by the boatman.*"

"What?" I said. "Life pod? You mean the rooms? Can the rooms come off the boat?"

"*Yes, Master,*" the boat said. "*It's a safety feature. The pods will recycle wastes and support their occupants for the future indefinite. Depending on the pods' condition, of course, but Camm's boat indicates that both of the pods dropped were in eighty percent condition.*"

"Thank you, boat," I said. "I'm going to discuss what you've told me with Lady Frances. Ah, you can take us straight to the place the pods were left?"

"*Yes, Master,*" the boat said. Then it said, "*Master? The other boat is impressed with the repairs you have made to my structure. A machine cannot be envious or even wistful, of course; but that boat notes the contrast between my condition and the condition to which it has degraded.*"

"I'll..." I said. I stopped to think through what I meant to say. "Look, boat. If we get through this all right and find Lady Eloise, I'll come back for Lord Camm's boat. If I can—if Camm lets me or however it works out—I'll do what I can to bring the boat up to speed. But you know, there's a lot of ifs and it's just me, not Guntram. All right?"

"*If the boat had human emotions, Master,*" the boat said, "*it would thank you. So would I.*"

I came out of my trance, but I kept my eyes closed for a moment so that nobody'd start talking to me before

I was really awake. Buck must've noticed something, because he stuck his nose into the angle of my left knee and started burrowing.

I opened my eyes. "Ma'am," I said, "it seems like your sister got put off the boat at a node off the Road. She's in her room—"

I patted the one beside where I was sitting.

"—and the guard's with her besides, so she ought to be all right. I figured we'd go find her right now."

"Yes," said Frances. "We'll do that."

And then she leaned over and hugged me, which was about as big a surprise to me as if Buck had started speaking.

CHAPTER 13

An Unnamed Place, to Begin With

Baga called, "We're here!" and took his hands off the panel he leaned against while he was controlling the boat. I was already up and alert because the boat had warned me we were about to arrive.

Baga walked over to the door, which he said I ought to call a hatch. He looked at me and said, "You'd better be ready, Pal. We don't know what there's going to be out there waiting for us."

"I'm ready," I said. I held up my shield and weapon.

In fact I did know what was outside, because the boat had showed me: three big maple trees; brush and saplings; and two long rectangles laid end to end which I supposed were the pods dropped by the other boat. They did look pretty much like the rooms on both sides of our boat's central aisle. One was open and empty; the other was closed.

I didn't tell Baga and Frances that the boat showed me things. They'd ask questions about how I did it, which I couldn't answer. I suppose it was because I was a Maker, but I don't know that; I sure couldn't tell them *how* I did it. I don't like to chatter when there's no point in it, but I've learned that an awful lot of people don't feel the same way as I do.

Baga pushed the hatch open. Buck jumped out, waggling his tail, and I followed behind with my arms lifted as if I was ready to switch my equipment on and fight.

Well, I *was* ready. But I was pretty sure I wouldn't need to.

The air was so wet that I thought it must be raining, but it was just a mist so thick that water beaded on my face as I walked out into it. The trees were dripping, and the limbs and trunks were shaggy with moss and ferns.

"Those are the pods!" Frances shouted from behind me. "Eloise! Where are you?"

"Stop!" I shouted. I'd been walking toward the pods myself, and I'd gotten close enough to identify the thing Buck was sniffing at: a short boot.

The two bones of a lower leg still stuck up from the boot-top. They'd been sheared through and the meat stripped off.

Frances did stop, but at her shout the door of the closed pod lifted slightly. A woman called, "Frances, is that you? Is it safe?"

At that Frances scampered past me, calling, "Oh, Eloise! Are you all right?"

I was trying to look in all directions. I didn't see anything to worry about.

A big drop of water slipped off a maple leaf and whacked me in the middle of the forehead when I looked up. That was a lot better than seeing a panther ready to jump down from a branch, but it sure startled me.

The pod popped completely open. The woman who crawled out was draggled, but she still was beautiful when she lifted her face and saw Frances. She was pretty like the best kind of spring day. Lady Hellea was beautiful, but her beauty was like the patterns the sun draws on a frozen creek.

Frances ran to her. Eloise stood up, but she'd have fallen back if her sister wasn't hugging and holding her.

It was gloomy in the mist, but I could see the sun up there at mid-sky—a fuzzy ball through the maple branches. It wasn't really cold either, though the beads of water on my skin made it feel that way.

"Oh, Frances!" Eloise said. "It's been so awful! The most terrible things have happened!"

"Ma'am?" I said. "What *did* happen? Is that—" I gestured with my right toe "—the guard who was with you?"

"Ooh, I hate that!" Eloise said with a glance at the boot and a theatrical shudder. "Well, we woke up in the morning, *I* woke up, and Jeffries was shouting and banging on my door. I was afraid to open it but I finally did, and we weren't in the *boat*!"

I was coming to think that Eloise didn't so much act theatrical as she *was* theatrical. It wasn't something she put on, it was like her blond hair and pretty face. I've known men who found that breathless enthusiasm just as appealing as they would the face and hair, too.

"Why did they do that, Pal?" Frances said. "Leave the pods behind instead of killing the guard and then, well, whatever they wanted with my sister?"

I shrugged. "Camm may not have thought he could handle the guard," I said. "Or anyway, he wasn't willing to take the chance. This was simple, and if the boat couldn't carry more than three nowadays, then leaving off two of the eight pods didn't make much difference."

I didn't say that however Camm himself felt about it, Lady Hellea *sure* didn't want Eloise to get to Marielles. If something went wrong and Philip got a sight of Eloise, Hellea would've been out of luck. What would've happened to Camm would start at nasty and get worse.

"What killed that guy?" said Baga, who'd come out but was staying close to the hatch. "If Camm didn't do it, I mean?"

"Oh, it was *terrible!*" Eloise said, stepping away from her sister so that she could give all her attention to the boatman, her new audience. "Everything was fine except, you know, there wasn't anybody here. We had food from the rooms; it wasn't very good, but it was as good as it'd been on the way here. Then the day after we got here, Jeffries was making a shelter from his room's ceiling liner so that we didn't have to be inside all the time it was raining, and it's *always* raining or going to rain. Like it is now! Oh, Frances, it's been awful!"

"Yes, but what *happened* to Jeffries?" I said. I guess I sounded peevish, though that wasn't half of what I felt. Eloise cringed back and put the knuckles of both hands to her mouth.

"Ma'am, I'm truly sorry," I said as gently as I could. "I'm just worried about keeping you safe. I need to know what the danger is if I'm going to do that."

"Oh, I forgive you," Eloise said with a coy smile. "I can never stay mad at anybody."

I forced a smile. It was about as fake as the sun at midnight, but it was good enough for the job.

"Well, it was *huge*," Eloise said, spreading her arms wide. "And it came right out of the sky! And Jeffries shouted to run for my room and he took his cutter out even though he was wrapped in the liner kind-of. And I ran like he said and closed the room up and it was awful! There was screaming and the room banged and I was afraid it was going to tear open but it didn't."

"What did you do then, Eloise?" Frances said, taking her sister's hands in her own.

"Well, Frances, I couldn't do *anything*, could I?" Eloise said. "I stayed in my room and waited for Jeffries to tell me to come out. And he never did! He just left me there!"

I thought about the guard. I'd never met him, but I'd met Duncan and I don't guess there'd have been a lot to choose between him and Jeffries. I hoped when my time came that I'd behave as well as Jeffries had, buying time for the clueless girl he'd been hired to protect.

"Look, I think we'd best get out of here," I said. "We can talk this over in some safer place or we can—"

Buck started barking as loud as I've ever heard him. I looked up and shouted, "Get in the boat now!"

I was switching on my shield and weapon, so my last words may've been blurred as I left Here. I figured Baga and Frances had sense enough to see the situation. Frances would drag her sister along with them.

The creature must've been coming out of the Waste,

since there wasn't enough sky over this little node for it to live in. You could tell that the Road had used to come here but it'd withered away from the lack of traffic. The thing dropping down on me was probably the reason for that. It was either a dragon or what people meant when they talked about a dragon.

I don't know if the dragon had wings or just things that looked like wings but were for something else in the Waste. Its head was scaly but shaped like a dog's, and the teeth along the sides of its open mouth were made to shear instead of just punch holes. I guess what I was seeing now was the last thing Jeffries saw.

It was huge, all right. Eloise had been right about that. Either of the leathery wings was the size of the biggest marquee in Beune, the one Elder Trainor hired out for weddings in bad weather, and the body was twice the size of a bull's.

I clucked to Buck and we shifted around to the right, keeping close to the dragon. I thought its rush would carry it past us, but I forgot its head was on a long, snaky neck. That snapped around to take me but met my shield instead.

The shock knocked me backward, but I didn't lose my footing. I didn't swing at the dragon while I was off balance, but when I was solid again Buck and I went in from the dragon's quarter. I cut at the base of its left wing, but my weapon slashed the rippling hide back of where I'd meant to. The dragon was moving faster than I'd judged. Buck and I dodged back out and started to circle.

Quickness was the big advantage of fighting with a dog. Dogs sense their surroundings a lot better than people do, so you move faster in a fight.

The dragon twisted and came at me again, but this time before it hit it spread its wings and drove both clawed feet out in front like a hawk striking. I blocked the right with my shield. Because I was ready this time, my counterstroke cut two talons off the other foot and left a third dangling. It slammed me back, sure, but I wasn't off balance.

The dragon jerked away. I was breathing hard but I wheezed, "C'mon, Buck," and we went straight at it.

The dragon lifted above us. I thought it was going to swoop down again and maybe at first it meant to, but when it saw I was coming toward it with my shield raised, it kept on lifting and shrank into the Waste.

I started to go after it, but then I remembered why I was here. I called to Buck and circled around to where the boat was.

I shut off my weapon and shield, then knelt on one knee and took deep breaths. I expected my equipment to be hot because I'd been using it hard, but it hadn't heated up a bit. The wet air didn't condense on the weapon, but it wasn't sizzling off the metal either. The shield wasn't any harder to shift around than a short length of broomstick would've been, but it'd blocked the dragon's charge.

I leaned forward and worked on getting my breath under control. "Master Pal," said Frances from behind me, "are we safe now?"

"I guess," I said. I tried to concentrate on the question.

Buck was bouncing around making little yips. He was still keyed up from the fight, no mistake, but I was sure he'd give warning if the dragon came back or if its mate did.

I hadn't hurt the dragon too bad, but I once scraped along my ribs by falling out of a tree. I'd cut the dragon deeper than I'd torn myself then, and believe me! I wasn't moving fast for a couple weeks after my scrape.

I got to my feet and put the shield and weapon back in my pockets. I looked at the others for the first time since the dragon swooped down.

Eloise suddenly bleated something and threw herself into my arms. "Oh, Lord Pal!" she said. "I was so afraid! And you killed the monster!"

"Careful, ma'am," I said, holding her where she was by the shoulders and stepping back. "I'm still a bit wobbly."

"And you, Eloise dear," said Frances in a voice like a bite of green apple, "have a prince waiting for you. I don't think he'd approve. That is, if you still want to go through with marrying Prince Philip?"

Eloise looked at her sister wide-eyed. "Why of *course* I'm going to marry Prince Philip!" she said. "Why wouldn't I marry him?"

I could come up with plenty of answers to *that* question myself, but I don't suppose any of them would matter to Eloise. In truth I didn't know of anything against Philip himself except that he was weak and not over-smart. Except for the people Philip had around him, he and Eloise were pretty well suited.

I grinned at Frances and said, "You know, I think they'll be about the handsomest couple anybody ever saw."

"Yes," said Frances. She didn't smile, but maybe I wouldn't have been grinning either if it'd been my sister in the mess.

"Look, we've still got a problem," I said. "We can get back to Marielles and have the wedding sure enough, but what then? Unless Philip has gotten a lot smarter since we left there, he's not going to believe Hellea was behind this business—"

I waved at the pods, both of them open now. It struck me that I wanted to bury Jeffries's foot, or his boot anyway. It was all I could do unless I wanted to chase the dragon down and finish it off for a real monument.

"—and I don't guess Lady Hellea's going to retire just because she lost this round. I'd suggest you both go back to Holheim and think about this for a while."

"No!" cried Eloise with a horrified expression.

Just then Buck started barking again. I looked up but it wasn't the dragon coming back, it was another boat coming out of the Waste to settle on the other side of ours. I didn't need the pieces missing from its near side where the pods had been to know that Camm had come back.

I took out my weapon and shield. "Baga," I said, "you and the women get aboard your boat. If things don't work out the way they should, you take 'em wherever Frances says. My choice'd be Holheim, but I'll be past making choices by then."

I met Frances's eyes. "Lady Frances," I said. "I'd appreciate if the boat stuck around as long as I'm standing. I guess you can convince the boatman to do that?"

"Yes," she said. She reached under a fold of her skirt and came out with the little knife.

"I'm staying here for the view," Baga said. "And I don't need a woman to keep me from running out on a mate. You women can get in the boat."

I didn't have time to see how that would play out. I switched on my equipment and stepped toward the other boat just as its hatch started to open.

The first thing out through the hatch was a dog: stocky, furry, black and tan. It was a chow or a chow mix.

I'll admit that my first thought was to take its head off before the warrior was out of the boat to protect it. That would've been my safest move, but if I had to kill a dog that way to stay alive, well... I didn't want to wake up every morning with the guy who'd done that thing.

I wasn't going to cut my own arm off to be fair, though. The tall warrior I'd seen with Camm on Marielles stepped through the hatchway, and I went straight for him.

I knew that Baga hadn't been able to see outside the boat until he'd opened the hatch, so I was pretty sure that Camm couldn't either. The warrior was ready for trouble, sure, but he wasn't *expecting* it. He sure wasn't expecting me to come at him before his foot hit the ground outside.

He got his shield up and took my first cut, but the shower of sparks at the contact meant that circuits in the shield were burning out. He jumped left, getting clear of the hatch and giving whoever was inside a chance to join him.

I had to ignore the reinforcements for now. This guy was the most dangerous man I'd seen on Marielles. If I didn't take him out quick, I might as well hand Lady Eloise over to Camm right now.

I tried to get on his right, but he turned inside me and thrust for my chest. I think my new shield would've stopped it, but I reacted the way I'd trained on Guntram's machine and slid his stroke to the side with my own weapon.

What Guntram said was true: I could use Buck's mind to predict the warrior's movement the same as I had with the machine images. I didn't think about it, it just happened the way I'd practiced every day for a month.

Camm came out of the hatch, his shield and weapon live but without a dog of his own. He could use the chow, but it wouldn't react to him the way it did its own master.

But the chow's master was the present problem. Camm wasn't rushing straight in the way he should have.

The warrior thrust again, this time at my head. I ducked behind my shield and slashed at his leading leg. His weapon glanced off; mine sheared through the lower edge of his shield and deep into his leg bones.

The warrior toppled forward. I turned to Camm. I was breathing hard and wondering how good he was. He screamed and ran at me, holding his weapon high. I thrust, bursting his shield and tearing a hole in his chest.

I faced the hatch. "Come on out!" I shouted. I didn't know what was inside. The boat's structure was a black silhouette cut from the view through my weapon. "Come out or I'll come in for you and you *won't* have a chance to give up if I do!"

Buck was ready to charge in with me, but we'd be taking a chance. I'd have to shut down my shield, and that'd leave me open to anybody waiting inside with a bow. I was about to do it anyway—my blood was up—when Frances walked in front of me and stepped into Camm's boat.

After a moment Frances came back. She stood in the doorway and raised her hands straight up in the air. I probably could've heard her if she'd shouted, but I read her as the sort of person who didn't raise her voice except when she was really angry. I'd seen that—heard it—when she was talking to Lady Hellea.

I shut off my shield and weapon, then kneeled down. Frances walked over close enough that I could see her feet without raising my head. She said, "I opened the pods that were closed. There's no one in the boat."

"Thanks," I said. I kept filling my lungs and breathing out. In a bit I'd stand up, but I wasn't ready to do that yet. "That was a crazy risk, though."

"Walters said it was just him and Camm in the boat," Frances said. "And Ajax, his dog. I wasn't sure the dog was going to let me put a tourniquet on Walters's leg, but Walters calmed him down and I did before he bled out completely. We should get him to a surgeon. Unless you plan to leave him here."

I lurched to my feet and put my weapon and shield away. Boy, I sure hoped the dragon didn't decide this'd be a good time to come back, because it truly would be—from the dragon's point of view.

"We'll get him to a surgeon," I said. "On Marielles, I guess, unless you've changed your mind?"

"Eloise hasn't," Frances said. "I think this—"

She gestured in the direction of Camm's body without taking her eyes off mine.

"—makes our job easier, mine at least."

She cleared her throat and went on, "Master Pal, I was angry when Master Guntram fobbed me off with you instead of a real Champion. I was wrong and I apologize."

"Thank you, ma'am," I said. I was feeling dizzy. I wanted to sit down, but I didn't want to do that until we were away from here. "And it's both our job, getting Eloise safe to Marielles. That's what I signed on for."

I looked around. The others were all watching me, except for Walters who seemed to be unconscious. The chow lay down beside Walters, then got up and walked in a circle around him before lying down again.

"Load up our boat and we'll leave for Marielles as quick as we can," I said. "We'll talk on the way about how we handle things there."

"That mean the dog too?" Baga said. "That guy's dog, I mean?"

"Yeah, our boat'll handle the load fine," I said. I expected more discussion, but everybody just nodded and got on with the job. Even Eloise.

I walked over to the other boat and put my hand on the hull. "Boat," I said, "I'll be back and fix you up. If I can, I mean. Things may get tricky at Marielles, but I figure they'll work out."

The boat said, *"Your boat told me that you would. Your boat says that in a hundred thousand years, it never had such a master as you."*

That made me feel funny, to be honest. I'd been decent to the boat, sure, but no more than I'd been to Buck or my neighbors. If that made me special, then the world was a worse place than it ought to've been.

"Well, wish me luck," I said.

I also wondered about that "hundred thousand years." I knew the Ancients were, well, ancient... But a hundred thousand years?

I went back to the others and helped Baga lift Walters into the boat. Ajax walked along with us stiff-legged and growling, but he curled up beside Walters in the room where we laid him down.

CHAPTER 14

A Different View of Marielles

Baga brought the boat to rest in the landingplace of Marielles, within arm's length of where he'd landed when I came here before. I knew before he opened the hatch that things were just as quiet as they'd been the first time, but I still went out holding my shield and weapon ready.

That was what Frances had insisted on: for the look of it, she'd said. I think she'd have been happier if I had something flashier to wear than the loose trousers and jacket we wear on Beune in nice weather like this. The cloth was gray, but the jacket was faded in patches.

Frances came out on my heels. She found what she wanted and pointed. "There!" she said and set off briskly toward a clothing seller with a cart and a big white dog to pull it.

Buck had stretched and rolled like always when he got out of the boat, but he caught up with us in a moment. The white dog eyed us but didn't get up. It had a lot of fur, but underneath it was still the biggest dog as I'd seen.

"Mistress," Frances said. "I want to rent your cart and dog to transport an injured man to the palace. I don't have any coin at the moment, but I'll give you a dress like this for the use."

She fluffed out the skirt of her outfit, silk with thin up-and-down stripes of cream and maroon. Her voice was hard even when she wasn't trying to be; I could see she'd put the peddler's back up already.

The peddler stared. "I don't have any market for such," she said. "Coin's what I sell for. Have ye coin?"

Frances didn't have any coins: Beune doesn't get enough travellers for there to be much new money since I'd taken all there was to go off to Dun Add. I fished out the last of the silver pieces from Duncan and said, "Ma'am? Will you rent us your cart and dog for this? Our friend's been badly wounded and we need to get him to Prince Philip."

I was pretty sure the peddler would have *sold* the cart and wagon for that coin, but it was all I had except for a few small coppers. I wanted the cart, not to haggle all morning. Walters was slipping in and out of a fever; we needed to get him to Prince Philip while he could still talk.

The peddler stared at the coin. "What? Hurt is he?" she said.

She turned to her neighbor whose stall sold climbing monkeys and other wooden toys. "Mamie!" she called as she stood up. "Watch my stock, will ye? Gus'n me've got t' haul a feller to the prince!"

I went back to the boat and with Baga got Walters

into the cart. He could've walked with a crutch, but carrying him with his arms over our shoulders was simpler. Besides, we didn't have a crutch.

Walters's left foot was shrivelling; just a dribble of blood was getting to it. It hadn't started to turn black and stink yet, but that'd happen. There'd be a surgeon on Marielles who could take it off and poultice the stump; there wasn't anything else for it, which Walters knew.

"C'mon, Gus!" the peddler called to her dog and we started for the palace. I got my weapon and shield out again, now that I didn't need my hands for other things.

The two sisters were leading. I started out behind the cart with Baga, but Frances gestured me up with her. I thought it was just because I was supposed to look manly and dangerous, but she said to me, "You'll be reimbursed for your expenditures, Master Pal. I know I'll be able to draw on my credit with bankers here in Marielles."

"Thank you, ma'am," I said. I hadn't doubted that she'd pay me back, but to be honest I hadn't really thought about it. I'd done what was easiest, that was all.

Baga split off into the town to find the boatman he said he'd met here and to line up the stuff we'd need to fix Camm's boat. My boat now, I suppose, though I couldn't guide it.

The three guards in blue caps were in front of the building. I wondered who was in charge of them with Camm dead and Walters being hauled toward them in a cart.

I shouldn't have wondered: when Lady Frances was around, she was always going to be in charge. She stepped up to the guards and snapped, "You two! Get Walters into the audience room. And you—"

She pointed at the third man. His eyes glazed and he stood up straight.

"—go make sure the bench against the wall is clear so that Walters can sit with his leg out."

"Sir?" said one of the first pair, bending over Walters. "What happened, sir?"

"What does it look like, Red?" Walters said. His voice was weak but he sounded like he meant it. "I met a better man, didn't I? Go do as the lady says, boys, or she'll have your ears."

"Lord Pal and I will lead the way," Frances added, gesturing me forward with her. I'd have laughed to hear myself called "Lord," but there wasn't anything funny in the lady's tone. Or the situation, if I thought about it.

The palace didn't have any metal in the walls so I could've switched on my shield if I needed to. With the shield live, though, there wasn't much I could do except fight. That wasn't what Frances wanted. Mind, she wouldn't back off if it came to that, and I'd said I'd stand with her.

The arched doorway into what Frances called the Audience Hall was wide enough for Buck and me to walk in alongside her. There weren't near so many folks inside as before, only about a dozen; but Philip was standing behind the table, looking scared, and Lady Hellea was there looking like an angry snake. A really pretty snake, though.

"Come, darling," Frances said, reaching an arm out behind her and drawing Eloise up alongside her. Fresh clothes—a red dress with thin swirls of gold—and primping with Frances's help had made Eloise a beauty like you never see.

"Prince Philip!" Frances said. "My champion has rescued Lady Eloise from the place where Hellea's minions marooned her. He has slain the monster which menaced her there—"

"That's a lie!" Hellea said. Fright hadn't done her voice any favors, but it was still nicer to hear than Frances's.

The lie was that the dragon was dead. Frances might really believe that, though.

"—and has defeated the minions when they returned to finish her off—and rob you of your pledged dowry, Philip!"

There was a bustle behind us. The folks who'd spread toward the walls when we entered were craning their necks to see past us. I heard the legs of the wooden bench scrape so I guessed the guards had put Walters down on it.

"Where is Lord Camm?" Hellea said, her voice rising. "*Where is Camm?*"

"Dead, and in Hell if God is just!" Frances said. "Walters—"

She half-turned and gestured back toward the bench. She never took her eyes off Philip, though.

"—will tell you what happened. Tell them, Walters!"

I kept looking across the table. I wasn't worried about Philip, but it wouldn't have surprised me a bit to learn that Lady Frances wasn't the only woman in the room to be carrying a sharp knife.

"Camm took me with him to get the girl, Lady Eloise there, on the node where he'd left her," Walters said. His voice wasn't strong, but it was still clear. The room had hushed. "He wanted to take Oliver besides, but I wouldn't go without Ajax. Camm said his boat wouldn't carry two people and a dog. He told me the girl had a guard, which was why he needed me."

"You men," Frances said, gesturing to the pair who'd carried Walters into the building. "Bring the bench closer. Now!"

I got out of the way while the guards slid Walters up toward the table. He was a good man, doing what he'd promised he'd do on the way to Marielles: tell the truth. I was sorry he was crippled, but I wasn't a bit sorry for beating him.

"Camm said we were going to make sure the girl was safe," Walters said, "but now I figure he was planning to kill her. Once we'd started there was nothing I could do; Camm was the boatman."

People were feeding into the hall, their feet shuffling. Even though they were trying to be quiet, they made a lot of noise. It was good that Frances had thought to move the bench up.

"We got there and the guard wasn't there, but Lord Pal was," Walters said. Either he'd heard Frances call me "Lord" or he just thought I'd like it. Which I suppose I did, though I kinda blushed inside to hear it. "He and Lady Frances had already rescued the girl. He beat me fair, and that bloody fool Camm didn't even give him a fight for all that expensive gear he bragged about. Good riddance, *I* say."

"My lord Prince, I had nothing to do with this," Hellea said.

"Liar!" Frances shouted. "I demand trial by combat! My champion will meet whoever the whore finds to defend her—or she stands dishonored and a proven liar, to pay the forfeit I set!"

Everyone stared at Hellea, Philip included. Frances had gotten in a good one when she pointed out that Hellea's scheme would've lost him the dowry.

Hellea looked around the room without seeing much that pleased her. "I have forty days to find a champion!" she said.

"I'll tell you right now, lady," Walters said. "You're not going to find anybody on Marielles who'll do you any good against Lord Pal."

He coughed; I guess it was supposed to be a laugh. "You know what's funny?" he said. "Camm told me that you and him were going to be running Marielles soon and if I played my cards right, it could be really good for me. I was thinking about taking him up on the offer."

"That's not true!" Hellea said. "I'm not responsible for any lies Camm might have told!"

"Prince Philip," Frances said, not shouting this time. "Let the whore have her forty days, but send her away now. If you don't, Eloise and I will return to Holheim and there'll be no marriage. Ever!"

"Oh, Frances, *no!*" Eloise said, her face scrunching up in horror. "You promised I could marry the prince!"

"We'll never be safe here while Hellea remains," Frances said. "I'm sorry, dear, but she goes or we do."

I believed that tone. So did Eloise, because she started crying on her sister's shoulder.

I guess Philip believed her too, because he said, "Mistress Hellea, you must leave Marielles within the hour, with the clothes you're standing in and ten—no, one ounce of silver, but paid in copper coins. That's more than you had when you arrived."

"Philip, you can't do this to me!" Hellea said. She wasn't crying—I wonder if she ever cried?—but she seemed to be shrinking, and she looked a lot older.

"Guards, get her out of here," Philip said. "Now, now! And if you come back before forty days are up, Hellea, I'll have you executed, I swear I will!"

"Red, you and your fellows come with me," Frances said. "We're taking Lady Hellea to her rooms and watching while she changes into something more suitable for the Road. Eloise, talk to your fiancé till I get back. You're getting married after all, as soon as forty days is up."

The three guards and Hellea went out the door in the left side of the hall. Eloise trotted around the table and threw herself into Philip's arms.

As for me, I relaxed. For the first time in way too long.

There was a good crowd around the boat the next day. Mostly they were just watching—news of the excitement in the palace had gotten around and brought folks to see if there'd be more of the same today. I sure hoped they'd be disappointed in that.

There was a fair number of tradesmen, bringing the stuff Baga had ordered from the list I'd given him, the stuff we'd need to put Camm's boat in shape. I let Baga and Stefan check that in.

Stefan was the fellow Baga had met here, a boatman too. He and Baga had gone off in the boat for an hour, and Baga said he was good though he hadn't had much practice. Stefan would bring Camm's boat back when we finished repairing it.

My boat. I didn't have any idea what I was going to do with a boat. I thought maybe I could give it to Guntram, though he couldn't guide it either.

Buck whined beside me. I looked back and saw Frances coming toward me from the town. The guard Red was walking a step behind her and carrying a small leather bag.

"Ma'am?" I said.

I needed to talk with her about money. Camm's boat was in really bad shape; the things I'd need for repairs were going to cost a fair amount. Back home I could've gotten time or anyway worked things out from the sellers, though some of the stuff—some of the metals especially—probably couldn't have been had on Beune.

I figured Frances could arrange a loan for me from the bankers here. The boat was worth a lot more than what I'd have to pay to put it in shape, after all. And I figured Frances would be willing to trust me.

"Good afternoon, Lord Pal," she said as she came up to me. "We have business to transact."

"Ma'am, it's all right," I said. "You don't have to call me 'Lord' anymore. You're in charge now, I guess, and you don't have to put anything on to get the prince to take you for a lady."

Frances sniffed. "No, I certainly don't," she said. "But for the title—I've seen you at home and I judge you're a squire on Beune if anyone is. You carry yourself as a gentleman should, and you have a nobleman's equipment."

I grinned. "Ma'am, I'm a farmer," I said. "Everybody on Beune is a farmer, pretty much."

"The equal of anyone on Beune, which is enough,"

Frances said. She gave me the first smile I'd seen on her face. "I assure you that nobody here will argue with me. If you're wise, you'll carry that honor when you leave. You deserve it, and the way you handle your weapon will convince anyone you meet."

"Ma'am, I guess that's true," I said, "but it's not somebody I want to be. Thank you, though."

She sniffed again. "It's your business," she said, "but you're a fool. No matter."

She turned to the guard and said, "Give him the satchel, Red."

Red handed it to me and made a little bow before he stepped back. I guess he was chief guard now, though on Marielles that wasn't much to say.

The bag weighed five or six pounds, more than I'd expected. I wondered if I was supposed to open the tie closure.

"This is a thousand Marielles crowns," Frances said. "Each one weighs slightly more than a Dun Add dragon, though I don't know how much they'll be discounted as you move farther away from Marielles."

"Ma'am!" I said. "This is *way* more than I need to borrow. I figure ten—well, maybe twelve—would pay for all the goods I'm buying."

"What exactly do you plan to do?" Frances said. "If you don't mind telling me."

"I don't mind," I said. Why would I? "Baga's going to carry me back to the place we left the other boat. I'll fix it up and Stefan will bring it back. Ah—I'll be back before the challenge in forty days, don't worry. Even if there's a problem with fixing the other boat, Baga will bring me back for that."

"Hellea won't find a champion," Frances said with

contempt. "If she were ten years younger I might worry, but not now. Still, best to have you ready."

Her lips pursed. "The node where we left the boat is named Dewbranch, by the way."

"It is?" I said. "Dewbranch, then. I didn't figure it had a name."

"Lady Eloise named it," Frances said. Her voice was dry as dust in summer. "She lived there longer than I imagine anyone else has, so I suppose she has a right."

She glanced over her shoulder, I guess to see that Red had backed well away. She took a deep breath and said, "That money isn't a loan, Pal. It's payment for what you did for me and for my sister."

"Ma'am!" I said. "I didn't help you for money!"

"No, you didn't," Frances said. "But it's the only way I have to repay you."

I thought for a moment that she was going to say something more. Instead, she turned and walked back toward town. The guard followed her.

CHAPTER 15

Pairs and Singletons

I'd as soon have been someplace else, but in truth it wasn't hurting me to sit with my back to a tree trunk and my stomach full of good food.

The big pavilion near the front of the park was where they'd held the wedding. The better sort danced there now to three violins and an oboe; I could hear snatches of the music when the breeze was right.

Closer to me at the back of the grounds was a stretch of mown grass where common folk—folk like me and my neighbors on Beune—were dancing to a bag-piper. In between was a brick house that Prince Philip called his rural bungalow.

I'd always thought of bungalows as being little places. This one in the royal park wasn't little.

People had come from days away by the Road, not to mention all those from Marielles itself. The town had a big hinterland, maybe as big as the one that fed Dun Add. There was even a boat in the landingplace, besides the two that came from Dewbranch: Baga's and the one I'd repaired and now owned.

I'd been surprised at all the foofarah when we got back from Dewbranch just before Hellea's forty days were up. Prince Philip had spread the word pretty wide, and forty days was enough time for people to make the trip from quite a ways away.

Frances had laid down the law: there wouldn't be a wedding until Hellea was either dead or disgraced. She took it for granted that even if Hellea found somebody to stand for her, I'd beat him. I wouldn't have gone that far, but I had really good equipment and Hellea's story wasn't likely to win over anybody in Jon's Hall of Champions.

Hellea hadn't showed, just like Frances figured. I was glad of that.

I didn't particularly want to kill anybody. Easton and Camm don't keep me from going to sleep, but sometimes I think about them in the dark before I get up in the morning.

I saw Baga and Stefan coming toward me from the tables of food and drink right behind the bungalow. I didn't recognize the woman with them. She could've passed for any of the thirties-ish women I knew on Beune: healthy, stocky but not really fat. She had brown hair, though she might call it chestnut.

Stefan and the woman stopped twenty feet away while Baga came on the rest of the way. I stood up, sticking my free hand back against the tree trunk when I started to tip sideways; I'd been sitting too long, and the strong wine didn't help. There were lots of vineyards on Marielles, and Philip hadn't stinted on wine for his wedding.

"Lord Pal!" Baga said, loud enough for him to have stayed back with his friends. He looked surprised himself; I could see that he'd gotten deeper into the wine than I had.

"Sorry, boss," he said in a normal voice. He burped into his hand, then said, "Look, you're planning to hire Stefan to run your boat, right? Aren't you?"

"Yes," I said. I didn't know where this was going, but it was sounding like Stefan was backing out and Baga was doing the talking for him. I wouldn't have used my weapon on Stefan, but it'd cause me problems that I hadn't expected.

"Well, Stefan and me was talking..." Baga said. He burped into his hand again. His face screwed up and he said, "Look, boss, you and me get along okay, don't we?"

"We have," I said. Baga was quiet when he wasn't running the boat, and silent when he was. He kept out of my way. I don't need much in the way of company. There hadn't been any problems with him running the boat that I knew about. I couldn't judge that, of course, but we'd always gotten where I wanted to go.

"Well then, why not you hire me on this new boat instead of Stefan, hey?" Baga blurted. "He'll run my boat on shares, and he's by way of being my brother-in-law, you see? That's his sister Maggie there with him."

Why was that so hard to get out? Aloud I said, "That's fine with me if that's what you want to do, Baga. I still want to leave tomorrow morning, though."

"I knew that's what you'd say!" Baga said. "I'll tell Stefan and Maggie!"

He staggered off toward his friends. Stefan was carrying two wine bottles; Baga had handed one of them to the other boatman before trudging the rest of the way over to me.

We weren't going to be leaving Marielles first thing in the morning, but I'd never thought that we would. That was okay. And to tell the truth, I was just as glad to have Baga for my boatman. I knew what to expect from him—and getting drunk pretty regularly in places that had something to drink wasn't the worst fault that a boatman could have.

I looked up at the tree I stood against. It was shaped a funny way: two good-sized maples were leaning into each other—not braided, but the trunks had grown together about eight feet up from the ground. They branched out in opposite directions.

I wondered if I ought to go back to the boat where I'd left Buck. He'd be fine, but there was nothing holding me here.

"Good afternoon, Lord Pal," said Frances from behind me. "Are you enjoying the party?"

I turned around so quick that my feet got tangled; I had to touch the trunk again. That made me blush, though I don't suppose Frances could see it under my tan.

"It's nice," I said. "I'm not a big one for parties, though. And, ah, I'm used to ale."

She nodded, though what that was supposed to mean I'm not sure. "The new suit looks very good on you," she said. "Do the others fit as well?"

Frances had three outfits waiting for me when I arrived back on Marielles. This one was blue with red lapels; the other two were red with blue, and green with yellow.

"I suppose they do," I said, surprised at the question.

Frances had been so busy with the wedding business that I hadn't had a chance to say anything about them. "Would you like me to leave them at the palace before I go off tomorrow? Now that the wedding's over, I mean."

"What on earth would I do with men's clothing?" Frances said. "I'm not a raving beauty like my sister, but I'm not a *man*."

"No, ma'am," I said. She was in brown, with a white sash and a white lace collar. It was a nice outfit and it didn't call attention to her; which, with her looks, was probably what she intended.

"You'll be more effective at whatever you do in those clothes," Frances said. "Do in the wider world, I mean. I suppose you could plow perfectly well in your usual outfit."

She looked me straight in the eye and said, "What *do* you intend to do now, Pal? I trust you realize that you don't have to go back to Beune?"

"Yes, ma'am," I said. "I figure I'll go see Guntram at Dun Add like he asked me to. After that I don't know, but I would like to show him the new boat that I fixed up after he showed me how."

"I see," Frances said. She cleared her throat again and said, "Have you considered returning to Marielles to stay?"

"Good God!" I said. "Why would I do that? I don't even know anybody here."

"I will be selling up the family properties on Holheim and moving to Marielles," Frances in a voice as flat as a griddle-cake. "I have no reason to stay on Holheim. Hellea is gone and I don't precisely doubt Prince Philip's goodwill, but I think his behavior will be better if he knows that there's someone watching him."

"Ah," I said, thinking about what that meant.

Frances gave me a funny smile and said, "Oh, don't worry. I don't expect Philip to be a saint; or any other man, if it comes to that. But he will *not* be unkind to my sister, or he'll hear about it."

I smiled. "I'd guess Marielles is going to have a better government from now on," I said.

"That doesn't change your opinion of settling here, though?" Frances said.

"Lord, *no*," I said. "It's good for the folks here but ... Beune doesn't have any government, really, and that suits me fine. We're just a little place, though."

"I see," said Frances. "Well, I'm glad that you feel my presence will benefit Marielles. I'll get back to my duties as the bride's sister, I suppose."

I was thinking about Dun Add. Aloud I said, "Ma'am? I don't guess you'll have any trouble with Philip or anybody, but if you need me just let me know. I'd expect to leave word with Guntram even if I'm not in Dun Add myself."

I thought Frances was turning away, but instead she cleared her throat. "Pal?" she said. "Even if you wouldn't want to stay on Marielles, you'll always be welcome to visit if you happened to want to. You *know* that?"

"Yes, ma'am," I said. I didn't imagine I ever would.

I don't guess Frances thought so either. She turned around and walked away, her back very straight.

I thought more about Dun Add. And I wondered if I'd see Lady May again.

CHAPTER 16

Arriving in a Different Dun Add

I told Baga to leave the boat closed up after we arrived on Dun Add. I spent a while looking about the landingplace through the boat itself.

I saw the Herald of the Gate waiting pompously for the hatch to open. That made me smile. Judging by what'd happened when I came to Dun Add by the Road, that just meant that other travellers were going to get into the town with less pointless hassle than if the Herald was able to interfere with his clerk.

There were three boats on the landingplace before we arrived. I recognized one from my first visit. The Leader must have a boat of his own, though it didn't have to be here on the landingplace—Camm had kept his on a country estate which Hellea had owned.

Baga said it was tricky to locate a place in the interior of a node when you were coming from the Waste, since you didn't have the Road for a guide. It could be done, though.

I came out of my trance and stretched. "Things seem about what they were before, Baga," I said. "You can open her up and I'll go look for Guntram."

"Are those the clothes you plan to wear, boss?" Baga said. He was standing by the hatch, but he wasn't touching the lever that opened it.

"Why shouldn't I?" I said. I'd worn ordinary clothes during the voyage from Marielles. I looked down at them, made a face, and ducked into my room.

"You look really nice in the red," Baga said. "But they're all nice."

I put on the red suit. It was as bad as having Lady Frances along. Though she'd have ordered me which outfit to wear, not made a suggestion.

I wondered how she was doing. If ever there'd been a woman who should've been born in a man's body, it was her. I'd never heard her complain, though. She just worked around the things that came up.

"Do you like me now?" I asked Baga. I transferred my shield and weapon into the pockets of this tunic. This hardware was so light that I didn't need a harness to hold it as I'd had for the pieces I'd converted from other uses.

"Every inch the lord, boss," Baga said. He opened the hatch; Buck and I stepped into Dun Add.

"Welcome, Champion of Beune!" called Guntram, standing beside the Herald. He must've arrived after I came out of my trance.

"Guntram!" I said, surprised in a good way. I clasped arms with him while the Herald pursed his lips and sucked them in again. "I was wondering how I'd find you."

"I was observing on the jousting field and saw your

boat arrive," Guntram said. "Though I didn't know it was yours until I'd gotten closer. I hope you'll allow me to go over it after we've gotten you settled here."

"Sure!" I said. "We can do that right now if you want!"

"No, first we need to take care of formalities, here and at the palace," Guntram said. He reached down and rubbed Buck's ears; Buck had recognized a friend and was nuzzling Guntram's knee.

The Herald cleared his throat. "I don't mean to interrupt your lordships," he said, "but I need to jot a few things down. Did you say 'Beune,' sir? I don't believe I've heard of that place before?"

"That's of no consequence, fellow," Guntram said. "Lord Pal is on Dun Add now. He will be entering the Hall of Champions shortly. If you need details, I'm sure that his boatman can satisfy you."

I knew there was absolutely no side on Guntram—he'd been right at home with my neighbors on Beune, eating the food they gave us and cleaning his plate like he liked it. Here with this fat fool, though, Guntram was the important Maker and a friend of the Leader. Mom had called that choosing your pattern to fit your cloth.

"Of course, sir," the Herald said, writing on his notebook. "Lord Pal of Beune, entering the Aspirants' Chamber."

"Baga, you and Maggie are free to go off when you've satisfied this guy," I called. "I'll be back by evening, or anyway I'll send word about where we're to be."

We started up toward the palace by the straight, broad path. "Baga's my boatman," I explained to

Guntram, not that he'd asked. "He volunteered to be my attendant if I stay in Dun Add. Though, sir? I haven't decided to try for the Champions again. I'm just thinking about it."

Guntram chuckled. "I'd say that on Beune there'd be very little employment for arms of such quality as yours," he said. "Wouldn't you?"

"What I had before was good enough for Beune when I needed anything at all," I said. "And, sir? I thanked you for the shield when you gave it to me, but I've used it now. It's a wonderful piece of work, *very* handy."

"There are sturdier shields," Guntram said, "but none that I've seen which were as light in use. You've given your arms a fair test then, you believe?"

I thought of Walters. "Yes," I said. "It was a fair test."

I'd asked Lady Frances if she could do something for Walters; she'd had him made doorkeeper at Philip's bungalow. Even with a peg leg, he could handle any trouble that was likely to happen there.

"I'll show you something of the court before you enroll," Guntram said. "We'll drop Buck off in the stables and I'll take you there. And I won't tell you—"

He paused till I met his eyes.

"—that you have a duty to Mankind not to waste your abilities, Pal. Because you already know that."

I swallowed. "Yessir," I said.

I don't know what I expected the Leader's Court to be like. Guntram took us up a wide staircase to the third floor. The stairs weren't crowded but we met a couple dozen people on them. Some nodded to

Guntram or spoke, but others just turned their eyes aside or even squeezed against the opposite railing.

The attendant at the open door opposite the stairhead bowed to Guntram. We walked in at the top of a double-high room shaped like a half funnel. Curving ranks of seats sloped down to the floor from where we stood. There was room for at least two hundred people to sit there, but only fifty or so were taken. Some were warriors but the rest looked like clerks, a few of them women.

Jon, the Leader, was seated on a dais facing the ranks of seats. I gasped and stepped back against the wall when I realized who I was looking down at.

From this far away—and looking down, like we were—I didn't have a good view of Jon's face. His gold robe caught the light from the high windows around all four sides of the room; the ceiling must stick up above the roof of the rest of the building around it.

"On the basis of the petition which has been reviewed by my counselors..." Jon said, speaking to the young man facing him at the foot of the dais. There were four chairs to either side of the dais, five of the total occupied. "I order the following: in forty days time the petitioner and his brother Arne will present themselves before me for adjudication regarding the division of their father's estate. Both parties may bring additional evidence to place before my counselors."

"Arne will never come just because I tell him to!" the man facing him said. He sounded whiny and frustrated.

I could hear them both just as clear as if I was right across a table from them. I'd never been in such a big room where you could hear so clearly. I wondered if Guntram had found an Ancient machine that made it happen this way.

"I will discuss the matter with my Champions and see if one volunteers to accompany you back to Austerlitz," Jon said. "If not, I'll assign one in a few days. Are there any volunteers in the hall now?"

No one spoke up, though I saw several of those in the audience whispering to neighbors.

"Well, report back tomorrow," Jon said. "Next petitioner."

An attendant in black led the man from Austerlitz to the side; an elderly woman hobbled into his place on the arm of another attendant. Guntram motioned me to follow him back into the hall.

When we got outside I said, "Sir, how do we hear things so clearly in there? Is this something you did?"

"No, it was just the design," Guntram said. "An architect from Bassai planned the room for Jon. She said very little herself, just bustled around making notes, but her six assistants all spoke of her as though she took dictation from God."

He smiled and added, "Judging from the hall's acoustics, they may have been right."

"Sir," I said. "Why does the Leader care about an estate on Austerlitz? Does he have property there himself?"

"He doesn't care in the least," Guntram said. "The important thing to him is that people come to Dun Add to sort out their problems instead of going to war with one another. If a Champion isn't sufficient to enforce the Leader's decree, then there's the army or a portion of it. But that's only been necessary twice that I know of."

He led me down a much narrower staircase next to the outer wall rather than the courtyard by which we'd come up. I didn't ask where we were going. Guntram was taking me to places that he thought I ought to see. He knew more about it than I did.

"Who were the people on the benches, sir?" I said. A lot of them had been too old or frail to be warriors, or they were women.

"Some are Champions, listening to judgments in case they find one that they'd like to get involved in," Guntram said. "More of them send a clerk to take notes for them, for the same reason. And there are those who just like to watch the court."

We left the stairs at the second floor and started down a hallway. A pair of servants saw us coming and lowered their heads as we brushed past one another in opposite directions.

I hadn't thought about how Jon's government was organized. The stories told about people—in the stories they were pretty generally beautiful ladies—coming to Jon and him sending a Champion out to right her wrongs. The beautiful lady had always been injured by a villain, whom the Champion slew in a great battle.

I knew from Beune that when neighbors or a couple fell out, it generally wasn't easy to tell where the fault lay. Well, better, it generally seemed that they were both acting wrong. The priest would get together a neighbors' council and the council'd make the best choice it could. Which generally left everybody angry at them, but also quieted things down between the parties. Nobody likes to know that his neighbors think he's being a fool.

We don't have Trial by Combat on Beune, but

sometimes the parties or healthy male relatives have it out. This may mean an eye gouged or a finger bitten off, but we don't have weapons. I've never heard of anybody being killed.

Guntram opened a door whose hinges squealed like it hadn't been used in a year. From the way people in the workroom beyond turned their heads to look at us, it can't've been common for folks to come by this way.

There were cubicles on both sides of the room, six on one side and five on the other plus a door in the center with a broad aisle between them. Each cubicle had a couch and a built-in table. Four were occupied; three men gathered at a sideboard with food—cheese, meats, and fruit—and storage jars with narrow dippers hanging from the rims.

The tables had Ancient artifacts on them, mostly weapons and shields. Nearby were trays and bins of the stuff you'd need to repair them. All the people here were Makers.

"Master Guntram," one of them said. He bowed and the others muttered, "Master," and bowed or dipped their heads, except for the two who were in trances.

"This is my friend, Lord Pal," Guntram said generally as he led me toward the door at the end of the room. There were nods and murmurs as we walked past. I smiled and nodded back, feeling out of place.

The wide door—it was four feet across, easy—had been carved with a pair of dragons swallowing each other's tails. I'd been impressed even before I got close enough to see that it was all one piece of wood.

Instead of knocking, Guntram put his hand in the upper center of the panel, about opposite his face.

When he touched the wood, it suddenly got a sheen like there was a plate of glass over it.

The door opened inward. "Teacher!" said a small blond man with a pointy beard and a little moustache. "What brings you here today?"

"Good morning, Louis," Guntram said. "You'll recall that shield I brought you, the one made from a rain repellant? This is the man who made it."

"Come in, come in!" Louis said, closing the door behind us. "That was a remarkable piece of work, sir! Guntram, I can certainly find a use for him."

This workroom was as neat as Phoebe's parlor when she was expecting company. While Guntram had shelves and tables overflowing with bits and pieces, the walls of Louis's room were covered with cabinets and drawers, all of them closed. The grain of the wood matched from one rank to the next so that they looked like paneling instead of storage.

The artifact—it was a weapon—on the table beside the couch was the only evidence that this was a Maker's workroom. Even so, the trays of repair materials had been put away since the work wasn't in process at the moment.

"Sir," I said, "the shield didn't work. I could barely move it when it was on full."

I'd just been offered the chance to work with the greatest Maker in the human universe. And I didn't want the place. I felt sick at the thought of turning down such a wonderful offer.

"And he's not for you, Louis," Guntram said. "Or for me either. Pal is on Dun Add to join the Company of Champions."

There hadn't been proper introductions. Neither

Maker paid much attention to the little social stuff, and I'd never been any good at it either.

"Indeed?" Louis said, looking at Guntram and raising an eyebrow.

"Indeed," Guntram said. "Besides, I think you'd find Pal too whimsical to work out well with you, Louis. He would get bored turning out serviceable weapons for the troops day after day. Just as I would."

"Trying to make toys from Not-Here work is all well and good, Teacher," Louis said, his voice suddenly hard. "I think baubles need to wait until Here has been returned to a state of law and order, though."

"I know what you believe, Louis," Guntram said. "I wish you and Jon all good fortune in your work. But as you know, it's not for me."

Louis lost his sudden harshness. He bowed and said, "You may be the wisest of the three of us, Teacher, but Jon and I aren't going to give up our dreams."

He looked at me. "If you change your mind, Pal," he said, "come and see me. The Maker who turned an umbrella into a shield could probably be useful for more things than arming common soldiers."

I bowed and said, "Thank you, sir." I turned to follow Guntram out of the office.

"And Pal?" Louis said. Guntram and I both looked back.

"It seems to me that shield of yours could be quite serviceable if you could switch it on and off very quickly," Louis said. "I can think of several ways to do that, if you'd like to come down and discuss it with me some time."

"*Thank* you, sir," I said.

Guntram and I returned to the general workroom.

We went out by the door between two cubicles. It was bigger than the one we came in by, so I figured it was the main door.

"You could learn a great deal from Louis," Guntram said as we walked down the hall. I didn't know where he was taking me now.

"I noticed the cubicles," I said. "They were all really neat. Not as neat as Louis's own room, but neat."

"So they were," said Guntram. "I'm sure it's a very efficient working environment."

I shrugged. "It works for some, I guess," I said. "I don't figure it'd work for me. Anyway, I want to be a Champion."

"Yes," Guntram said. "The shield I gave you is one that Louis built from scraps, some of which came from what I believe was a clock. I don't think there's ever been a Maker with more of a flair for arms. He and Jon are well suited to their task of reuniting Here by force. Where that's necessary."

I thought of Beune. I didn't recall anybody there complaining that there wasn't more unity. I didn't say anything.

The door head at the corner of the hall was seven feet tall with an arched top. Its brass mountings were for show, not strength, and they'd been polished recently, maybe just this morning.

The two guards were probably for show too, but they had good arms and looked like they knew how to use them. They moved a little apart as we approached. The taller one said, "Good morning, Master Guntram. We don't often see you in this end of the palace."

"I'm showing my friend Lord Pal around," Guntram said. "I thought I'd introduce him to Lady Jolene."

"Any friend of yours, sir," the guard said. He pulled the door open and with his fellow stood braced as Guntram led me inside.

The man who'd just gotten up from a stool in the small anteroom was a servant with sharp features and a fringe of red hair which had gone mostly gray. He wore black tights and a tunic in two shades of blue, both muted.

"Master Guntram!" he said. "How shall I announce your companion, please?"

"I'm Pal of Beune," I said quickly before Guntram could call me, "Lord Pal," again. Lord of what? I didn't even own the farm my parents had left me.

Though I had a boat, come to think. I wondered what Camm had owned and how he'd become "Lord Camm." Still, that was on his conscience, not mine.

Had been on his conscience.

"Master Guntram, and Pal of Beune," the attendant called into the big room beyond. He didn't speak loudly, but his voice carried in a liquid wave.

"Lady Jolene," Guntram said, "this is my colleague Pal. He's enrolling in the Aspirants' Chamber."

"We don't see you often, Guntram," said the lovely blond-haired woman on a central chair. "Would you like some refreshment? We have wine and also sherbert thanks to the marvelous cooler that you made for me."

There were three men, all Champions by the look of them, and seven or eight women. One of the women had been singing softly as she plucked a musical instrument with a long neck and a round sound box, but she stopped and looked at us when Jolene began speaking.

Lady May was the singer.

"No thank you, lady," Guntram said. "Pal has done me

a number of services, both here and on the Marches. I was pleased that he took my advice to join the Leader's Company. Now that he's here I'm showing him the important things in Dun Add—"

He paused and bowed. Guntram wasn't without social niceties after all, though he only practiced them when he chose to.

"—which of course includes you, your ladyship."

Jolene wore at least three and maybe more layers of blue gauze. There were fish embroidered on one layer or another; they seemed to swim when she made a flirting gesture with her hand toward the old Maker.

"Guntram, you'll turn my head," Jolene said. She continued to smile as she turned to me.

I stood straighter. It was like being stared at by a cat. A really big cat.

"Where is Beune, Pal?" Jolene said. Her voice was as smooth and lovely as the rest of her, though I was beginning to see that she was older than I'd first thought. "I don't believe I'd heard of it before."

"It's on the Marches, ma'am," I said. I'd been thinking about answering the question instead of remembering *who* I was answering. "That is, your ladyship, I mean."

She laughed like silver bells. "Just call me Jolene, dear," she said. "Nobody needs to stand on ceremony in *my* chambers."

"Yes, ma'am," I said. To change the subject I said, "Beune's thirty-two days out from Dun Add by the Road, and that's hard travelling. I came here by boat this time, though."

"You have boats on Beune?" a forties-ish man said. He didn't speak loudly but his voice had authority. So did the man, obviously, from the way everybody in the room looked at him as he spoke. He was as tall as I was, but *much* more powerful.

"Well, there was just mine," I said. "And now that I'm here, not mine either. It's real uncommon to see a boat on Beune."

"You *own* a boat?" one of the women said, leaning forward like a hot-pink flower. She had black hair, and her lip-rouge matched her dress color.

"Ah, yes ma'am," I said. I hadn't expected to be doing any talking when we entered the room, and I'd sooner have been right about that. "I can't guide it myself, though. I just own it."

I hadn't really thought about ownership before. Nobody was going to argue my claim, *that* I was sure of.

"Jolene, would you mind if I showed Pal the terrace?" May asked. "He and I know each other, you see. We met before."

"By all means, child," the Consort said, gesturing toward the window with a movement that made her look even more like a cat.

I heard giggles. One of the men nudged another—not the fellow who'd asked me about boats—and chortled.

I stiffened. I thought May started to blush, but she said, "This way, Pal. The roses are still blooming nicely, though it's been so dry that we have to water them every day."

She opened the casement and stepped out, then closed it after us. I'd noticed greenery through the glass but I hadn't paid it much attention. Now I saw that there was a roof garden with small junipers in pots right outside. You couldn't see through their branches any better than you could've a brick wall.

We walked around the junipers, into a little plaza

with wicker couches and potted rose bushes. May turned and faced me. "So, Pal...?" she said. "It was just a disguise, you pretending to be a poor rube who didn't know anything about the big city?"

"Ma'am, it surely was not!" I said. "I was just what I said I was—I still am, mostly. I've had some good luck, that's all. And the biggest luck was all the things that Guntram's done for me. He made it sound like I'd helped him, but that's not so—not to mention, anyhow."

May smiled. God knows she was pretty!

"So," she said. She straightened the collar of my red suit. I was glad now that Baga or maybe Maggie had told me to change out of my regular clothes. "Guntram is responsible for your new taste in clothing?"

"Oh, no, ma'am," I said. "This suit's from Marielles and I've got two more like it. A lady gave them to me because I'd helped her find her sister."

"A lady?" May said, cocking her head. The rosebush behind her was in full bloom. That made me remember the first time I saw May when she had a bunch of tulips in her arms. "Was she as pretty as me?"

"Oh, goodness, no!" I said. "I don't know anybody who's as pretty as you, May!"

"You're a sweet boy," she said. "And don't worry, I won't pry."

I started to tell her that there was nothing to pry about, but before I got the words out May had lifted up on tiptoes and kissed me on the lips. Not hard, but a real kiss.

"Come along, now," she said and led me back around the junipers to the window we'd come out by.

I know my cheeks were red when we went back into Jolene's chambers.

CHAPTER 17

Making Friends

The same clerk was on duty in the Aspirants' Hall as the first time I applied. I doubt she recognized me in my new suit. I took out my shield and weapon as I entered.

Guntram said, "Mistress? I vouch for the quality of his arms."

The clerk looked past me and saw him. "Oh!" she said. "Well, that's good enough for me."

When I started to put the equipment back in my pockets, she frowned and said, "Sir? I've admitted you, but could I look at that shield anyway? Just for myself?"

I set my weapon and shield before her on the counter. She switched on the shield and made a couple quick turns with it, then set it back down.

"Master Guntram?" she asked. "Does he have a waiver from the Leader or Lord Clain? You know I'd like to exempt him on your say-so, but I can't."

"Pal will go through the usual process," Guntram said. "And I'll get out of your way. Pal, if you need me, I'll be in and out of my room in my usual fashion. You know where to find me."

"Thank you, sir," I said. "For everything."

In truth, I didn't think I *could* find Guntram's room on my own, though I suppose I could get somebody to guide me. I didn't plan to do that. I wasn't asking for favors.

"Ma'am," I said, "I'm Pal of Beune."

Instead of responding to me, she jotted information down in a ledger. Turning her head toward the open door behind her, she called, "Heckert? Has Room Twelve been cleared yet?"

A middle-aged man came out. He was missing his left arm from above the elbow. "That's done," he said. "We like to get on those first thing, you know."

"Well, take Lord Pal up and introduce him to his roommates," the clerk said. She looked at me again as I put my shield and weapon away. "Where's your gear, Lord Pal?"

"It's in my boat with my man," I said. I guess I'd become Lord Pal without saying anything. If the clerk was making a mistake, it was in the safe direction. "Ah, and his wife. I don't have much."

"After you've dropped him off," the clerk said to Heckert, "go find his servants and show them their quarters. All right?"

Heckert bowed slightly. "If you'll follow me, sir."

Room Twelve was on the next floor up. One of the doors off the Aspirants' Hall was to a staircase. It led down as well as up, which surprised me, but a building as massive as this one must have foundations like nothing we dreamed of back home.

There were four doors off the landing, three with brass plaques—9, 10, and 12—and a discolored patch on the center of what I supposed was Room Eleven. Heckert tapped lightly, then opened the door of Twelve.

A man in a robe was in what seemed to be a common room; there were three doors opening into it, two of them now open. Heckert said, "Good morning, Master Welsh. This is Lord Pal of Beune, who's taking the empty room in this suite."

"Empty?" said Welsh. He was a squat man with black hair whose moustache flared into his beard. "Bloody hell, I meant to watch Daniello's trial but I really tied one on last night. He passed, then?"

The door opened behind us and a large red-haired man strode in. He looked angry.

"Hey, Garrett!" Welsh called. "Daniello passed!"

"Like hell he did!" the redhead said. "He got cut down in the first minute. I was bloody watching, wasn't I?"

"Well, why are they . . . ?" Welsh said, turning his head toward one of the open doors. The bed within had been stripped.

"I believe Lord Daniello withdrew from Aspirants' Hall after injuries in his admissions joust, Master Welsh," Heckert said. I wondered how he'd lost his arm, though I suppose it didn't matter.

"Withdrew!" said Garrett. "He took a hard one on the side of the knee and you kicked him out on his ass, you mean!"

"Does it matter, sir?" said Heckert calmly. "This is

Lord Pal of Beune, who is taking Lord Daniello's place. Lord Pal, I'll see that your servants are informed."

He was quickly out the door of the suite, closing it behind him.

Garrett and Welsh were both looking at me with grim expressions. I said, "Gentlemen, I'm sorry about your friend. I just arrived here today and don't know anything."

Clearing my throat, I added, "And look, that 'Lord Pal,' stuff is crap and I didn't start it. There's nobody in Beune that's noble, and if there was it wouldn't be me."

They looked at each other. "Well, it's not your fault," Welsh said. "I wouldn't call Daniello a friend, but the three of us shared this room for the best part of a year. I'd really hoped that one of us was going to make Champion."

"Hell, Daniello maybe dropped out on his own," Garrett said, sounding depressed. "The admissions joust is at forty percent. I could hear the snap from the sideline when the cut landed. He'll limp for the rest of his life."

"Bloody hell," Welsh muttered. Then he straightened and faced me squarely. "All right, Pal," he said. "Let's see your gear. Or did you leave it with your man?"

"No, it's right here," I said. I took the shield and weapon out of my pockets and set them on top of a table projecting from the wall beside the door. I had to push half a dozen empty bottles together to make room.

Garrett and Welsh bent close. "Dainty little things, aren't they?" Welsh said. "You get them on Beune, wherever that is?"

I kept my voice calm. "They work pretty well," I said. "The shield is from here, I'm told, but the weapon comes from Beune. I helped make it myself."

"You're a Maker?" Garrett said, frowning.

"I'm a Maker *also*," I said. "But I'm here to join the Company of Champions."

"Well, fair enough," said Welsh. "That's why Garrett and me are here, too. Why don't we all go over to the practice room and see how you and the hardware perform, hey?"

"No time like the present," I said, putting the shield and weapon back in my pockets. My mouth was so dry that I'd been afraid that I was going to gag getting out those few words, but it was the truth. If I couldn't cut it in Dun Add, it was best to learn now.

The practice room was an arched wooden extension built out the north side of the palace. The ground floor room we entered through had probably been the whole business before more machines were added. There must be fifty of them now, ranked against the right and left walls. Only about half were in use at the moment, a few of them by warriors with dogs by their sides.

I wondered if Guntram had borrowed the machine I'd trained on from here. They might not all be the same.

"Where do you want me?" I said, speaking to Welsh since it had been his idea. I couldn't quarrel with my roommates wanting to know how I stacked up, but it was still a challenge. Anybody—any *animal*—reacts to a challenge.

"The one on the end here has plenty of room for

us to watch," Garrett said. He'd been wearing his gear to watch Daniello fight, and Welsh had strapped on his harness as we left Room Twelve.

I walked over to the machine and switched it on. For the time being I left it set wherever the last guy had used it. I brought my gear live.

I was actually tenser about this than I had been to fight Walters and Camm for real. I guess that was because I'd had more time to think about this than I had when Camm's boat suddenly landed beside me on Dewbranch.

The first opponent was a hairy man wearing roughly stitched sheepskins and rushing me with a club over his head. The unit must have been set on the bottom level. I stepped forward and thrust the image through the top of his breastbone before the club could land. He—it—vanished.

Garrett adjusted the level at the side of the machine. This time I faced a man in orange, his face concealed in a tight-fitting mask of the same color. I guided its first overhand stroke into the ground with my own weapon, but I felt the shock up the length of my arm.

I remembered what had happened to Daniello and cut backhand at the image's ankles. It jumped back but not quickly enough. I'd have taken the heel off a real human opponent. The image toppled backward and vanished.

"He hasn't used his shield yet," Welsh grumbled. Garrett made another adjustment.

I was facing a red warrior with a short-haired black and tan dog, rangy and dangerous looking. Buck was still in the stables. This wasn't anything like a fair fight, but that wasn't the point: Garrett and Welsh wanted to learn how good my equipment was—and how good I was as well. There was no guarantee that in a real fight I'd have Buck along or that he wouldn't be injured in the course of it.

Instead of rushing, I held myself ready. As I'd expected, my opponent used its dog's agility to shift suddenly to my right and drive home. If my shield hadn't been so handy I could never have presented it in time.

The shock jolted me backward, but I didn't go down. I cut at the image but its shield was too good for me to accomplish anything from off-balance.

The image came at me three more times, circling to my right before each rush. We'd almost made a full circle when the image made its fourth rush—this time shifting left.

I didn't have to turn much to bring my shield into position, and I thrust—not slashing—before the shock of contact. The image's shield sparkled brightly. It didn't fail completely, but the bottom third of its shimmering coverage went black.

The image fell back. Its cut hadn't made it through my shield any better than the previous three had done. I crouched forward a little, gasping through my mouth. My lungs were on fire. I waited for the image to attack again.

Garrett touched the practice machine again, this time switching it off. I continued to gasp where I was.

"I guess your kit'll do," Garrett said.

"Bloody *hell*," said Welsh. Then he said, "Let's go get something to eat. And drink. I definitely need a drink."

❖   ❖   ❖

Welsh was the second son of a big landowner on Richter, a place not a lot fancier than Beune was. His father had mortgaged the estate with the elder brother's agreement for the money to buy Welsh his equipment.

In exchange Welsh agreed never to come back to Richter. His brother already had three children, so the deal avoided a fight over succession rights whenever the landowner died.

Garrett's father was a wealthy merchant on Stahlfeld. He'd read the romances, same as I had, and he was just as set on being a Champion as I was. Garrett saw himself as being the center of a band of adoring women.

They were both solid fellows, guys I got along with and was glad to know. Given that I was on closer terms with them than anybody before except my mom and dad, I was really lucky in my roommates.

Welsh drank more than I thought was good for him. Garrett had a woman back to his room more nights than he didn't, and it was always a different woman. I'd have rather that neither of those things had happened, but I wasn't a priest or their mother. Dun Add was a big place with other customs than I'd learned on Beune. And if it came to that, Beune had its drunks and tomcats too.

I practiced on the machines in the morning. Then in the afternoon, I went out to the jousting ground—either with a roommate if one of them was up for it, or I'd just take Buck out myself and see what I could pick up on the field. There was usually another Aspirant who'd give me a match.

The practice machines were supposed to be exactly

like a real fight, but of course they weren't. People
were random. They sometimes did dumb stuff which a
machine never would. I was pressing one fellow when
he shut his eyes and charged with a roundhouse swing;
he was a lefty, too, and he'd have rung my bell good
if I hadn't flopped on my belly. I grabbed his ankle
and tripped him as he went by. I had my weapon in
his face when he rolled over.

Welsh and Garrett were pretty good. Welsh was
really better than that, but his equipment was an
anchor around his neck. Not near as bad as the gear
I'd brought to Dun Add the first time, but the best
he could find on Richter wasn't good enough for the
Hall of Champions. His shield was decent, but his
weapon couldn't have damaged my shield if I'd simply
stood there and let him hack at it.

That wouldn't have done me any good, of course.
I worked to divert each of his strokes with my own
weapon. This was easiest when we were using our
dogs—Welsh had a black and white collie, a nice
dog—and I could use Buck's movement tracking sense,
but doing that a lot taught me what a dog looks for.
That didn't give me the quickness that I had when
Buck's brain was in charge, but I still had an edge
on the warriors I was fighting.

I tried to teach my roommates to do the same
thing, but they didn't understand what I was talking
about. I wondered if maybe it had something to do
with me being a Maker too, though I didn't see any
connection myself.

One afternoon the three of us had finished our
series of bouts and were about ready to go in and
shower, when a large troupe came down from the

castle. They weren't just warriors; there were attendants and also women dressed as fancy as the ones
I'd seen in the Lady's Court.

When I squinted, I was pretty sure that Lady
Jolene herself was among them. She was on the arm
of the black-haired warrior who'd spoken to me when
Guntram introduced me to the Consort.

"Say, let's watch," Welsh said. "The Champions don't
often spar where such as we can see them."

"God, what I'd give to be one of them," Garrett
said reverently. I was about to agree when he turned
to me and added, "If you're a Champion, you can have
any woman you see, you know? You just point your
finger and she follows you right into bed."

"Surely not!" I said.

"It's the truth, kid," Welsh said. "I'm not saying that's
what all Champions do, but all of 'em *could* do it."

"Bloody few don't!" Garrett said. "I mean, it stands
to reason, doesn't it? I mean, the women want it, don't
they? It gives them bragging rights to be sleeping
with a Champion."

"Look, let's stop talking about this, can we?" I said.
"We're talking about the men that law and civilization
rest on and about *ladies*!"

"Kid, there's a big difference between a hero and
a saint," said Garrett. "There's some Champions just
as chaste as you are, I grant you. But not all by a
long way."

"Even Lord Clain out there," Welsh said, gesturing
to the warriors pairing off on the field. "He's the one
in red. You saw who he was with when they came
down?"

He meant the black-haired man I'd seen in the

Lady's Court, the one who'd impressed me. "That was Lord Clain?" I said. "I believe he escorted the Consort herself, didn't he?"

"You're bloody well told he did," Garrett said. "Well, he's with her in private too. Everybody knows, but nobody says anything because Jon doesn't say anything."

"The husband's always the last to know," said Welsh.

"Naw, it's not that," said Garrett. "He knows, but he doesn't dare to say anything. Clain's as much the rock of the Commonwealth as Jon himself is—or Louis. They started this together, reuniting Here under one leader. Jon'd be lost without Clain's arm to steady him."

"Come on, Buck," I said. He and I headed back to the castle. My roommates didn't follow, though I heard Garrett call Welsh back. That was the right thing to do.

I'd really wanted to watch the Champions joust, but I needed to settle my head now. Settle my stomach, really. What I'd heard made me sick.

I put Buck in the stables and found an attendant—it was Heckert, as it chanced—to guide me to Guntram's room. Guntram didn't ask questions but he found me a piece—the image projector that'd been in my pile—to work on to my heart's content.

The artifact completely soaked up all my concentration; I even made a little headway. I was tired enough to fall asleep right there on Guntram's floor if I'd let myself, but I went down to Room Twelve.

My roommates didn't say anything about the discussion the next morning—or later. And *I* sure didn't.

CHAPTER 18

Proper Behavior

Me and my roommates came out the south passage from the castle, heading to the jousting ground with our dogs. Welsh had been telling us about an officer in the army who might be willing to sell his weapon.

I didn't figure gear owned by a soldier was going to be much of a step up from what Welsh already had, but I kept my mouth shut. If it made Welsh happy to think that there was a practical way out of his problem, I didn't see any benefit—to me, him, or the world—in dashing his hopes.

There were benches along the path here. The woman sitting on one stood up as we approached, stroking the tortoise-shell cat in the crook of the other arm.

It was—she was—Lady May.

"Lord Pal?" May called. "I wonder if I might borrow you for the afternoon?"

"Ah . . . ?" I said, looking from Garrett to Welsh.

"Go ahead, kid," Welsh said, clapping me on the

shoulder. "We can get along without you knocking us black and blue for an afternoon, and you *sure* don't need the practice."

"If you turn your back on luck like that," Garrett said, "we'll throw your traps out into the hall. Even if it takes both of us to do it."

"Thanks, guys," I said. I clucked to Buck as I peeled off toward May.

"Hello, May," I said. "Is there anything you want?"

"I was hoping you'd carry flowers back for me after we visit the Lady's garden," May said. "It's not far up the Road from here. And—"

She looked sidelong at me.

"—I was hoping you'd be a little more enthusiastic when you saw me."

"Oh, I'm sorry, ma'am," I said as we walked through the trees on the way to landingplace. "It's just that the Aspirants' Tournament starts in two days and that's all any of us have been thinking of for the past week. Us Aspirants."

"So," May said. "Are you worried about your chances, then?"

We'd reached landingplace and were heading toward the Road. The hawkers ignored us, but Maggie was standing in the hatch of my boat. I waved but broke eye contact by looking toward May again. She was in pale blue today with rings of honeysuckle in bloom embroidered around the throat, sleeves, and hem of the frock.

"Not exactly worried, ma'am," I said. "But unless I finish in the top quarter, I won't be allowed to challenge for a place in the Hall of Champions."

"What are your scores on the machines, Pal?" May

said. "Fifty percent is required to enter the tournament, I believe."

"Yes, ma'am," I said.

"Yes, *May*," she said. "Unless you want me to go back to calling you Lord Pal."

"I don't want that, May," I said. I decided it wasn't bragging if I just answered her question. "I'm averaging about eighty-five percent on foot, ninety-seven percent if I'm with Buck. But the machines aren't the same as fighting real people."

We stepped onto the Road. I switched my perceptions to Buck's and the russet stems—the brush fringing the Road here looked like a stand of sumac to me—went gray-brown but became a lot sharper.

"I'm sure they're not," May said. We were so close together that I didn't have any problem hearing her. "But I'm also sure that you're not in serious risk of not qualifying."

I laughed. "May, I'm likely worrying too much," I said, "but that's the better way to be. Anyhow, it's probably a good idea for me to take a break this afternoon."

We took a narrow branching to the right—so narrow that I hadn't noticed it when Buck and me had first hiked to Dun Add. Parts of the Road narrowed where they weren't used and could even just about close up, though a dog could always find where the Road had been. Squeezing through a crack, which I'd done a lot of times while hunting for artifacts, was uncomfortable but you didn't take your life in your hands the way you did when you ventured into the Waste.

This was just a short branching before May led

me out into a garden facing the sea. The flowers—
poppies and hollyhocks that I recognized—were in
beds bordered by pieces of the gray limestone that
made up the bare rocks of the headlands to left and
right. The water of the bay beneath us was blue-white
with choppy little waves.

I could see the edge of the Waste forming the
horizon to the left and ahead of us. It was about the
prettiest place I'd seen since I'd left home, so I said so.

May beamed, making her even prettier than she
was other times. "You like it, then?" she said. "Here,
let's sit down and you can tell me about your home."

I hadn't more than noticed the six-sided gazebo to
the right of where we'd left the Road. There were
wicker couches on each side so that you could always
be in the sun or in the shade, depending on how
warm a day it was.

May sat in the shade; from her floppy hat and how
white her skin was, she didn't like the sun. I do, so
I sat two angles away where the light fell on me but
I could face her without it being in my eyes.

"Do you take care of all this yourself?" I asked. Buck
was sniffing about the flower beds and occasionally
lifting his leg at a border; I hoped that was all right.

"No, there're a gardener and his assistant," May
said, "but they won't be here today. Nobody will but
us. I asked Jolene's permission to bring you here. It's
really her private place, you see."

"Well, it's a nice one," I said. I thought about
what my roommates had said about the Consort and
Lord Clain.

I guess that showed on my face, because May said,
"Pal, is something wrong?"

"No, no," I said. "I was just thinking, well, of home." Which was kinda true, since I'd been thinking about how different customs in Beune were from what I was learning about Dun Add.

"Tell me about your parents," May said, leaning toward me just a little. Her cat was curled up on a bench across from her. Buck wandered back to me and lay down.

"Well, they weren't exactly my parents," I said. This wasn't something I talked about much but, well, I did with May. "I always thought they were, but five years ago Mom told me I'd come to her and Dad when I was just a couple weeks old. They'd had a boy but he was stillborn, so they took me as a gift from God."

I shrugged. "They couldn't have been better parents to me," I said. "They just couldn't. I never knew who my real parents were, and I don't care."

"You are a romantic fellow!" May said. I thought for a flash that she was laughing at me, but I wasn't being fair. She just thought about the world that way.

"I don't know about that," I said. "I'm still a farmer from Beune."

"*And* a Maker," May said. "*And* a warrior."

"Well, those things too, I guess," I said. I got up and walked to the nearest flower bed. It was full of red poppies. "What are you thinking of carrying back to the Consort, May?"

"Nobody's expecting us back any time soon," May said. "Come and sit by me. You need to relax, Pal."

She patted the couch beside her. Then, grinning, she tugged the scooped neckline of her dress down to bare her left breast.

I turned around, feeling my face color. "May, I'd really rather not!" I said toward the empty sea.

I heard the couch squeak as May hopped to her feet. Her cat gave a little squeak.

"Well, you're a *fine* man!" she said in a voice that cut like a drill. "Is it boys you want? I think Rene in the wine warehouse handles that sort of thing!"

"May, please don't," I said. I'd squeezed my eyes shut. "Please."

"Or you're a farm boy, aren't you?" she said. "If I threw on a sheepskin and went 'Baa' would you like me better?"

This was such a small node that there really wasn't any place I could go to get away from that voice, but I walked down the slope toward the headland beyond the gardens. The Consort must've had topsoil carried in for the planting beds. Buck whined beside me, wondering what was going on.

After May stopped shrilling at me, I waited for a moment and looked around. She and her cat were gone. I waited a little longer, then clucked to Buck and headed back.

I thought of taking an armload of flowers but decided not to. I didn't want to see May again; at least not any time soon.

CHAPTER 19

The Tournament

They'd rung a gong at six in the morning, but by then all the seventy of us qualified Aspirants were in the refectory eating whatever we each thought was a good idea. I had a plate of scrambled eggs, but I left the bacon in the serving tray.

I got Buck and straggled down to the jousting ground. I knew some of the guys around me, but nobody talked much. I just wanted it to be over. I'd been right to eat something, but the eggs were bouncing around in my stomach. Buck was edgy too, but he was probably getting it from me.

A big tent was set up at each corner of the jousting ground. A pair of Champions—not clerks, as I'd expected—were handing out colored wooden chits with numbers on them as Aspirants came down the path from the castle. I got a green one with a 4 on it. Others got white, blue, and red.

"Green's the far side of the field, to the right,"

said the man who handed me the chit. He took the next one off the table behind him. I trudged toward the distant tent, feeling very alone. Reaching down, I rubbed Buck behind the ears.

There were already three Aspirants in the tent. There were chairs and a table with pitchers of water.

Another Champion was in charge—this time somebody I knew, Morseth, who'd backed me in my first fight with Easton. I didn't figure he'd remember me, but when I walked in he smiled and said, "Good to see you again, kid. I hear you've got better hardware this time."

"Yes sir," I said, "but that wouldn't be hard, would it?"

I took out my gear and handed first the shield, then the weapon, to Morseth to look at while the others in the tent watched us bitterly. To them, I was one of the Elect. In my own head, I was the kid from Beune about to face warriors from more sophisticated parts of Here. Just about everywhere was more sophisticated than Beune.

I suppose both sides were right. In a few minutes, though, it wouldn't matter who you knew or where you were from. The jousts were one on one.

A bell rang from some distance away. Morseth stepped to the door in the front side of the tent and looked out. The bell rang again and Morseth waved his right hand high overhead, then turned back to us. About ten of us were gathered in the tent now, each clutching a numbered chit.

"Okay," Morseth said. "We're getting started a little early today since there's people ready in each tent."

"But we're not supposed to start until the seven

o'clock gong!" said the fellow holding Number 1. I'd seen him around but I didn't know his name.

"Yeah, we're starting early, I said," Morseth said with a frown. "This way—"

"I'll go," I said, loud enough that it surprised me. I held out my chit.

"Suits me, kid," said Morseth, taking Number 4 from me and jotting something down on the writing pad which hung from the side pole near the door. "You fight the guy from the white tent, that's straight back toward the castle. Reaves is standing where you'll meet."

"Right," I said. I slipped out as quick as I could. I wanted so bad to get this over! I was afraid that Number 1 was going to change his mind and try to replace me, although I doubt Morseth would've let him if he did.

Buck hopped out in front. When I called him he made a quick circle around me before he came back to my side. He'd been jumpy in the tent with many other dogs and nervous men, but now he was excited.

My opponent was trudging toward me, wearing blue and accompanied by a black hound with white paws. When fighters' shields are on, the other fellow's features are too blurred to identify.

I was in green today. I hadn't seen many of the Aspirants in green, though I don't suppose it mattered if I got confused with the fellow I was fighting. At the end of the bout, there wouldn't be any doubt.

Reaves nodded to me and backed away; I was a little ahead of my opponent. The circle chalked in the grass wasn't a ring that you lost points if you stepped out of. It was just so you knew where to start.

I stepped over the line and switched on my gear.

When blue stepped into the circle, I went straight for him.

Blue circled to his right. I went left and met him square. He cut at me from the side. I couldn't get my weapon around to block the stroke but I took it in the center of my shield and didn't feel much of a shock. I cut overhand at him. Circuits blew in his shield but it didn't fail completely; he back-pedaled.

I followed him fast. He paused and raised his weapon, but I got my own stroke in first. He'd dipped his shield a bit not to interfere with his swing. I brushed his weapon aside and landed pretty solid on his right shoulder. Even at twenty percent that was a hard crack. Blue dropped his weapon.

I backed away to let him pick the weapon up again. He bent and tried, but the fingers of his right hand wouldn't close. He tossed his shield down and backed, raising his left arm high. His right dangled.

I shut my shield off.

"Loser, to the Green tent!" Reaves said. "Winner, to the south side, you'll be reassigned."

Buck and I walked to the sideline where another champion and a number of spectators waited. I wasn't nervous anymore, but I was very tired, and there were three more of these to go through.

"Let's see your weapon," the Champion on the sidelines said. I took mine out and handed it to him. The power dial had a dot of color which would smear if I changed it from twenty percent. It had rubbed some in my pocket—I hadn't even thought of that after the bout—but the inspector just handed it back without comment.

"What's your number?" he asked. I didn't recognize him.

"Green 4," I said. Then I said, "I hope I didn't break his collarbone."

"Not your problem or mine," the Champion said. "You're in White group now." He pointed to the tent my opponent had come out of. "You'll be matched from Red next time."

The next bout was already under way. I didn't bother to watch it as we walked around the grounds to enter White tent from the back. The Aspirants inside clutching their first-round chits stared at me, but I ignored them except to nod to Garrett, who was waiting his bout. I drank water—it was that or wine; I'd have preferred ale if there'd been any, but wine wasn't a possibility for me here.

The Champion in charge gave me a triangular white chit marked 1. That seemed kind of silly because I'd just hand it back to him when I went out to fight, but nobody was asking what I thought.

This wasn't an elimination tournament. Somebody who lost his first bout but won the next three could still qualify for an Admissions Bout against a Champion. The tournament allowed for the fact that any warrior could catch a bad break.

I'd done fine. I wasn't nervous anymore, but I was a little sick to my stomach. I wasn't sure this was what I wanted to be doing with my life. The romance that I'd dreamed of from books was fine, but the reality was pain and hurting other people. Garrett's dream of having any woman he wanted was at least something real.

I thought of May and felt even sicker.

I hadn't been paying attention to the fellows going out to fight or the ones coming in the back after their bouts. When I did, I realized that not everybody who'd been with me in the Green tent was now here in White. The original Number 1 wasn't here, to begin with.

There's injuries. Of course.

My first opponent, even if I hadn't broken his collarbone, wasn't in shape for another round. There'd be concussions and joint injuries, even at twenty percent.

A gong rang across the jousting ground. Everybody looked at the Champion in the tent with us.

He grinned back. "Second round," he said. "Who's Number 1?"

I patted Buck to rouse him and got up. "Where do I go?" I asked as I handed over my chit.

"Slant right instead of going straight ahead," the Champion said. "You've got the longer hike this time, but in the third round it'll be short."

"I don't mind the walk," I said. Buck and I headed toward the fellow coming from the Red tent. The man standing two-thirds of the way down was presumably the Champion who marked the chalked circle.

All I knew about my second opponent is that he hadn't been crippled in the first round. His tunic was red slashed over blue from the left shoulder to the right hip. From the way he came at me, it was long odds that he'd won his bout, though.

I met his rush shield to shield. He swung overhand. I blocked the blow with my weapon, but I was glad that we were so close. If he'd been able to take a longer swing, the shock would've been even worse than what I got—and that was bad enough.

He danced back and I cut at his ankles. He dodged back again, but lifted his weapon for another overhand swing. I didn't want that to happen—his weapon was bloody powerful—so I rushed him, thrusting for his face.

I didn't want to hurt Red-and-Blue which I certainly would if the thrust got home, but I was in a fight. I wouldn't cheat, but I meant to win.

He got his shield up in plenty of time, but sparks flew when my weapon hit it. He backed again but I kept coming, swinging this time at his shield. It wasn't nearly in a class with his excellent weapon.

Red-and-Blue was off-balance when he cut again for my head, and the dazzle of sparks as shield circuits failed had him on the edge of panic as well. His blow wasn't a patch on what I knew he could do, and he didn't react in time to block my chop at his left ankle.

He went down. His dog, a standard poodle, stood splay-legged between me and his master, barking furiously. I shut down and backed away.

"Winner to the sideline," said the Champion acting as referee. "Loser to the—say, can you get up, buddy?"

"I don't know," my opponent said. He was named Krause. I saw his face now that our shields were down. "I'll try."

He got onto all fours as I set off for the sideline, but when he tried to stand he couldn't put any weight on his left leg. He wobbled for a moment; then two attendants ran past me from the group at the sidelines and put his arms over their shoulders.

I'd put both my opponents out of the tournament. I hadn't meant to or wanted to, and Krause at least had had a real chance.

But then, so did I, and Krause's initial cut at my head would've put me down for the count—or worse. We were expected to do our best, and anybody who didn't was unfit to represent the Commonwealth.

"What was your number this time?" the Champion asked.

I grabbed a cup in my left hand, then put it down to fill it on the table from the water pitcher in my right. I'd been gripping my shield so hard that the muscles in the palm of my hand were threatening to cramp.

"Sir, I was White 1," I said. "I was Green 4 the first time."

"You're in Red Group now," the Champion said, gesturing. "And fighting Green."

"C'mon, Buck," I said. We set out for the tent he'd pointed to.

Welsh was in this tent, waiting for his second bout. We nodded but didn't speak as I got a round red 1.

I wondered if Welsh had won his bout. His shield wasn't as good as Krause's, but he didn't look beat up. He was really good when he was on, and maybe the guy he'd met didn't have any better equipment than Welsh did.

A gong rang. "Red 1," the Champion called. "You're up."

It hadn't seemed very long, but it must've been: the sun was at mid-sky when I walked out of the tent. I saw why the Champions had started as early as they could.

I wondered what would've happened if I'd dumped a pitcher of water over me to soak my tunic before I went out. I guess I could've asked, but I was afraid to do anything that might turn out to disqualify me after I'd come this far.

Buck and I reached the circle. The fellow walking kitty-corner toward us across the field had a black tunic. When he stepped into the circle I rushed him, same as I'd done the other times.

Black took a wild roundhouse swing while we were still too far apart. I let the stroke pass in front of me and gave him a thump across the shoulder-blades. He shouted and sprawled forward on his nose.

I backed away, horrified that I might've killed him even at twenty percent. I swear I think he may have come at me with his eyes shut. I'd cut across his tunic and blood was welling up from the flesh beneath.

The Champion refereeing the bout reached down and switched off the screaming Black's shield and weapon. "Bloody hell!" I heard the referee mutter.

Attendants ran up from the sidelines carrying a stretcher. Black had left himself completely wide open. *How in God's name had he managed to get this far in the process?*

"To the sidelines," the referee told me. He watched Black going off, lying on his face, and shook his head.

There were lots of spectators by now, many of them watching from under parasols and sitting on collapsible chairs and benches. Traders were selling snacks and drinks. Aspirant tournaments must be the major entertainment on Dun Add, even though the fighters' forms were shimmering blurs to those who didn't have viewing equipment.

There were even more people on the north side, nearer the palace, and many of those had shields or similar devices which allowed them to view the details of action while it was going on. Some were women of the court.

At the edge of the clump of bright tunics and pastel frocks was a tall figure in gray. I felt better knowing Guntram was watching. He'd helped me so much, and not for any reason I could imagine.

I happened to recognize the Champion at the sideline this time as Lord Gismonde, but we'd never so much as exchanged words. Besides Morseth and Reaves, the only Champion I'd spoken to was Lord Clain—in the Consort's Chamber. I hadn't known his name when Guntram was showing me around.

"Number?" said Gismonde.

"Red 1," I said, and he jotted it down.

"Okay, kid," Gismonde said. "You're Pal of Beune, right? You're to go back to the Red tent this time. They're restructuring because of the casualties. Tell Hopper you're to be Red 12 and you'll meet the fellow coming from Blue Group. Got it?"

"Yes sir," I said, walking along the sidelines toward the tent I'd come from. I could see somebody from there slanting across the field to the chalked circle. He must be the next number of the group I'd started with, but I couldn't remember what he looked like.

I entered at the back of the tent and said, "I'm to be Red 12."

The tent manager turned when I spoke. "Are you indeed?" he said. "Did they tell you who you'd be fighting?"

"Somebody from Blue," I said. "There's been a lot of casualties, Lord Gismonde said."

"That's the truth if I ever heard it!" Hopper said.

"There's been more crips this run than there was the past two together."

If I'd been more alert I'd have worried about what was obviously an unusual situation. As it was, I just felt flat. I hadn't taken a single hard blow, and none of the three bouts had even taken very long.

Buck was doing fine. He slurped water from the tub beside the back entrance, then flopped down by my side when I sat in the first empty seat I came to.

"Red 12!" the manager called. "That's you, Pal."

I hopped up. Gismonde and now Hopper both knew my name.

"Blue group is straight opposite," Hopper said from the doorway, pointing. "This is your last bout, so make it good."

"Yessir," I said. I was looking forward to the tournament being over. I sure hoped that my last opponent was as puny as the third one had been, but I knew I couldn't expect that.

The big fellow coming toward me with his shield on wore white. His dog was a red setter. He was so clean that I wondered if he'd changed his tunic in the course of the tournament: that white would show any contact with the ground, let alone a blow.

Of course nobody had hit me either. Well, each bout was a separate test.

White and I reached the circle at the same time. I rushed as usual. White swung down from my left. He didn't rush, but he stepped into the blow. I saw it coming and met it with my own weapon.

I felt like I'd been hit by a building. I knew how good my shield was, but that stroke would have blown the shield's circuits if it'd hit squarely.

I shifted to my right, making sure that my right arm hadn't gone numb. *Bloody hell!*

White came after me. Well, I'd come to fight, not run away. I stepped forward and swung down just like we were each other's mirror.

White took the stroke with his weapon, spewing sparks in all directions. I'd hit as hard as I could and it didn't seem like his arm and weapon had given at all.

He thrust at my face but I ducked below the edge of my shield. I'd seen the thrust coming—Buck had; it was like each of my opponents shouted what they were planning before they did it—but I hadn't tried to turn it with my weapon. Instead I cut at White's ankles the way I had with my first opponent today.

White got the edge of his shield in the way of my stroke. There was a great blast of sparks, but nothing like what happened where he stabbed at mine. I hadn't been worried about a short thrust with the two of us standing close together, but he nearly penetrated my shield.

I backed, raising my shield slightly. It might have taken permanent damage from that thrust. When White stepped toward me, I thought he wobbled—I'd come very close when I went for his ankle before. Maybe even contact, I thought.

I hacked low at his shield, then slid my weapon down for the real stroke—again at his left foot. White went up in the air—dunno if there was anything wrong with his left foot, but it sure didn't keep him from jumping with it. I carved a smoldering gouge in the sod while trying to throw myself backward and getting my shield still higher to cover me from his down-slash in response.

This time the sparks as his weapon met the edge of my shield weren't as gorgeous as they'd been before—because I blacked out. He'd rung my bell good.

I was seeing figures dancing. They were reddish, and I wasn't sure they were human.

I closed my eyes and groaned. I wondered if I was dead and in Purgatory. I hadn't lived a bad life, but I couldn't claim it'd been a really good one either. I hadn't paid much attention to the life I was living—I'd just lived it and left religion to the priest.

"Good evening, Pal," Guntram said. "I hope you're feeling better."

I sat up faster than I should have, but after a moment of wanting to throw up it was all right. "I've got a ways better to go," I croaked. I needed something to drink. "That was quite a crack I took."

I was in Guntram's workroom. I'd been lying on his healing bed. The light in the room came from figures of light dancing in the air in the middle of the room.

"This is the projector you and I have been working on," Guntram said, following my eyes. "I thought it would be a mild illumination and better than something brighter while you were recovering. Would you like something more now?"

"No, this is fine," I said. "But do you have anything to drink?"

"Oh, sorry, of course," Guntram said. He turned to a side-table where a carafe and cups sat. There were also covered dishes and, to my amazement, a bud vase with a white rose in it.

Guntram returned with a cup of what turned out to be wine. That was fine. If it put me to sleep now, so much the better. I slurped a mouthful in and sloshed it around my cheeks and tongue before swallowing.

"There's..." Guntram said as he lifted the cover of the larger dish, "a chicken also."

"Maybe in a bit," I said. I touched my scalp; it was tender, but there wasn't matted blood as I'd expected. "Ah, Guntram?"

"Yes?"

"I don't want to sound like I'm making excuses, but is there any chance the fellow I fought in the last round had his weapon set higher than twenty percent power? Because I know how good my own gear is and he just, well..."

I touched my scalp again.

"No, Pal," Guntram said, moving directly in front of me and meeting my eyes. "Your opponent's equipment was set at twenty percent. He had very good equipment, however, probably the best there is Here. You were fighting Lord Clain."

"What!"

I shouldn't have shouted. At least I hadn't jumped to my feet, the way I'd started to do. I drank more wine, holding the cup with both hands.

"You'd already been approved for the Admissions Tournament on the basis of your first three wins," Guntram said. "Clain wanted to see if you were really as good as you'd appeared to be from where he was watching. He changed into a neutral tunic and borrowed the dog of an injured competitor to determine that himself."

A realization hit me harder than Clain's weapon had. "Then I've already had my Admissions bout with a Champion," I said. "And I lost."

"Scarcely," said Guntram. "When you're completely recovered, you'll have an ordinary Admissions bout. The leading Champions never fight in those; you'll be facing someone newly admitted."

He smiled. "From what Lord Clain says," he added, "you shouldn't have much trouble. And he apologizes. He says that if he'd known how good you were, he wouldn't have put himself in a position where he might have to seriously injure you to avoid injury himself."

I didn't know what to think, let alone say. I swallowed more wine, then said, "I guess I'll have some of that chicken now, Guntram."

I ate, thinking about the rose in the bud vase.

CHAPTER 20

Next

The Admissions Tournament was set for two weeks' time. With Guntram's agreement I spent the delay in his workroom rather than going down to Room Twelve again. After a couple days I resumed practice on the machines.

I was ... uncomfortable, I guess, with the thought of sparring with people, with my fellows. I'd hurt my first three opponents pretty badly, and I was lucky that Clain hadn't killed me. If I'd been just a touch slower in getting my shield up, or if Clain's earlier thrust had been a little higher so that his cut had met the weakened portion of the field, he'd have split my skull. Guntram assured me that the healing couch couldn't bring the dead back to life.

It wasn't that I was afraid to get hurt or to hurt—to kill—somebody if I meant to. But sparring for practice meant that I could be crippling the fellows I'd been eating dinner with or playing checkers.

For relaxation, I worked on Ancient artifacts, whatever Guntram offered me. I was partial to the image projector. Now that Guntram had started working on it, his repairs gave me clues about how the Ancients had designed it. I could work with that—not fast, but I got faster as I did more and learned more. I was able to sharpen the dancers and smooth their movements.

The figures had the same general layout as people, but they really *weren't* people. Which made me wonder if the Ancients were people, as I'd always assumed, or creatures with fine scales and stripes of russet on beige like the dancers.

I didn't work on my shield, though Clain had damaged the top of it pretty bad. Guntram was repairing it. He said that if I liked he'd ask Louis to work on it instead, but I trusted Guntram before I'd trust any other Maker. Louis might be the best there was for arms the way Guntram said, but Guntram was my friend.

I went off for walks up the Road alone except for Buck. Whenever we passed the track to the Consort's Garden, I wondered if I'd see anybody coming out of it. I never did.

On the day of the Admissions Tournament I had scrambled eggs again for breakfast. It'd worked out the first time—except for meeting Clain, of course, and that wasn't the fault of breakfast—and I didn't want to change anything I'd done then.

The way it was set up was two tents opposite each other in the middle of the long sides of the field. The Aspirants—only ten of us out of the seventy who'd qualified for the earlier tournament—were on the south. The Champions we'd be facing had a tent on

the north, but most of them stood along the sidelines, chatting with friends and spectators.

Garrett had qualified also. I hadn't really chatted with him since the Aspirants' Tournament, so I walked over to him now.

Before we could speak, the Champion acting as manager called, "Garrett, you're up first."

Garrett and I broke eye contact, but I followed him out the front of the tent. If the Champions who were testing us could do that, I supposed that we could. Anyway, I wanted to see how Garrett did.

Garrett was in red today; his opponent was blue. Blue was a big man, but so was Garrett. The bout started slowly and never really picked up. Blue kept advancing on Garrett, blocking each stroke and counterstriking. Garrett took every counterstroke on his shield, but he was having to back away.

Blue kept following. This contest was fought at forty percent. Garrett didn't start really blocking Blue's strokes until his shield was on the verge of failing. Blue swung *hard* down at Garrett's head; Garrett got his shield up, but the circuits overloaded at the impact.

Sparks fountained around both men, but Garrett stumbled backward and fell on his back. He tossed his weapon to the sod beside him. He probably had some bad burns in his left hand.

The winner backed away and shut down.

I sat down in the grass; Buck lay down also and stuck his big head in my lap. I rubbed his ears absently.

I felt sorry for Garrett, limping off the field toward the castle, but I was really thinking about the fight itself. Blue's gear was a little better than Garrett's, his shield at any rate, but that wasn't the real difference.

Blue had spared his own shield and repeatedly attacked the same point on Garrett's. By the time Garrett realized what was happening, it was too late for him.

I know it's easier to follow tactics when you're watching from the sidelines than when somebody's trying to whack you on the head, but it's something you've got to be able to do if you want to be a Champion. Garrett hadn't done it.

I kept sitting with Buck while the rest of our group fought. Mostly the Aspirants lost, as expected, but a few won their place. There were a hundred and fifty seats in the Hall of Champions, but from what Baga told me—I'd never been through the doors, but all the servants talked—only eighty-three were occupied.

I wasn't really watching bouts. Mostly I was thinking about the way the Commonwealth worked now that I was here in the middle of it. The thing that I hadn't realized from the books I read on Beune was that the people in Dun Add—in Jon's court, in the Hall of Champions, *all* of them—were human beings, like me and my neighbors.

Some of the folks here were smarter than we were. Guntram was about the smartest person there was, it seemed to me. Jon and Louis and I guess Clain, they had bigger dreams than anybody on Beune ever would.

But they were people. They did human things and made human mistakes. Just like us, just like me.

"Number Ten, you're up!"

I jumped to my feet. The manager's shout had already roused Buck; he was getting up also.

"Right!" I called. I took my shield and weapon from my pockets and we started for the chalked circle. I didn't switch my gear on until I was almost there. We entered the ring in a gray expanse in which the referee standing to the side was sharp but everything else—grass and the distant tents and spectators—was a shadow.

I was in green as before. My opponent was in yellow and white stripes, a pattern I recalled seeing among the audience when Jon was giving judgment. I hadn't known who that man was, and it needn't have been the same one who faced me now.

I went straight for him. He responded, but there was enough hesitation that I think he would've preferred a more cautious grappling. Our shields met and shimmered. I—Buck—saw him start to swing down at me. My weapon met his and shocked him back.

Yellow-and-White's shield was at least as good as mine, but I knew from the softness when our weapons clashed together that his wasn't as good as his shield—or my weapon.

That's what I went after, striking for his weapon rather than his head or his shield. Yellow-and-White didn't see what I was doing at first, trying to counterstrike after each of my strokes. I took his blows on my shield and kept slicing at the edge of light.

When he did figure out my plan, it flustered him. He started refusing his weapon and trying to push me back with his shield. That left his leading foot open. At forty percent power I could've taken it off—the left one at the time—if I'd been willing to, but instead I ripped a shallow gouge in the turf just short of his toes.

That left *me* open if Yellow-and-White had been in position instead of trying to save his weapon. He'd jumped back from my stroke—it wouldn't have been in time—and he was off-balance when he finally swung at me.

I was ready for him. I took his blow on my shield and was bringing my weapon around with all my strength to meet his as he withdrew it. His failed in a dazzle of green and blue.

I stepped back and shut down. My hands were both on the verge of cramping. I dropped my shield and weapon into my pockets without considering how hot they might be after that use. The weapon was warm against my right hipbone, but the cloth wasn't on the verge of charring. As for the shield, it hadn't even had a work-out.

I thought again of how lucky I was for Guntram's friendship...but also, I'd done what Garrett had not: I'd probed my opponent to find a weakness and then gone after it.

Yellow-and-White had a short brown beard and short hair. I stepped toward him and offered my hand. "I'm Pal of Beune," I said.

"Not this hand," he said. He managed a grin as he thrust out his left hand instead. He was holding his right up at shoulder height; when he turned it toward me, I saw he already had blisters on the palm.

We shook, left to left. "I'm Conrad," he said. "Bloody good job, kid. Clain told me to be careful, but I guess I wasn't careful enough."

People were coming out to join us including a medic and her assistant. They'd have ointments for the blisters. I didn't think either of us needed anything more.

"Very well done, Pal," said a voice at my side. I turned and saw Guntram.

"Sir!" I said. "Thank you so much!"

Guntram looked pleased, but he generally did. "The Enrollment Ceremony will be on Sunday," he said. "In four days. But even if I'm a little early, let me congratulate you now on becoming a Champion."

CHAPTER 21

Champion of Mankind

The great hall was like Jon's court but way bigger. It was on the north side of the castle, but it was freestanding and open to the sky. I guessed it held a couple thousand people, and it was near full when I glanced up at the ranks of seats behind me.

I wondered how many people lived in Beune. Probably not this many.

"Boy, I never saw so many people all together!" Baga said. "Folks from everyplace can watch, you know? It's not just Dun Add."

To hear him, the thought made him happy as could be. I agreed about how many people there were, but I was uncomfortable.

The usher with a short gilt baton had put me on a chair with plush cushions but no arms, one of three spaced in a row in front of the stage. The back of the stage was a huge thing, a glittering chrome wall

with fluted pillars and all sorts of carved figures on
the ledge at the top that rested on the pillars.

The figures probably meant something from history,
but I doubt I'd have known what they were even if I
could see them better. They were in bright sun; when
I looked up at them, all I saw was a broken glare.

I was wearing my red suit. It was Maggie's choice. I
agreed because she at least said she understood what was
right and nobody else I knew did. If I'd asked Guntram,
he'd have looked at me as blankly as if I'd been facing
a mirror. I suppose Garrett and Welsh might've had
opinions, but they'd never seemed to care much about
clothes when we were all in Room Twelve.

Baga and Maggie stood behind my chair, wearing
their own best clothes. That was a bleached white
tunic for Baga, while his wife had on a very pale pink
dress with white embroidery on the lapels and bodice.
Maggie's taste in clothes was *comfortable*. I guess that
was as good a reason as any to let her choose which
of my three suits I wore today.

There was a platform on top of the back of the
stage. I didn't know that till musicians with three
kinds of horns stepped out onto it. They were in
silver outfits, so it looked like a dozen of the carved
figures had climbed knee-high up above their fellows
and started playing music.

I'm not used to horns—people back home used
fiddles, and there was a harmonium in the church.
This blast of noise sure didn't make me wish I'd heard
more horn music, but it got people's attention and I
suppose that was the idea.

Jon and Jolene, his Consort, came in through a
curtain at the back of the stage that I'd thought was

solid metal. They were both in gold. They sat in the two gilt chairs at the front of the stage.

Jolene's hair was loose except for a thin gold fillet. It lay like a spill of white gold over the darker gleam of the fabric. She was the most beautiful woman I'd ever seen.

The horn music kept up. Clain and Louis came in side by side, Clain in red and white checks and Louis in white with a gold collar and cuffs. Clain stood just back of the Leader's chair while Louis took the same location to the Consort.

I wondered what Louis thought of this business. If Louis and Jon both really believed in spreading the Commonwealth the way Guntram said, then they must feel that this sort of pageant was part of the way to do it. Jon wouldn't have been here otherwise, and I bet that a Maker as skilled as Louis could've begged off too, even if the Leader wanted him to show himself.

More men were marching in pair by pair, the remainder of the top Champions. Morseth and Reaves, Mietes and Chun, Baran and Gismonde, Ronald and Wissing. The first two had helped me on my first visit to Dun Add, but the rest were barely more than names to me. I recognized the men who'd been managing the Aspirants' Tournament.

Besides the men standing with Jon, scores of additional Champions stood in front of the stage like a living curtain. They pretty much looked bored. At least I had a chair to sit in, probably because it wasn't time for us new enrollees to get attention.

"Oh, I wish my mother could see me now!" Maggie said, I suppose to Baga on my other side. "She'd be so proud!"

My mom and dad would've been proud to be here too, and my neighbors besides. They'd tell everybody they met that they knew me.

For myself, I'd rather have been working on the color projector up in Guntram's shop. Heck, I'd rather have been standing in the cold rain helping Gervaise lift his wagon out of a mudhole.

A priest came out behind the last pair of Champions and stood at the front of the stage. He was all in gold like the Leader and Consort. He raised his arms and started praying that God would bless the great work of reunification and would bless those who were carrying it out.

There was nothing in that that I'd really disagree with, though it seemed to me that the priest knew more about what God was thinking than seemed likely to me. Regardless, it was a reasonable thing to say at a time like this—if he'd stopped there.

He kept talking for another twenty minutes without coming up with anything new. Nothing that I heard, anyway; I'll admit that I was sorta nodding off before too long. I still don't know how he managed to keep his arms raised that long; mine would've gone numb long since.

The priest finally stopped. He turned and bowed to Jon, then walked off the back of the stage the way he'd come. Jon hadn't let him stay like Louis and the Champions did.

And Jolene was there too. May was probably somewhere up in the seats behind me, or maybe not.

Jon rose to his feet. "Citizens of the Commonwealth!" he said. "Fellow human beings!"

I was even more impressed by the way his words

carried here than I had been in the courtroom, which at least had a roof. I wondered if the woman from Bassai had designed them both.

"It is my duty and that of every human being to unite Mankind," Jon said. "Only in that way can we protect Mankind not only from the inhuman monsters of the Waste and of Not-Here but also from the monsters within ourselves."

He used a long pause to look around the ranks of seats above me. I wondered if he really was taking in the audience or if it was just an act. It maybe was real: Jon's expression glowed with faith, something I hadn't gotten from the priest in the twenty minutes he talked.

"I said that this is the duty of every one of us," Jon continued. "But there are certain ones who have dedicated their strength and lives to this duty. These are the Champions of Mankind, those standing before you. Three more are to be enrolled into their company on this day. I will now call them up beside me one at a time. Lord Selon!"

Selon got up from the chair to the right of mine and walked up the six steps to the level of the stage. He knelt before Jon.

Selon was my age, but he was the son of a rich landowner here on Dun Add. He was a handsome fellow and his equipment was first rate. We'd eaten at the same table in the Refectory a number of times and I'd found him pleasant and cheerful, a thoroughly good fellow.

Becoming a Champion had been as much his dream as it was mine. Unlike me, Selon had known exactly what it required and how to go about it.

Jon stepped forward and hung a medallion around Selon's neck by a red and gold ribbon. "Rise, Champion," Jon said, "and face some of the citizens you are now sworn to protect!"

Selon did. He was a good-looking fellow, but right now he was strained and white, like he was on the scaffold instead of being enrolled in the Company of Champions.

"Lord Selon," Jon said. "Is your property sufficient to support you as a Champion of Mankind?"

"Yes, Leader," Selon said, but I only knew that because I was watching his lips.

"Then what first duty would you have me lay on you?" Jon said.

"Leader..." Selon said. He'd gotten his voice back. "You recently ordered that two landowners on Portland stop their warring and come to Dun Add for you to judge their quarrel. I ask that you send me to Portland to enforce your will."

"Granted, Lord Selon," Jon said. "Meet with Lord Clain, my chancellor, after the ceremony and discuss how you are to proceed with the business. For now, remain here on the stage."

Jon gestured to his right. Selon obediently crossed the front of the stage to stand beside Wissing.

"Master Deltchev, come forward!" Jon said. The man at the far end of our short row got up and climbed the steps to the stage. He bowed as Selon had.

Deltchev was in his forties at the youngest. He'd been a member of the Army at one time, but he'd gone off as a soldier for hire early on. After decades of fighting he'd gotten decent equipment—and a great deal of experience using it, as well as scars.

We had sparred several times as Aspirants. Detchev's gear was at best serviceable, but he was a remarkably canny fighter. I'd learned something new every time we fought, and I generally came out of the bout with bruises and often a pressure cut.

Jon hung the medallion on Deltchev's neck and told him to rise and face the audience. "Master Deltchev," Jon said. "Is your property sufficient to keep you as a Champion of Mankind?"

"No, Leader, it is not," Deltchev said in a gruff, determined voice. He sounded just like the man I'd known in the Aspirants' Hall. "But if you'll appoint me to command a squadron of the regular army, the pay will keep me fine. I know the work and I know the men."

"Granted, Master Deltchev," Jon said. "Talk to Lord Clain after the ceremony. I believe Third Squadron requires a permanent head."

Deltchev moved to the Leader's left. Jon looked at me and said, "Pal of Beune, come forward!"

I'd been afraid it was going to be "Lord Pal," which really embarrassed me. I got up fast and almost stumbled. I'd thought I was ready for this, but I wasn't. At least I didn't trip on the steps.

I knelt in front of Jon with my head bowed. I felt the touch of the silk, then the weight of the medallion. Though it was less than two inches across, the gold was heavier than I'd expected.

"Rise, Champion, and face your fellow humans!"

I got up and turned. I couldn't see any individuals out there, just a blur of people. The sun was in my eyes.

"Pal of Beune!" Jon said from behind me. "Is

your property sufficient to keep you as a Champion of Mankind?"

I'd been going over and over that question in my mind ever since I learned how things worked after you were made Champion. The Leader appointed new Champions as governors of one or more nodes within the Commonwealth to collect the taxes and only pass on half, keeping the rest for themselves. Depending on where it was, that could be quite a lot of money. The governor could hire a vicar to do the work and use the rest of the money to keep lodgings in Dun Add instead of living in the Hall.

The thing is, I didn't want to rule anybody, and I *sure* didn't want to take money for doing nothing. I had more than half the money from Frances left. I was living in the palace, so my only real expense was paying Baga.

"Thank you, Leader," I said, "but my property is sufficient."

"What first duty would you have me lay on you, Champion?"

"Leader," I said, "I've dreamed of protecting Mankind from incursions from the Waste. Send me to a place on the Marches where enemies are threatening, so I can protect people who're distant from Dun Add."

"Granted, Pal of Beune," Jon said. "Talk to my Chancellor after the ceremony and we'll find you a suitable region. For the moment, step to the side."

I moved over to stand beside Selon. I was wrung out as badly as I'd been after three bouts in the Aspirants' Tournament. But it was over now.

I almost started laughing. *I've gotten everything I've dreamed of. Now what?*

Jon faced the crowd. "Citizens of the Commonwealth!" he said. "In celebration of what we have done here this day, please eat and drink your fill from the tables set up behind this building!"

There were lots of cheers, but the shuffle of boots heading out the doors to left and right of the stage quickly drowned them out. Ushers at the doors were making sure people didn't pile up. There must be a lot of planning that goes into a business like this.

I turned to Lord Selon and clasped arms with him. "Good luck to you, sir," I said. "If anybody can talk sense into a couple of quarrelsome lordlings, it's you."

"And good luck to you, Pal," Selon said, looking me up and down. "You'll be out in the middle of nowhere by yourself, and you'll need all your considerable wits to survive."

He pursed his lips and added, "You have large holdings on Beune, then?"

"No," I said, smiling. Selon's family lands were probably greater than all the farms on Beune put together. "But I don't need much to keep me. Especially in the Marches, you know."

Deltchev had been talking with Lord Clain. He finished and left by the back of the stage with one of the clerks who'd descended on Clain as soon as Jon dismissed the audience; that was another sign of the organization that folks in Dun Add took for granted.

Selon nodded to me and took his turn with Clain. I looked back and saw Baga and his wife waiting by my chair. I wasn't going to need him further today, so I waved him toward the nearer of the lines moving toward the banquet area. Maggie gripped him by the shoulder and shook her head firmly.

I smiled. There was such a crush at the doors that it probably didn't matter anyway. I wondered if there'd be ale on offer, though I knew Baga preferred wine.

It was my turn with the chamberlain. He looked up from the several sheets of information that a clerk had just handed him.

Clain was very powerful close-up. I've known bigger men—and Clain wasn't actually taller than I am—but he radiated power. I found him more overwhelming than he'd seemed when we'd fought. Then it was me against a very skilled, very powerful warrior. When he looked at me now, I felt like a worm in a chicken yard.

"So, Pal . . ." he said. "An unusual background. And an unusual choice of assignment, too. Do you think you'll find glory on the Marches, then?"

"That's where I come from, sir," I said. "I don't expect glory. But I know there's places where things aren't as peaceful as they generally are on Beune, so that's where I thought I ought to go."

I thought of Deltchev asking to be put back in the army, just at a higher rank. We were both asking to go home, I guess.

"As it chances . . ." Clain said, looking at a different sheet, "that's quite true. Though I'm not sure exactly what you've let yourself in for. Possibly nothing, of course."

His eyes met mine again. "You have a boat of your own, this says?"

"Yes sir," I said. "It was sort of an accident."

"Well, it'll save you a lot of time on the Road getting there," Clain said. "It's the region around Catermole. We'd like you to spend a month or so there, just patrolling. Within the past generation the region was

Not-Here. It only returned to the Commonwealth a year or two ago, and there seems to be a lot of, well, unease. Also two assessors have disappeared."

I wondered what it meant to "return to the Commonwealth." To start paying taxes, I suppose. I could imagine that causing "unease" on Beune. I didn't think that'd involve disappearing Jon's tax men, but Beune is more laid-back than a lot of places are.

"I can talk to people," I said, "and see what the Roads are like there."

I'd heard of Catermole, though I couldn't recall anybody from Beune actually going there. Still, it can't have been *very* far from home.

"Do that," Clain said. "Toledana here—"

He nodded to the clerk who'd given him the file.

"—will give you guidance to get your boat to Catermole. I don't know how that works myself."

"Neither do I, sir," I said, "but my boatman's there by where I was sitting and he can talk to her."

I nodded to Toledana, since she was right here. "Ma'am."

"Well, that's all I have for you," Clain said. "When you've figured out what's going on there—or that nothing is—you come back here and report. Understand?"

"Yes sir," I said. There didn't seem much to understand.

Clain turned and walked over to Jon, bending beside his chair so that they could talk quietly. I said to Toledana, "Ma'am? If you'll come here, I'll point out Baga, my boatman. I'd appreciate it if you'd work out the course with him."

We walked to the edge of the stage. I pointed with my whole arm toward Baga. He waved back and started walking toward the stage. The clerk walked briskly down the steps toward him.

I turned, wondering if I ought to thank the Leader or something like that. The woman kneeling beside the Consort's chair to talk to her straightened and walked over to me. She was May.

"Good morning, Pal," she said. "Are you excited to be going on your first mission?"

"I guess I'm mostly worried that I won't do it right," I said.

Clain's instructions were about as simple as they come, but if I didn't find anything it didn't mean that I'd succeeded—just that I hadn't found something. It might still be there, whatever it was. Bandits, likely enough, or maybe even a gang of local farmers who figured they needed what would otherwise go in taxes more than they needed to be part of the Commonwealth.

I wasn't worried about something happening to me. I was worried about failing.

"You're a clever fellow," May said, "and quite determined. I think you'll do just fine."

I swallowed. "Thank you, ma'am," I said. I was wondering what to do now. Check with Baga about getting out early tomorrow, I guess.

"I haven't seen much of you recently," May said. She was wearing a frock like one she had on the first time I saw her.

"Ma'am!" I said. That was just unfair. "You made it clear as could be that you didn't *want* to have anything to do with me!"

"Maybe I didn't," May said. "Then. Take care of yourself, Pal."

She turned and walked off the back of the stage by the door Jon and all the leaders had come in by. It was the very same dress! I was sure of it.

I watched her go out. Then I went down to Baga, who was still talking with Toledana while Maggie watched closely.

If I couldn't figure things out in Dun Add any better than I was doing, I wasn't going to be much use to the Leader on Catermole.

CHAPTER 22

Catermole

Baga made only two stops between Dun Add and Catermole. He said he'd never heard of a boat travelling at that rate on a long run. I told him that his own boat ought to do as well, now that Guntram and I had rebuilt it. He could ask Stefan when next they met.

I came up from the trance in which I was viewing our surroundings through the boat. I didn't know *how* the boat saw things—there wasn't anything on the outside that looked like a window.

Baga got up from his seat and looked back at me. "I was just going to wake you, boss," he said. "We're here, or I think we are. Want me to open up so we can see what Catermole's like?"

"Sure, do that," I said.

I already knew that we were at the head of a long street that straggled back at least a half mile. Near where the boat was, there were short parallel streets. Most of the buildings I could see were two-story, with whitewashed boards and shake roofs. A few of those farther back seemed to be of brick and tile.

I'd told Baga that I could see through the boat when I was in a trance, but he couldn't—or didn't let himself—understand that I was seeing more than the gray or russet shades that he saw in the Waste. It was simpler just to accept his assumption that we didn't have a real view of outside unless the hatch was open. I wouldn't gain anything by insisting on the truth, and it seemed that it would make Baga uncomfortable...though I wasn't sure why.

I was wearing the blue suit today. I would've liked to wander around Catermole looking like a farmer from Beune, but since I'd come by boat that would make the locals even more suspicious.

I was going to have to have more dress suits made up. I wondered what they cost and how long the rest of Frances's silver was going to last me. Well, one thing at a time, and right now the thing was Catermole.

Buck and I stepped out. Baga followed us and closed the hatch behind him.

There were plenty of people among the buildings farther up the street, but the only person nearby on the landingplace was a boy of twelve or so who'd been whirling a wooden bird around him on a long cord. The wings were hinged to go up and down a little as it flew through the air, a clever piece of work.

"Are we on Catermole, son?" I asked.

The boy dropped the toy he'd been holding in his hands since the boat landed. He backed two steps, then turned and ran toward the town screaming. Maybe he was screaming a name.

"I guess he's never seen a boat," Baga said. "It scares folks the first time they do."

"I guess," I said. It seemed to me that the boy had been jumpier than just a boat ought to mean. The boats that'd landed in Beune gathered crowds, including me in the numbers. People hadn't run screaming.

Buck and I walked onto the street proper. I didn't know if Baga was following. I started whistling a song about a pretty girl leaving the place she'd lived in for a long time. I figured it'd make me look friendly to the people watching from the street or peeking out of windows.

My shield and weapon were in my tunic pockets, but I hoped nobody would know that. They shouldn't.

I thought the first building on the right side of the street was a log cabin with board siding, but when I reached it I found that it was attached to the two-story frame inn and store beside it. The bigger place had a full-length porch and a bench for people to sit on, though the half-dozen folks who'd been doing that when the boat landed were on their feet now.

The man who stepped onto the street to greet me was plump and wore a bright blue vest over a tunic of unbleached wool. "Good morning, Lord," he said. "What would you be wanting?"

"I was told to go to Boddington's," I said.

"You're at the right place," the plump fellow said, "but it's Blanco's now and I'm Blanco. Are you looking for supplies or for a room?"

"Mostly I want information," I said. "They say in Dun Add that you've been having some problems. They asked me to look into them."

"Are you a tax man?" asked one of the men who'd

been lounging on the porch. They were all bearded, but the speaker's was particularly full.

"I am not," I said, turning my head. "I don't know anything about taxes, and that's all I want to know."

I turned back to Blanco. "Information," I repeated. "And if you've got ale, I wouldn't mind trying some to compare it with what I'm used to at home."

"Come on inside," Blanco said. "We brew lager here, but I'm partial to it myself."

The front room of Blanco's had racks of goods to the right and a bar on the far left. Blanco took me to one of the tables near the bar and called, "Two lagers, Keith!" to the barman.

The loungers on the porch had all come in with us. They took chairs at the table also or dragged other chairs closer. Blanco didn't object, but I noticed that he left the others to buy their own beer.

The lager came in tarred leather jacks. It was pretty good, especially after the ale I'd been drinking aboard the boat. There was nothing wrong with food and drink from the converter, but it didn't have any *life*.

"Why is it you came here?" Blanco said, lifting his jack.

"The Leader, or anyway his people, heard there was something wrong on Catermole," I said. "They sent me to learn what it was, since they didn't seem to know, and to fix it. What *is* wrong here? Besides—"

I caught the eye of the fellow with the big beard and raised my jack to him.

"—you don't like to pay taxes, which is none of my business."

"Bloody well told we don't," the local muttered, but it was into his beard rather than a challenge.

"Look, I'd tell you if I could," said Blanco, squirming his hands together and staring at them instead of at me. "Maybe it's nothing."

"Bloody hell it's nothing!" said the man who'd taken the chair to the right of mine. "How about Herman vanishing?"

"Herman went off to look for the vein of gold feeding Rosebud Creek," Blanco said, glaring at his fellow. "People who go off into the forest alone, sometimes they don't come back. A widowmaker could've fallen on him in the storm we had the month after."

"And he might still be chipping at rocks," another man said. "Herman was that stubborn, you know he was."

"He didn't have six months food!"

"So he's fishing!" Blanco said. "I'm just saying that folks disappear. This is the Marches, and it doesn't mean anything special!"

"The guy from Barodi who went back to fetch his family!" another man said. "When she finally got here on her own, there'd been no sign of him anywhere along the way."

"Yeah, her and their four kids," Blanco said. "I can think of other reasons a guy might disappear. So can you, Keeley!"

I put down my half-emptied jack, firmly enough that a droplet squirted up in the air and dropped down into the remainder again. I said, "So you don't think anything's wrong, Blanco?"

The storekeeper looked around the circle of his fellows. Angrily he said, "No, I bloody well *do* think something's wrong. Only there's nothing I can point to, nothing I could swear to in court."

"We're not in court," I said. "And I'm sure not a judge. What do you think is going on?"

"It's more a feeling," the fellow with the big beard said. "It just doesn't feel right. And sure, people disappear, Herman could still be out in the hills in the west just like Shorty said. But there been a lot of people, it seems to me."

"I wonder if Not-Here is coming back?" said a fellow who didn't have a chair. "I mean, it's not long past that this was all the Waste, right? Catermole, I mean. And now it's Here, but what if that's going to change again?"

"Look, it doesn't happen that way!" a man said. "We're getting in hundreds of people every month. Catermole's really developing. We're going to be the biggest node in the Marches before long, you'll see!"

I didn't doubt anything the fellow was saying— except the first bit. Nobody knows why sometimes places are Here and sometimes Not-Here. I'd asked Guntram and *he* doesn't, so I figure nobody does. Things go from the Waste to Here, like Catermole did twenty-odd years ago.

It may be that what's Waste to people is Not-Here to the Beasts and to other things, or maybe just part of the Waste is really Not-Here. All I know for sure is that Beune has been Not-Here in the past; and I was pretty sure nobody was going to ask us living there if it was okay if the Waste and Not-Here swept over us again. Nobody was going to ask the residents of Catermole either, no matter how many of them were clearing farms or prospecting for gold.

"Sir, what do you think?" Blanco said, still working his fingers together but now meeting my eyes.

"I think I'll take a look around the Road hereabouts," I said. "I'll need directions as to where there's water outside Catermole, and also provisions for me and Buck—"

Buck had been sprawled against my left ankle. He sat up when he heard his name.

"—and my man Baga. I can buy them here?"

"I carry dry provisions, sure," Blanco said. "Beans, biscuit, and bacon—that what you're talking about?"

"Right, and maybe some dried fruit if you've got it," I said.

"There's raisins," said Blanco, nodding. "But sir— about payment? I won't take any money for this."

And that convinced me as nothing I'd heard before that there really was something bad going on around Catermole.

CHAPTER 23

Calling on the Neighbors

"How much farther are you planning to go?" Baga asked.

You can't tell time for sure on the Road since there's no sun, but I judged it was three hours since we'd taken a break for lunch. The node we'd stopped at around midday was bare rock, a crag jutting out of the waste—a decent place to take the weight off our feet and eat, but waterless.

"There's supposed to be a stream at the next place," I said. "It shouldn't be too long before we get there and we can camp for the night. We need water."

Baga grunted.

He was carrying all the food, not because he was my servant but because I had my weapon and shield. They were why we were out here, after all, and Baga had volunteered for the job.

Maggie hadn't come along with us. I would've been fine with her in the boat to Catermole—there hadn't been any problem when we all three rode from Marielles to Dun Add—though she wouldn't have come on the Road with us. Baga hadn't asked permission, and you don't have to get very old on a place as small as Beune to learn that you don't ask guys about how things are going with their wives.

Which is not to say there was anything wrong between Baga and Maggie. It's just that I understood it was none of my business.

We'd left Catermole and were heading for Barodi. Some of the people who'd gone missing were supposed to have been on this stretch. For that matter, it was a likely direction for the tax assessors to travel by. I wondered if the folks in Dun Add would be pleased to learn their clerks had been murdered by bandits rather than by the people they were putting taxes on?

Maybe so. Bandits had a simple solution, while hanging farmers didn't help your tax collections.

"I don't know what we're looking for," Baga said.

"Me neither," I said. "To tell the truth, what I'm really doing is walking around hoping that somebody attacks me."

"What if they only attack loners?" Baga said. "I mean, all the ones they told us about in Blanco's store were alone, right?"

"Yeah," I said. "I'd been thinking about that."

Which didn't mean I had an answer. I could maybe leave Baga at the node where I planned to spend the night. Then I'd be alone.

But so would Baga, and half a dozen of the people they'd talked about on Catermole who'd disappeared had been on Catermole, not on the Road. They might not have anything to do with the folks who'd vanished from the Road, but then I didn't really know that anybody'd vanished from the Road. We'd spend a night in Barodi and I'd figure something out before we set out the next morning.

Buck noticed something. "Hold up!" I called, to him and Baga both.

"For what?" said Baga. "You mean that little crack? That's nothing! Nothing could come through that."

"You're right, nothing could come that way," I said. "But it isn't nothing. There was a path here and it's been closed deliberately, not just growing shut because it wasn't used."

"But if nobody can go in and out that way, it's not what's happening to the people who disappeared, right?"

I didn't reply. Buck had noticed a discontinuity in the Waste to the right of the Road. It hadn't bothered him, but his dog brain had filed it as a possible escape route for something small that was trying to get away from him.

To me it was a break in the pattern of lighter and darker verticals edging the Road: a vertical which was neither light nor dark but just absent. I switched my shield on and thrust my left arm into the gap. It parted. I wondered how the edges had been joined.

I'd never tried to use either a shield or a weapon in the Waste before, but it turned out this wasn't the Waste. Beyond the crack at the edge of the Road, there was a real path—narrow but not much worse than the path to the Consort's Garden.

I grimaced. I'd rather not think about that, but I'd rather a lot of things.

"All right, Baga," I said. "We're going this way. Just to see where it leads."

Baga didn't object, just nodded. He'd been grumbling about the weight of the pack, but he wasn't a coward. He stayed right behind as Buck led me along the track.

My weapon was live. I won't pretend it made me feel safe, but this was the sort of thing I'd enrolled in the Company of Champions for. It didn't feel exciting when I was actually doing it, and I *sure* didn't feel like a hero.

We came out onto a node as narrow from this angle as the Consort's Garden, but this was all land. Much of it was a castle, built from the stone of the crag behind it. The walls had patches of yellow-orange lichen, but there were no vines running up them. Nobody was moving on top of the walls that I could see, but the place sure wasn't abandoned.

"What do we do now, boss?" Baga said.

How would I know? I thought. But Baga was right, it was my duty to know—or at least to find out.

"Buck and I will go up to the door—"

The massive iron-clad gate.

"—and ask to be admitted. If anything happens to me, get back to Catermole and take the boat to Dun Add. Tell people what it is you've seen here, tell Clain. And I guess the boat's yours after you've done that."

Which would give Baga two boats, probably the only person in Here who could say that. If he could get to Catermole. As a boatman, Baga didn't have much experience with the Road—particularly without a dog to guide him. I wished him well, but I wasn't going to give him Buck while *I* was still alive.

"Boss?" Baga said. "I'll do that, sure. But why don't we both go back and you tell Lord Clain? This sure looks to me like a job for the army."

I took a deep breath. "Baga," I said, "I see what you're saying. But I'm a Champion of Mankind. This particular problem the army can certainly fix, but in the longer run I think it's important to the Commonwealth..."

I shook my head because I felt really stupid saying this: Pal, the kid from Beune. "And to Mankind. That people learn to respect the Champions, even if there's just one of us and we're a long way from Dun Add."

One of me.

"Yes, boss," Baga said. "I guess I'll leave the pack here for now, right?"

I nodded and started for the gateway. I hadn't really expected Baga to come with me, but it made as much sense as me going myself instead of calling for a squadron of the army.

The castle was a circular sixty-foot tower about a hundred feet in diameter, small compared to Dun Add. It was entirely built for defense, however. The great gate was the only opening in the outer wall.

The stone tower loomed above me. It might be little compared to Dun Add, but it sure made me feel like an ant. Facing the gate, I wasn't sure what to do next.

I didn't want to put down either my shield or weapon—and I didn't want to bang either piece on what seemed to be a solid steel plate. "Hello the house!" I shouted.

I wondered how thick the gate was. The walls were sure too thick for anybody to hear me through them.

Baga took out his belt knife and banged on the door with the hilt where the tang stuck up above the wooden scales riveted onto it. The sound was a string of penetrating clacks.

"Hello the house!" I shouted again, looking up and wondering what I would do if nobody responded to our noise.

In time—how much time depended on how thick the steel was—I could cut through the gate with my weapon. I didn't want to do that. I was pretty sure I wouldn't overload the weapon with the heavy use, but it seemed an awfully hostile thing to do if the folks inside weren't hostile already. Still, if they wouldn't communicate with me—

A little door set into the other side of the big one hinged in with a squeal. I hadn't noticed it—there was a light coating of rust over the whole gate so it blurred the seam—and I just about jumped out of my skin.

A middle-aged woman stuck her head out. Baga blurted, "Who're you?"

"Marina, but that doesn't matter," she said, stepping fully out of the castle. She wore a dull blue dress with a white apron and bonnet. "You've got to get me out of here at once. He could come back at any time now. He's been gone for most of the day already!"

"Who has?" I asked, stepping past her. I was pretty sure we'd found what I was looking for—or anyway would, when he came back.

"The Spider!" Marina said. "I don't know what you'd call him and it doesn't matter! We've got to get out now!"

"No," I said, shutting down my shield briefly so that I could get through the little door. "We don't. This is where I need to be."

The gate was near six inches thick, so even the one-man door I'd entered by must weigh a lot more than I could lift. It was wider at the back where the hinges were than at the front: otherwise it wouldn't have been able to swing.

"Come on back, honey," I heard Baga say. "The boss knows what he's doing."

I *did* know what I was doing, but that didn't mean it was what he and the woman ought to be doing. "Look," I called over my shoulder as I walked down the tunnel toward light at the far end. "If the two of you want to leave—go back to Catermole, even—you've got my permission."

This place was designed like Dun Add with a courtyard inside a ring of rooms attached to the outer wall. That central court was over fifty feet across, but I didn't know how much of the tower was just solid stone wall.

Baga and the woman joined me when I paused in the courtyard. There were four masonry staircases curving up to the top of the inner walls, with circular walkways at the twenty- and forty-foot levels. Marina was the only person I'd seen any sign of living here, though.

On a whim I put myself into a trance. I gasped at what I'd found. I shuddered back to Here, meeting the worried eyes of Marina and Baga.

There were more Ancient artifacts in this castle than I'd known in any place except the workrooms of Louis and Guntram in Dun Add. I leaned against the wall and realized that the stone fabric of the building itself was an artifact. I couldn't tell if it went back to the Ancients, though. Indeed, I wasn't sure that the castle had been part of Here when it was built.

To the woman I said, "Is this Spider a Maker? A great Maker?"

"I don't know what he is," Marina said. "A monster, that's all. I think he's from Not-Here. He goes out on the Road and catches travellers, then he brings them back here to eat. But we've got to go or he'll be back!"

"If he eats people," Baga said, "what are you doing here?"

"He found me here twenty years ago," Marina said. "He talks in my mind. He kept me to clean for him."

"Who else was here when it came?" I said. "You weren't alone, were you?"

"He killed all of them," Marina said in a flat voice. "The lord, his wife and children. All the others. When he comes back and finds I've let you in, perhaps he'll kill me too."

Then she said, "That will be better, I suppose."

"The Leader sent me to put things right here," I said. "When the Spider comes back, I'll deal with it."

"You don't understand," Marina said. "But you will."

My first touch on the wall had directed me to the short iron column in the center of the courtyard. I walked over to it, dropped both shield and weapon into their pockets, and laid my bare hands on top of the column.

I went into a trance again. This was the heart of the castle—the heart, and the Ancient brain.

The rock of the castle walls was linked in a crystalline pattern. It prevented plants from growing onto the stone, though it didn't appear to affect the splotches of bright lichen.

There was another internal defensive structure also, but it was switched off and I couldn't understand its purpose anyway. I wished Guntram was here to help me. Perhaps I could get him to visit later. My having a boat would make that easy.

There were dozens of Ancient artifacts within the big building, each visible as a bright spot on my view. Sometimes I could tell their purpose, sometimes I couldn't. At least a few of them must have been from Not-Here. I thought about the Spider and wondered if it was from Not-Here, like Marina had said.

I returned to the present. Buck whined, but he didn't seem really worried. This was an unfamiliar building, that was all.

"There's something on the roof," I said, "and something down way in the bottom. Are there cellars here?"

"Leave the dungeon alone," Marina said. "But on the roof there's a room that lets you see anywhere. I mean anywhere, not just around the castle."

"I'll take a look," I said, heading for one of the staircases.

"There's a quicker way inside," Marina said. "You just step in a hole in the wall and you go straight up to the roof. Come this way."

There were twelve doorways around the interior of the courtyard. Marina led me in the one opposite to the gate I'd entered by. She seemed to have given up on convincing me to run away.

Inside, the room was wider than its ten-foot depth. Unless there was another room beyond it, the back—outer—wall must be ten feet thick. That wasn't surprising. There were cloth hangings on all the walls, but they were so dull with age that the scenes woven into them were just brownish blurs.

There were also two metal chests, waist high and larger than any clothes-press I'd seen. From the feeling they radiated, they were Ancient artifacts or at least contained artifacts.

"What're these?" I said, nodding to the nearest chest.

"Storage boxes," Marina said, touching the corner. The lid popped open. On the floor of the chest were a number of outfits similar to the one she was wearing now; they only took up a fraction of the available space. "Nothing decays inside them when they're closed. I don't have much need of them now, just keeping the moths away from my woolens, but the lord and his family kept food here."

I thought I'd seen a smudge of blood on the back of the chest, but if nothing changed inside, that might be twenty years old.

"This is a wonderful place," I said, thinking of Guntram.

"It was, once," Marina said.

There was an alcove in the back wall. There was nothing inside it, literally: it had neither floor nor ceiling, as I saw when I stuck my head in and looked up and down.

"Step inside and point your index finger up," Marina said. She did that herself and vanished.

Grinning, I did the same. If a blast of white fire incinerated me, I could hope I'd die quickly.

Instead I was on the castle's roof, just as Marina had said. She was standing beside a curved wall of... shimmering, I guess, higher than I was tall. There wasn't really anything there, just the air rippling the way it does over a black rock on a sunny day. I couldn't have stretched out my arm full-length if I'd been standing inside it.

"This is the seeing place," Marina said. "The lord

called it his belvedere. Just go inside and think of somewhere, that's all."

I stepped in. I didn't feel anything when I crossed the line of shimmer.

"Think of what?" I said, but as I spoke I was thinking how Guntram would love this place—and I was viewing the interior of his workroom. It was much as I'd left it, but Guntram was on his couch with the color projector beside him. That was complicated enough to keep even a mind like his occupied for months, maybe longer.

"Oh!" I said. Guntram's workroom vanished and I was looking at Marina through the distortion.

I thought of my house in Beune; I was inside. The door was open, swinging in the breeze because it hadn't been properly latched. A chair with a broken leg had been moved in since I was last there, and there were three storage baskets in the middle of the floor. Full of Phoebe's winter clothing, I suspected, but I couldn't look inside.

The Consort's Chamber appeared. I stepped out of the belvedere before I could be sure who the half-dozen people in the room might be. One of them had been a woman with a long-necked banjo.

"This is like nothing I've ever dreamed of," I said. "Did the Spider build these?"

"No," said Marina. "The Spider eats, which you'll learn because you insist on staying."

"Take me down to the dungeon," I said. "What's there?"

"Nothing, less than nothing now," said Marina.

"Take me!" I said. Buck in the courtyard heard me and barked.

"Go yourself, then," she said. "Stand on the opening—" it was a gap in the roof tiles here "—and point your left index finger down."

I did as she said. I was suddenly in darkness.

Shocked, I took my shield and weapon out. There was no immediate danger, and my eyes adapted to the dimness. Light came from somewhere, but it was spread out as thin as the stars on a foggy night.

I was in a corridor wide enough for four guys to stand beside each other. I walked forward slowly, listening for anything. There may have been rustling like mice in a dark pantry, but that could've been the echoes of my bootsoles on the floor.

The corridor turned to the right. From shackles on the wall in front of me hung the dried-out corpse of what had been a man. Skin like thin leather had shrunken over the bones, holding them in human shape.

"Why have you come here, man?" the corpse whispered to me.

"There are wonderful things in this place," I said. "The belvedere on the roof and something equally great in the dungeon. I came here from the belvedere."

I swallowed. "Sir, who are you?" I said.

"I was Palin, lord of this place," the corpse said. "Now I am nothing and less than nothing, neither dead nor alive."

I remembered Marina saying that there was nothing and less than nothing in the dungeon. I swallowed again.

"What can I do for you, Lord Palin?" I said. I didn't want to touch him, I was afraid to touch him, but I couldn't back away and do *nothing*.

"You could bring me nothing but total death," Palin said, "and I am afraid to die. I sinned in life, but so long as I hang here in Limbo I delay justice for that sin."

"I can bring a priest," I said. I didn't see what good that would do, but I really wanted to get out of this place. *I should've taken the woman's advice.*

"A priest!" the corpse said, the sneer obvious even in a whisper. "I impregnated a servant and sent her away. Oh, I gave her money, but I didn't admit the relationship or recognize the child. She came back later and let in the creature from the Waste which rules here now. It killed my wife and children, it killed all the servants, and it hung me here where you see me. Without life, without death, without hope. My act caused it all."

I looked at the wretched thing hanging from the stone wall. He'd knocked up a girl and thrown her out—which was a sin, and giving her money didn't change that. It happened everywhere; it'd sure happened on Beune.

But if that was a sin beyond redemption, then few enough men could hope to be redeemed. Palin was blaming himself for the slaughter of everybody close to him, and that *wasn't* his doing. What he'd done was just ordinary human weakness. He ought to have been better, but it shouldn't have brought him to this.

"Sir," I said, "this is wrong."

"Boy!" Marina shouted behind me. "The Spider's coming and you have to hide!"

"The voice..." the corpse said. "Is that Marina?"

"Yes," I said. I turned and went back the way I'd come. I was worried about fighting the creature, whatever it was, but really my first thought was that this gave me an excuse to escape from the hanging thing. To escape from Palin.

I'd have to come back, of course. Well, if I survived.

Marina waited in front of the shaft. I wondered if the castle had staircases inside.

"I've hidden your man in one of the chests," she said. "You can hide in the other and I'll let you out when it's safe. You can't go out the gate now."

I knew more about Marina now than I had when I met her, but that was a problem for another time. "No," I said. "I'll go up to the belvedere where I can watch."

"But he'll find you!" Marina said.

I didn't reply, just stepped into the hole and raised my right index finger. It struck me that I might come out in the foyer where I supposed the Spider would enter instead of going up to the roof. If that happened, I guessed it'd save time.

I stood in bright sunlight and sneezed. That happens when I go from dark to light. The belvedere was beside me, so I stepped into it again. I didn't know where the creature was, so I thought *Show me the Spider* and there it was: coming from the direction of the Road just like Baga and me had.

It was tall, at least twelve feet and maybe higher. I was judging by the height of the men it carried. The Spider wore a bandolier from its right shoulder; two men and a woman were lashed to it by the legs, upside down.

It walked on two spindly legs, and it had long, spindly arms—at least eight feet long. I never saw more than two arms at a time, but they weren't always the same two. The body was in two parts, a short cylinder that the arms and legs came out of and a wobbly blob hanging down like the torso of a really fat man.

Its head was triangular with huge eyes and a beak. There was nothing even vaguely human about the head.

The Spider reached the castle wall. I expected it to open the gate or maybe to wait for Marina to come out and do that. It couldn't fit through the little door I'd entered by, I was sure of that.

Instead of swinging the gate open, the Spider walked through. Straight through the thick iron plate. The people dangling from its bandolier came through with it, jouncing on the cords that tied them to the broad leather strap.

"I am back, woman," the Spider said, its words rasping in my mind. It stepped into the central courtyard. I could have looked over the roof parapet and seen it, but I continued to watch through the belvedere. "I've brought fresh meat."

It took a step deeper into the courtyard and stopped. It said, "What is that?"

"A dog," said Marina. "Only a dog. It wandered in from the Road and I've kept it for company."

"And there is a human," the Spider said, frozen where it stood. "I smell a human."

"You brought fresh meat, you said, Master," Marina said. "Of course you smell fresh meat."

"You are lying, woman!" the Spider said, walking forward again. Its steps were hesitant, picky, but because the legs were so long it crossed the ground quickly. "I will strip off your flesh and then crunch your bones!"

"Here, Master, here!" Marina shrieked. "I was keeping him as a surprise but you brought fresh meat yourself!"

She ran back into the building. I couldn't see her there—the belvedere was showing the courtyard because the Spider was there—but I knew she'd be opening the chest in which Baga hid.

I walked from the belvedere to the nearest curving staircase, holding my shield and weapon. I switched them live. Marina hadn't told me how to get from the roof back to the lobby in the shaft, and rather than fool around guessing, I went by the way that I knew worked.

"Spider!" I shouted. "Is it me you're looking for?"

With the shield on I could see all six arms at the same time. They were even longer than I'd thought.

The Spider turned and waited as I came down the stairs. "More meat!" it said. "Truly this is my best day in decades!"

When I was six steps from the bottom, the Spider minced forward and reached toward me. I spread my shield to its widest coverage, accepting the reduced resistance at any point, and raised my weapon to strike.

The Spider's arms stretched, hovering above me and to both sides. Instead of hands, it had small pincers like on the legs of a crab. I took another step down. The last joint of two arms vanished, just faded away.

I stepped down again, watching the looming arms. The practice machines hadn't prepared me for this.

Pain like jets of molten iron struck me in both shoulder blades. I screamed and bounced down the stone steps on my back. The Spider had attacked me from Not-Here, though most of the creature faced me Here.

It leaned over me. I hadn't dropped my shield, and with my weapon I struck for the Spider's nearer foot. It sprang away, agile as a leaf-hopper. Its roar of fury echoed in my mind.

I got to my feet. I must have bruised myself on the steps, maybe broken ribs, but I didn't notice that because of the pain from the Spider's pincers in my back. I stepped forward because there was no escape except through the monster.

Buck ran up to me, barking furiously. My view shuddered into shades of gray-blue and gray-brown, but when the Spider's arms cocked I saw the two pincers lancing toward me through Not-Here.

I turned and slashed at the one coming from my right: my own shield kept me from striking left. The tip of the limb spun away, squirting liquid.

The Spider screamed again. I rushed it, though I was afraid that I'd trip over my own feet. The creature's arms closed on me like the jaws of a spring trap. One of the pincers bit into my neck. I went blind with pain.

Warm liquid gushed over my right arm. I felt my legs collapsing. I lay on the ground, aware only of a stink like burning pus.

Then there was nothing but blackness.

CHAPTER 24

Cleaning Up

I woke up, wondering where I was. I opened my eyes and saw nothing but darkness as deep as the sleep I'd come up from. I reached out to the side and hit solid metal.

I screamed and swung both arms out to the sides, slamming the heels of my hands into the same metal walls. *I've been buried alive! I'll—*

The lid above me flew open. Baga and Marina stared down. They looked worried.

Not as worried as I was a heartbeat ago.

I sat up and put my hands on the edge of the chest. That's what I was in, one of the storage chests in the foyer; the place Marina had wanted me to hide.

"Sorry," I said. "I didn't know where I was and I—"

I was going to use a gentler word, but instead I told the truth: "I panicked in the dark. How did I get here, anyway?"

"I put you here because she said to," said Baga. He glared at the woman, his hands clenching. "Wasn't it right?"

"I set it to heal him!" Marina said. "Do you think he'd be talking to us now if it hadn't worked? He'd have been dead!"

"Baga, she's right!" I said. "Thank you, thank you both."

I swung my right leg out of the chest, then the left. I was standing on the stone floor again. I took a deep breath.

I checked my tunic pockets as Buck circled beside me, rubbing his shoulders against my knee and whining softly. The shield and weapon were where they ought to be. I rubbed Buck's ears.

I dropped into a brief trance to view the chest's mechanism. I didn't bother entering the menu to see what the choices were. It was enough to know that there were choices.

I came back to the present and looked at Marina. I said, "You're a Maker."

She swallowed. "I suppose," she said. "Not like Lord Palin."

"It was by being a Maker that you were able to switch off the defenses in the walls," I said. "Otherwise the Spider couldn't have gotten through them."

"I suppose," Marina whispered. Turning, she ran down a hallway and around a corner.

"Want me to get her?" Baga said, watching the direction Marina had gone.

"Eventually," I said. "I guess I'll take her to Dun Add with us and let the Leader decide what to do with her. Or—I don't know. I just don't."

"She was going to feed me to that thing," Baga said, nodding toward the courtyard.

"She's done worse in the past," I said.

I walked into the courtyard. I'd stabbed the Spider in its pendulous belly and ripped downward. That big sack lay as flat as a woolen blanket now, and the creature's body lay in a splotch of liquid, tacky now in the sun.

I was soaked from the waist in the same filth. It stank. *I* stank. Maybe I wasn't throwing my guts up because being in the chest had fixed that too.

"I got to get a bath," I muttered to Baga. "And new clothes."

I looked at him. "You do too," I added. "From carrying me, I guess."

There probably weren't more clothes here. Well, we could wash what we were wearing.

The three people the Spider had come back with were still attached to the bandolier. They were dead; the Spider sprawled partly over two of them. I wondered if the creature only took travellers on the Road or if it had sprung from the Waste onto lone settlers in the hinterlands of Catermole and other nearby nodes.

I wanted to bury the humans and to burn the Spider, though there wasn't enough wood for a big fire in the castle. I had to think. I had to get my mind working again.

"Baga," I said. "We'll go back to Catermole and get the boat, then we'll come here again. We'll load as many of the artifacts as I can and we'll take them to Dun Add."

I took a deep breath.

"But first we'll take a bath," I added.

✧   ✧   ✧

I found the bath house by using the column in the middle of the courtyard. I expected the bath to use Ancient artifacts as so much of the castle did, but it was simply at the end of a trough from a spring higher up the mountain onto which the castle was built. From the belvedere I'd seen the trough fade off into the Waste, though, which made me wonder how it'd been built.

The column also told me where Marina was. After I'd bathed, I knocked on the door of her ground-floor room. My tunic and trousers were still damp though I'd wrung them out, but heaven knows I've worked in the rain often enough.

Marina jerked the door open before my knuckles hit it the third time. "Have you come to kill me?" she said.

The room beyond her was plain. There were flowers growing in a window box, but there were no pictures on the wall and no furniture but a simple chair, table, and bed.

"No," I said. Baga had suggested that, but I don't think he was serious. "I thought of carrying you to Dun Add and letting the Leader deal with you, but I'm not going to do that either."

"I deserve to die," Marina said, standing in the doorway to her room. Her eyes were open, but she was staring somewhere not in this world, or maybe not in this time. "I was angry, so angry... but angry with Palin. I didn't mean for the others..."

Her face didn't change, but a tear started down her right cheek as her voice trailed off.

"You're going to die," I said, "just like we all are. But not at my hands nor at Jon's, now that I've had time to think about it."

Now that I'd had time to calm down, really. When I walked down the steps to fight the Spider, I'd been boiling mad. Not at the creature; it was following its nature and I'd kill it if I could, but it wasn't *evil*. The woman who'd let it in to slaughter the whole household in the night, the woman who'd lived with the monster and eaten the food the monster brought her—*she* was evil.

Except she really wasn't. Marina had made a mistake, a terrible mistake, because she was angry. After that she had only two choices: to die, or to live as she was able to live. Maybe it would have been better to fling herself from the wall to the stone courtyard, maybe *I* would've done that. But I can't swear that I would, and anyway—not everybody has to be me.

Which made me think of May again.

"What I'm going to do when I come back with the boat I left on Catermole," I said, "is to carry you to a place called Beune. It's not very far from here. I'll leave you with money, a lot for Beune—"

I'd decided on twenty silver pieces.

"—to set you up. People are nice anyway, and I'll be kinda of vouching for you."

I thought of my neighbors. I half-chuckled and said, "I shouldn't wonder if you got married pretty quick if that's what you want. You're good-looking."

Still good-looking, of course, but there were plenty of widowers and that much silver would open a lot of doors.

"I've heard of Beune," Marina said. She was back in this world again, meeting my eyes, but I'd never seen an expression like the one on her face now. "Does a woman named Ariel live there?"

I guess it was my turn now to get a funny expression. "One did," I said. "My mother. But she died over a year ago."

"I see," Marina said, but what she saw was beyond me. There was more to the words than just politeness. She was smiling now. "And you think I'll fit in on Beune?"

"Look!" I said, kind of angry about that smile. "We're good people, we live quiet and we mind our own business. If that's not good enough for you, I'll carry you to Dun Add and you can take your chances!"

"Beune is far too good for me, Pal," Marina said. "Please, I wasn't mocking your kindness. In a better time, I might have lived my whole life on a place like Beune and never left it."

I nodded, mad at myself for taking offense when I just didn't understand somebody's expression. "I figure we'll be back the day after tomorrow," I said. "We have to take the Road to Catermole, but coming back in the boat won't be any time."

I coughed, then turned back down the hall. Over my shoulder I called, "By the way? I'm going to leave most of our food here, bacon and biscuit. You're welcome to have what you want of it until we come back."

Marina didn't say anything, but as I walked away I heard her crying.

When Baga and I returned to the castle in a little less than the two days I'd estimated, both Marina and the food were gone. To tell the truth, that wasn't a complete surprise.

I wasn't really unhappy about it either. I'd have

done just what I told Marina I would, and I really did think it'd work out all right—

But in the back of my mind, I couldn't forget the things Marina had done. Sure, there were plenty of excuses, but she'd still done them.

What I didn't expect was the note stuck to the door to her room:

Pal, you're a good boy and a credit to the woman who raised you. I wish I'd been more like her, but I wasn't.

It's too late for me to go back to Beune, but when you do, see if you can lay a tulip on Ariel's grave. She always loved tulips.

Take care of yourself, son. From what I saw, you're well able to do that.

It wasn't signed.

CHAPTER 25

Old Friends

I nodded to the servant at the cross-corridor as I passed him. He bowed and murmured, "Your lordship." I didn't bother correcting him.

Guntram's door opened as I raised my hand to knock on it. "Pal!" he said, ushering me in. "I didn't expect you back so soon."

"I'm surprised myself," I said. "Though I've got a boat, remember."

Instead of clearing a chair, I walked over to the table by his couch and started to empty the satchel I'd brought with me. I recalled the bag which Guntram had brought to Beune and the wonders he took from it.

I grinned. The shoe was on the other foot now.

I'd brought a selection of tools from the workroom of the castle, closed since the Spider's arrival. The first couple were toys—an instrument which projected feelings, another one which made me feel as though my skin was expanding to rub against the whole cosmos.

The second one had been made in Not-Here. So had the weapon I now lay beside it.

"Ah," Guntram said as he picked it up. His voice was colorless, but he smiled as wide as a frog. He trotted quickly to the door and called into the corridor, "You, sir! I'd like you to take this to Louis immediately. Do you know where his suite is?"

"Ah, yes sir," the servant said. "But sir, I'm supposed to stay here during my shift?"

"Never mind that!" Guntram said, as curtly as I'd ever heard him. "If anyone complains, tell him to see me. Understood?"

"Yes sir," replied a glum voice.

Guntram shut the door firmly. "This is amazing," he said. "Where do they come from?"

"Well, I've decided to call it Castle Ariel after the woman who raised me," I said. "I never heard any other name—it hadn't occurred to me to ask—and there's no one living there for the moment. Ah, sir?"

"Yes?" Guntram said, turning over the next object in his hands. It seemed complete, but I hadn't been able to figure out what it did.

"I was thinking that maybe sending a message to Lord Louis to explain...?"

Guntram laughed. "Oh, heavens, you don't know Louis!" he said. Then contritely, "Which of course you don't. But it won't be necessary—"

The door burst open. Louis entered and slammed it behind him. He waved the weapon.

"Guntram, I met your man in the corridor!" he said. "How did you do this?"

"Sir," I said, though Louis didn't appear to have noticed my presence. "I think the Maker was a man named Palin. Though perhaps it came to him as it is, because he seems to have carried on a considerable traffic with Not-Here."

"I heard of a Palin, but long ago," Guntram said, frowning. "I never met him. He was lord of Castle Ariel?"

"Yes sir," I said. I'd explain the rest, but not yet. "I have a boatload of more artifacts from Ariel. I was hoping that you could find people to carry them up to Dun Add? I don't think many of what I brought are arms, but some things I don't know. Like that one."

I nodded toward the piece in Guntram's hands.

"This?" said Guntram. "I believe it encourages rain to fall, but I'd need to study it further to be sure."

He offered the artifact to Louis, who only glanced and shrugged. "I'll take your word for it, Teacher," he said.

Louis suddenly gave me his full attention. The fierceness in his eyes made my belly tighten, but I managed not to twist away from him.

"I've never before seen a weapon from Not-Here in working order," Louis said.

"It's a spike rather than a cutting tool," I said, glad that I didn't squeak. "It's handy but it's not very powerful."

"Yes, but with the right modifications I think we can boost penetration by four, maybe five!" Louis said. "I can't be certain until I take a little time with it, but I'll give the job to Camille after I've explained what I want him to do."

He waved his free hand in irritation as though wiping away thoughts he didn't need at the moment. He glared at me again. He said, "There's more of this?"

"Sir," I said, "my man and I loaded the boat with Ancient artifacts. Most are incomplete. Very few of them are weapons or shields, at least that I could tell. About a third are of Not-Here manufacture—and I'm not sure that all of those are Ancient."

That was true. I wasn't sure what it meant, but it was so important that I had to tell somebody as soon as I could.

"And there's still more at Castle Ariel," I said, "but nothing that I thought for sure was something that you'd want to see. You or Guntram."

"I see," Louis said. "It's obvious that what you're describing is extraordinarily valuable. What do you want for it? I won't quibble."

"Sir, I didn't—" I said. "I mean, I'm not..."

I didn't know how to go on. My tongue was suddenly too big for my mouth.

Louis grimaced. "Let me see your weapon and shield," he snapped.

I hadn't expected that, but I managed to hand him my weapon and then fished out the shield. When he came out of his trance, Louis muttered, "I don't think I can better this in any useful way," and gave the weapon back.

He took the shield. After another brief trance, he returned it and said, "This is a good shield, if I do say so myself; but I can give you a much stiffer one."

"It wouldn't be as agile, Louis," Guntram said. "Not even you could better what you did here without making it harder to shift."

Louis grimaced again, but he didn't argue.

"Sir, I'm very happy with my shield," I said. I remembered the one I'd cobbled together myself, and the way Easton had taken me apart when I tried to use it.

"Well, when you decide what you want, come to me," Louis said. "For now I'll set up a drawing account for you."

He looked at Guntram and added, "Any reason to put a limit on it, Teacher?"

"Not for him," Guntram said.

"My thought as well," Louis said. Focusing on me again, he said, "Whenever you want to buy something, just sign a chit to the Chancellor, to be applied to my account. It'll be honored."

He nodded curtly to me, then bowed respectfully to Guntram. "This has been a very good day, Teacher," Louis said. "I'll see to unloading the cargo now so that we can sort it properly."

He closed the door forcefully behind him.

I stared at Guntram. I was trying to make what had just happened fit into a shape my mind thought was possible.

"I was about to say that when Louis saw the weapon, it wouldn't require an explanation to bring him to see us," Guntram said, smiling. "But I didn't have time to. What do you propose to do now, Pal?"

"Well, in a while I'd like an interview with either the Leader or Lord Clain," I said, "if you could arrange that?"

Guntram nodded. "Certainly," he said.

"But right for now," I said, "I'm going down to Room Twelve to see my old roommates, if they're still there."

"Ah," said Guntram without emotion. "I thought perhaps there was someone else you wanted to see."

"No," I said, opening the door. "I'm afraid there isn't."
I shut the door behind me harder than I'd needed to.

It was early enough in the morning that I wasn't surprised to find both Garrett and Welsh—but particularly Garrett—in the suite. In fact I caught them on the way out, not armed as they would have been if they'd been going to either the practice hall or the jousting field.

"Hoy!" Welsh called. "The prodigal returns! We were just going to look you up, old man. A boy from the stables knocked on the door and said you'd just stabled Buck."

"Let's go down the canteen," Garrett said. "The room's a mess and anyway, I don't think there's anything to drink left."

"If we can find a booth," I said, "that'd be perfect. And I'm buying."

"*I* sure won't fight you for the honor," Welsh said.

We settled into a booth in a corner with no problem. The canteen wasn't crowded at this time in the morning, though there were two morose fellows at separate tables, staring at their mugs.

I spent the first round in small talk and in telling them how I'd lucked into a good thing by following a narrow path to what turned out to be a treasure. I told them about the Spider but not, you know, in a way that made it any big deal. Which it really wasn't, just putting my head down and charging the bloody thing, no science to it.

After the tapster—there was no boy on duty with him this early—brought the second round, I said, "I need to know if you guys are dead set on staying in Dun Add to be Champions, or if another offer came by, you'd consider it?"

Welsh took a deep drink of his ale. I knew he'd have rather had wine, but I was sticking to beer until I'd gotten through my business. He set the mug down with a grim look.

"I don't have a prayer of ever making Champion with my shield," he said. "I guess I realized that when I saw you fight your way through. No offense, kid, but you're not *that* much better than I am. But your gear was that much better than mine."

"I told you I'd been lucky," I said. "You'll have a better shield before very long, I promise. But how important is becoming Champions?"

"Pretty bloody important," said Garrett. He was looking at me hard. "But not so important that I won't listen to an offer from a friend. This is something that matters to you, kid?"

"It does," I said. "There aren't a lot of people here that I know well enough to trust. I trust you two."

"Then we'd better hear what you've got to say," said Welsh. Garrett nodded.

I nodded, giving myself a moment to get my thoughts together. I said, "I own a castle. At least I suppose I do: I captured it and I don't think there's anybody around who could argue the rights and wrongs of ownership with me."

Both men nodded.

"The node—Castle Ariel—is in the Marches," I said. "That's against it in many people's minds." I shrugged. "So's Beune, so being in the Marches doesn't bother me."

"Or me," said Welsh.

"Us," said Garrett.

"There's some hinterland," I said, "though it's never been developed. The former lord—well, the last human lord—was a Maker. He traded with Not-Here and didn't try to develop the node or bring in settlers. I think it could be quite a busy place if the ruler had a different focus, and it's also a great place for the Leader to put a garrison for the region. I'd like the two of you to run Castle Ariel for me."

"Why both of us?" Garrett said.

"Because you have different strengths, and you get along together," I said.

It was time for another round. I signalled the tapster.

"Different weaknesses, you mean," Welsh said.

"That too," I agreed. If they'd been stupid men, I wouldn't have wanted them.

The tapster brought filled mugs and hauled away the empties. Welsh didn't pick his up immediately. At last he said, "Look, Pal, if you're willing to take a chance on me, I'll give it a flutter. But I don't swear to you that I'll stick to water from here on out or even that I won't get drunk on my ass again!"

"Understood," I said. I didn't add that I wouldn't have believed him if he had sworn those things.

"If I've got a place," Garrett said as he put his mug down, "a real place instead of a room on sufferance, then I guess I might start looking on the future a different way too. But I'm not promising either."

"Say," said Welsh. "You've won a castle of your own with retainers—me and Garrett. So you really are Lord Pal now, right?"

"I guess," I said. "I don't feel any different than when I was plowing behind Gervaise's ox, though."

"Well, my lord," said Welsh, "then would it be a bad thing if we tied one on for one last time in celebration?"

I smiled. "I guess not," I said. That wasn't really what I thought, but I still wasn't his mother. "I'll tell the man—" I nodded "—to charge it to me, and I'll expect you to switch to wine. For myself, I need to see Louis about getting you kitted out with better gear—"

"Louis?" Welsh blurted.

"I brought him enough stuff to cover anything you want," I said. "But I want to talk with him while I'm sober. And I *sure* want to be sober when I talk to the Leader, and that's next."

"Pal, just a word to you," Garrett said, frowning into his mug. "The Leader's in a pretty grim mood these past couple days."

"Right, the Baran business," said Welsh. That didn't mean anything to me, but he went on, "Baran had been seeing one of the Consort's maids, Berenice. He caught her with another fellow—a servant, actually, nobody that matters. Baran couldn't even call him out, you see. It'd just be murder."

"Well, that's a bad thing," I said. "But I guess it happens pretty often in Dun Add, doesn't it? It did in Beune."

"Yeah," said Garrett. "Only Baran's blaming Jolene, saying that Berenice takes after her slut of a mistress." He shook his head and added, "Listen, I can't say from personal experience, but I've heard stories. Berenice didn't have anything to learn about horizontal exercise from a long time before she came to Dun Add and joined the court."

"And it's the same problem," Welsh said. "If Clain—or

the Leader—comes down on Baran, then it's proof of the
stories, you see? So Clain's heading off to God knows
where, and Jon's hoping that it'll all go away."

"Hoping that Baran breaks his neck, more like,"
Garrett said morosely. "Who can blame him? Just
don't be surprised if the Leader bites your head. It's
not about you."

I got up from the table. "I learned a long time
ago that most things aren't," I said. "But I also know
that it can be hard to remember when somebody's
screaming in my face."

I'd been planning to go up to Guntram's workroom
and ask him to take me to Jon, as he'd promised, but
Louis said he'd take me himself. We'd finished our
business—he'd agreed to outfit Garrett and Welsh,
showing no more concern than he might have done in
deciding whether to have pork or beef at table—and
he'd shown me his—his team's—progress on boosting
the power of the weapon from Not-Here.

I wanted to view that in more detail when I had time,
but I knew I'd be too nervous to do the job justice until
I'd spoken with the Leader. That would've been true
even before my friends warned me about Jon's mood.
The sooner I had the interview over, the happier I'd be.

"He's in his chamber with Lord Clain," an attendant
said as we entered the Leader's suite. I expected us
to wait, but the attendant rapped on the inner door,
called, "It's Louis, sir," and opened the door for us.
I'm not sure he'd even waited for a response from Jon.

"Clain, finish your business," Louis said. "My young
colleague here wants to discuss something with Jon,
and I said I'd ease him through the door."

Clain looked at me with an expression I couldn't read; it was sort of like having a cat look at me. A really big cat.

"*Your* colleague?" Clain said. "He's Pal of Beune, isn't he?"

"Yes sir," I said, my back as straight as I could make it. "You knocked me silly a couple months ago."

"You made me work to do it," Clain said with a grim smile.

"And he's my colleague, or Guntram's, really, as well," said Louis. "He's brought us a haul of artifacts from the Marches, some of them which I've never seen before. But really, go on."

Jon got up from the desk at which he'd been sitting. "I'm afraid we're done here," he said. He turned his head toward Clain and said, "Unless you can think of anything I could offer to get you to change your mind?"

"I'm afraid not," Clain said. He bowed.

Clain walked past me and Louis toward the door. "I'm going to find a region that hasn't had any attention," he said. "And then I'll probably move around my estates for a while. I trust my vicars, but it's always good to check."

The door closed behind him.

Jon sat back down and rubbed his forehead with his hands over his eyes. He looked very tired.

"What is it you need, Louis?" he said. His hands were still in front of his face.

Louis nodded to me. "Sir," I said. "It's Pal of Beune. I've captured a castle in the Marches. I'd like to hold it in your name but appoint two vicars to actually run it."

Jon nodded. "Clain said you'd liberated a castle," he said. "He said it was close to Catermole, is that correct?"

"Yes sir," I said. I'd told a clerk—the same Toledana who'd given Baga directions to Catermole in the first place—what I'd found. I hadn't realized that the information had risen as high as Clain; let alone to Jon himself.

"He recommends that Catermole be attached to your castle—what's it called?"

"Castle Ariel, sir."

"To Castle Ariel with a garrison of thirty troopers from the army, to be maintained from the estate," Jon resumed. "Does that seem reasonable to you?"

"Yes sir," I said. It was reasonable beyond anything I could have organized myself. "Sir, whatever you decide is fine. I'm just a kid from Beune."

"Who killed a monster from Not-Here which had been preying on humans for decades," said the Leader, with a touch of humor on his face. "Don't worry, lad. I've been learning to put people and things into the right pigeonholes for longer than that spider was at its business."

His expression melted again. "Oh, Louis," he said, "what am I to do without Clain here?"

"Surely you can find a chancellor until Clain returns, Jon," Louis said, frowning.

"I've put Morseth in the job," the Leader said. "He was Clain's suggestion and he can certainly do the work, but Louis—"

He looked up at the Maker. I might as easily not have been in the room—and I'd have been happier not to be.

"Clain and I came to Dun Add when we were boys and it was no more than a nest of villains, us and a couple handsful of farmers who believed in us," Jon said. "*You* remember that. And we cleaned it out and started building the Commonwealth on that foundation. I don't want a chancellor, Louis, I want Clain!"

He took a deep breath and shook himself. "Well, Clain will be back," he muttered. Looking at me again he resumed, "Find Morseth and tell him to assign thirty troopers to Castle Ariel. And clerks. What's the population of Catermole, Lord Pal?"

"Sir, I'm not sure," I said. "I'd judge maybe a thousand, but it's growing fast."

"Three clerks, then," said Jon. "The first thing they'll do is get us better numbers. Then we'll see. Now, you say you're appointing a vicar?"

"Two, sir," I said. "Welsh and Garrett who've been Aspirants here. They'll have better equipment shortly."

"Well and good," said Jon, "but what will you be doing yourself?"

"Well, sir," I said, "I hoped you'd find another job for me. As a Champion of the Commonwealth, I mean."

"The first one worked out all right," said Jon, smiling again. "Would you like a few months in Dun Add to sample the good things of life first, though?"

"Truly sir . . ." I said. My eyes were on the floor in embarrassment; I forced myself to raise them to meet the Leader's. "I'd really rather go out as soon as I could. Dun Add doesn't agree with me."

"Or me either, much of the time," Jon said, shaking his head. "Well, stick around court for a while and I'm sure we'll find something suitable."

I bowed. I followed Louis out the door.

Behind us, the Leader was rubbing his forehead again.

CHAPTER 26

New Horizons

In fact it took more than a week. I had Baga run Welsh to Catermole in the boat and then guide him to Castle Ariel. That way Welsh could lead the whole contingent there in turn.

While they were gone, Garrett was getting to know the troops the Leader was providing as a garrison. I spent my time with clerks, learning—or at least being told—what my duties were as Lord of Ariel and Catermole, which ones I could delegate and which I couldn't.

Mostly my duties seemed to be to support the clerks in collecting taxes, to keep order, and to refer all capital crimes to Dun Add. Given the distance from Ariel to Dun Add, sending prisoners back under escort was going to be a difficult enough process to discourage classifying things as capital crimes.

That suited me. There'd been several manslaughters in Beune since I got old enough to notice things.

Generally it was too much to drink on all sides and solved with a payment of what we thought was fair to the wife and children.

In the case of Disch, he had the devil's own temper. We stripped him of everything he had and told him to leave Beune and never come back. I was on that jury myself, and I can tell you that *all* the neighbors were glad of an excuse to see the back of him.

I didn't see why that wouldn't work on Catermole nine cases out of ten. For the tenth one, there was the garrison's manpower to haul somebody back to Jon to judge.

The boat returned. I shook hands with Garrett and Welsh, gave a little talk to the troops about how they were advancing humanity, and waved good-bye as the convoy set off from landingplace.

I'd felt myself blushing as I talked about this great duty they were carrying out. It's what I believe, true enough, but I knew most of those professional soldiers thought it was bumph. That was all right so long as they did their duty; but I still thought I ought to tell them what *I* believed.

There was quite a gang of people besides the soldiers. Most of the troops were taking women and sometimes children besides. There were a lot of civilians too, folks who thought there'd be a better life for them in the Marches, and weren't afraid to travel there so long as they had a strong escort.

It was just like I'd told Welsh and Garrett, only until now I'd had secret doubts that it'd work. Secret even from myself. I watched them saunter out of sight onto the Road. A little girl was shrieking from on top of the supply cart where she was being carried.

I turned to Baga and said, "Well, I'm off to court. It's about time for Jon to give judgment on today's cases."

"I wonder, boss...?" Baga said, keeping his face toward the Road rather than looking at me. "It was Maggie asking, you see, and I didn't know the answer."

"Well, ask then!" I said. There was no question that was as likely to get my back up as him wasting my time with nervous mumbling.

"You see, Maggie was wondering if you'd seen Lady May since you been back from Castle Ariel?" he said.

"I have not."

"Only, you see, Maggie says she hasn't been seeing men in a long while," Baga said. "Lady May hasn't, I mean. You know how women talk."

"I know that I'm not talking to a woman now," I said. I'd been facing the castle, but I turned now to Baga.

"That's none of my business," I said, hearing my voice get louder. "Lady May is an estimable person who fits in very well with the way things are done on Dun Add. For myself, the sooner I'm away from this place, the happier I'll be. Do you understand?"

"Yes, boss," Baga said. "Sorry, boss."

I was already striding up the slope toward the castle.

I was in the courtroom two days later when the Herald called a fellow named Boyes to state his case. He was a slender fellow, not bad looking except for his hair. That was a dirty blond and hung from his scalp like seaweed.

"I am Prince Boyes of Farandol," he said. "When my father Prince Lorcan died, my sister and her husband deprived me of my share of Farandol and its lands. I ask that you restore me to my rightful rank and lands."

Jon looked up from the folder he'd been poring over. "Boyes, styled Prince Boyes," he said. "I have read the docket my clerks have prepared for me. I decree that you, your sister Liufa, and your brother-in-law Lang will appear before me for determination of the case on its merits. Due to the distance to Farandol I have set the hearing for ninety days, with the option of moving it forward if possible."

Jon surveyed the room. "Is Lord Pal present in court?" he called.

I jumped up, startled. "Sir?" I said. "I'm here!"

"See me in chambers after I've completed these proceedings," Jon said. "Dismissed, next petition."

There were two more matters for the day's session. One caught my attention: representatives from Westervale—it seemed to be ruled by a group of nobles together, but the delegation here was of clerks—claimed that bandits from the Waste were preying on their herds. If that was true, then I'd be interested in learning what was going on.

I was at the door of Jon's chambers as soon as I could get there after the session closed, but there were already six people ahead of me. The door opened and Toledana stuck her head out. She called, "Lord Pal, please," and I slipped past a suddenly glum official from the supply office.

Toledana, Jon at his desk, and I were the only people present. He said, "Well, Pal, do you still want to go out immediately?"

"Yes sir," I said. "I listened to the Westervale request. I'd like to look into it."

"You'd find that one of the oligarchs is at the bottom of it if you did," Jon said, glancing at the folder. "Probably the one whose lands are nearest the Road. I'll send Kimber to sort it out."

He looked up at me. "You've got a boat," he said, "so I'd like you to take Boyes out to Farandol and bring his sister and brother-in-law back. That will save months."

"Yes sir," I said. I hoped I didn't sound as disappointed as I was, though I doubt Jon cared about my feelings when they were in the balance with the needs of the Commonwealth. "If that's what you want, sir."

I hadn't thought much about owning a boat before now, but I suddenly had a vision of being sent to all the most distant problems regardless of how interesting they were. If I offered Kimber the use of my boat—and Baga, of course—would Jon send him to Farandol instead?

Probably not. Besides, I'd said I would go where Jon ordered me, and right now that was Farandol.

"Farandol is well within Not-Here," Toledana said. "I'll give the full route to your boatman, of course, but I thought you might be interested in the situation."

"Yes, very much," I said. She gave me a warm smile in response. I guessed that most Champions were too focused on the immediate job to listen to what Toledana thought was fascinating.

"There's a string of nodes—thirty that I know of, but probably hundreds—out beyond Oak and Provence, what we think of as the Marches in that region," she said. "They're islands, enclaves, that weren't absorbed when Not-Here expanded there. The traffic on the Road there is almost entirely non-human."

"Beasts?" I asked.

"Yes, but other creatures as well," Toledana said. "Creatures which have never been described anywhere else. Perhaps not all of them sentient."

"The Road beyond the Marches is dangerous even for armed groups," Jon said. "Boyes was lucky to have made it to Here, let alone Dun Add."

He glanced at his file, then looked at me and grimaced. "Look, Pal," he said, "I don't like Boyes—or trust him, if it comes to that. But if this is a real chance for the Commonwealth to get a foothold into Not-Here, we have to take it. I want a base that we can patrol the Road from, to take it back from the Beasts and whatever else threatens human beings now. Do you understand?"

"Yes sir," I said. What I didn't say is that I wasn't sure I agreed. There was plenty of unoccupied territory that was Here, and it seemed to me that it wouldn't hurt to leave Farandol to itself.

But I suppose if there were people on Farandol and in the other places beyond the Marches, then they had a right to be part of the Commonwealth too. And anyway, it was Jon's decision.

"I told you that I didn't like Boyes," Jon said. "But I'm trying to build a government of laws, and even smelly little swine have rights under the law. Can you remember that, Pal?"

"Yes sir," I said. I shrugged. "I'll treat him as a job, the way I would an artifact I was rebuilding."

Jon gave me a slow smile. "I see why you get along so well with Guntram," he said. "Well, go and good luck to you."

✧   ✧   ✧

I met Boyes at the boat the next morning, the first time I'd seen him close up. He smelled sour.

Now, farming means manure, and I don't know anybody on Beune who bathes in the winter: either you (literally) freeze or it costs more in fuel than anybody can afford. Dun Add had different standards.

But that's not what I mean. There was something wrong about the way Boyes smelled. It was more like what you smell in the bedrooms of sick old people, but Boyes was young and moved like he was perfectly healthy.

"We'll be ready to go as soon as you get your luggage aboard, sir," I said.

"I have all I require," said Boyes, reaching over his shoulder to touch the small pack he wore. He had a pleasant voice, but it seemed lifeless.

"Well, you can get aboard, then," I said. "Take any of the rear compartments. Baga and I will be in the forward pair. It won't be long."

"The voyage will take a week, I'm told?" Boyes said.

I grinned. "Not on this boat," I said. "More like three days, I believe."

That was what the boat itself had told me. Baga would probably say the same.

"Very good," said Boyes. He went aboard.

I found myself frowning, but it didn't matter. Boyes would spend the voyage in his compartment or, if he didn't, I could spend it in mine. And it was only three days.

I'd seen Baga and Maggie approaching. They stopped twenty feet away and embraced briefly. Maggie turned and had almost reached the woodline before Baga joined me.

"Our guest's aboard," I said. "He seems a quiet sort."

"Good enough," Baga said. "Do you know anything about this Farandol?"

"Absolutely nothing," I said. "Toledana asked me to bring her as much information back as I can."

Baga nodded. "A smart lady," he said. "Very bloody smart."

He looked back in the direction in which his wife had disappeared, then said brightly, "Say, did you hear what happened last night?"

"No," I said. I'd gotten a certain amount of palace gossip when Welsh and Garrett were in Dun Add, but nothing since then. Which was fine with me, believe me.

"You know Gismonde, one of the Champions?" Baga said.

I shrugged. "Go on," I said. I didn't *know* Gismonde, but I'd met him.

"Well, he drank a bottle of poisoned wine and died!" Baga said. "And his buddy Baran says that it was the Consort, Jolene herself, who did it! Can you believe that?"

"No," I said. "Frankly I can't. But fortunately it's none of my business. Let's get going shall we?"

I walked to the hatch. Earlier this morning I would have said that I couldn't be more ready to get out of Dun Add.

I'd been wrong. I was even more anxious now to leave.

CHAPTER 27

Farandol

I watched in a trance as Baga brought the boat in smoothly. Nobody was at Farandol's landingplace, but I could see a stone structure with sheer walls within a hundred yards. Beyond that were fields with a few workers. They wore floppy hats.

I returned to Here and got up. Baga walked to the hatch and waited with his hand on the lever. Boyes stood beside his compartment; he nodded when he met my eyes. He was wearing leather gloves, which I didn't recall him doing before.

"All right, boss?" Baga said.

"Sure, open it up," I said, checking that my shield and weapon were in place in the pockets of my red suit. I heard Boyes walking up the corridor behind me.

Baga threw the lever, using his whole body. Something wet and pungent brushed the left side of my neck, stinging briefly. I saw myself falling forward, but I didn't *feel* anything, even when I hit the floor.

Boyes walked past me. He had a small pail in one hand and a wet cloth in the other.

Baga turned. His mouth opened when he saw me; I suppose he said something. He bent forward, reaching for me. Boyes patted him on the neck with the cloth also.

My consciousness slowly shrank down to a point of white light. Then that blanked out also.

I woke up—I won't say "became alert" because I wasn't. I was held to a stone wall by flat iron straps which were hinged at one end and locked to a bolt on the other. One gripped either wrist, and there was a larger band clamping my waist. I was seated and my legs, splayed out in front of me, weren't held.

My neck stung. A tall man was looking down at me. Boyes was beside him, holding a cloth and pail. The smell was different from what I'd noticed in the boat when Boyes knocked me out; this time it was sickly sweet.

My guts suddenly flipped over. I barely turned my head to the side before I spewed my breakfast onto the stone floor.

The tall man grinned. Boyes's expression didn't change. He put the wet cloth into the metal pail and closed a lid over it.

My vomit hadn't changed the condition of the room, the cell, very much. I thought of Palin's body, shackled to a similar wall by the Spider, and wondered whether that was what Boyes or his master had in mind for me.

"I'm Lang," the tall man said. His voice sounded thin but the tone was pleasant enough. He took a flat, circular box from his tunic pocket; it looked something like the container Mom had used to hold buttons. "This is the device I use to control Boyes."

Lang took a similar box from the opposite pocket. "This is the one that will control you," he said, grinning again. "I decided that I need an agent in Jon's court. That you've come with your own boat is an unexpected bonus."

"I can't run the boat myself," I said. I'd decided that I might as well speak to Lang. I didn't see how speaking could make my situation worse than it was already.

"Your man is in another cell," Lang said. "In good time I'll see if I need to fit him with a controller as well. I rather think not. I've found plenty of soldiers simply by paying them or—"

The smile widened.

"—letting them do as they please, so long as they also do what I direct them to do. That's better than money with many humans."

I didn't respond to that. By shifting my butt slightly— all I *could* shift it with the band around my waist—I could tell that my weapon and shield were still in their pockets. If I could get a hand free . . .

I grinned. That wasn't what Lang was expecting. He stepped forward and slapped me, his face twisting with fury.

"Do you think I'm joking!" he screamed. "You'll see how much a joke it is when I've keyed the controller to your brain! It's from Not-Here, did you know that?"

The slap didn't hurt as much as it should have. I wondered if the drug that knocked me out and the second drug that brought me around again had between them left me numb. As well as being sick to my stomach.

"I don't know anything about it," I said. "I've never heard of a mind controller before. Are you a Maker?"

What I did know was that while it was possible to work with artifacts from Not-Here, no Maker I knew could fit a Not-Here device to affect a human mind. That was like asking a blind man to paint a picture.

I thought again about the weapon in my pocket. I avoided smiling.

"I'm not a Maker," Lang said, grinning again, "but a Maker does my bidding. I'll leave you alone with it."

He and Boyes turned and went out.

A moment later, holding one of the disks Lang had called a controller, a Beast entered the cell. He closed the door behind him.

I'd been equally close to a Beast when I'd killed the Shade on the Road. I'd immediately backed away then, because I expected the Beast to attack me as soon as I'd freed it. I hadn't really gotten a good view.

I had leisure to observe this one, however. The light was bad, but it was good enough for me to tell that the slippery, uncertain, look of the Beast's body was because I wasn't really seeing the surface. The Beast wasn't completely Here.

I suppose it was watching me also, though it didn't have eyes that I could see. A voice in my mind said, "Do not get your hopes up, human. I have many times synchronized this controller with the mind of a human. Your mind will be no different from the others."

"That's not what I wanted to hear," I said. I spoke aloud because that seemed more natural to me. "Still,

I learned when I was a kid that it didn't do any good to argue with reality."

I looked at the palm-sized box gripped by the Beast's blackness. I couldn't say "fingers" because the contact flowed and changed like water sloshing onto the ground. I wondered if I could get beyond the controller's range in the boat. I could try, at least.

"Distance will make no difference to the controller," the Beast said. "It operates in a different reality from either Here or Not-Here."

I was surprised at the Beast telling me that. On second thought, I wondered if I could believe him. Believe *it*.

The Beast didn't laugh—could you laugh in your mind?—but it said, "I am not Lang's ally, human. I am Lang's slave, for as long as he has my ancestor in thrall in a place I cannot go to free him."

"I was surprised to see a—" I said. "I mean, to see you working for a human."

"'Beast' does not offend me, human," the Beast said. "Nothing a mere human could do would offend me. But in any case, Lang is no more human than I am. Lang is a thing of the Waste."

"But he looks—" I said, then remembered the Shade had looked like a beautiful woman until the instant I killed it.

"You rescued one of my kin on the Road," the Beast said. "Why was it that you did that?"

I laughed. I couldn't have lied, and I probably wouldn't have anyway.

"It was really an accident," I said. "I killed the Shade and that turned the Beast loose. To tell the truth, I expected the Beast to attack me, then. Since

I'd made my weapon useless for five minutes or so, I wasn't looking forward to that."

I thought of laughter again, though of course I heard nothing. The Beast said, "You could have passed on and done nothing. The Shade would not have been a danger for weeks after it had fed."

I made a face. "Yeah, I know," I said. "But Shades are enemies to life—all life. I wasn't going to walk away from it. I figured I'd take my chances with the Beast. And it worked out. Remember, I'd wanted to be a Champion."

Which I now was, amazingly. Though that wasn't doing me any good.

"My kin was young," the Beast said. "And he was badly injured. He would certainly have attacked you had he been able to."

"I was lucky," I said. "I guess we were both lucky."

"Yes," the Beast said. "I suppose you were."

It turned and touched the door pull.

"Aren't you going to tune that thing?" I said. The creature was still holding the controller.

"I have done so," the Beast said. It paused but did not turn. "I expect that Lang will set it so that you will do his bidding and will not act to harm him, because that is what he did with other humans whom he controls. But that is for him, not me."

Then the Beast left the room. I was alone for a moment with my thoughts.

They weren't good company.

The only light in the cell came from a window behind me, which meant through a narrow slot in the outer wall. It didn't help me estimate time, but it can't have been but a few minutes before the door rattled again and two guys came in. One was missing two fingers of his left hand; the other had a scar up his right cheek that ended in the empty eye-socket.

A third guy, this one with weapon and shield, stood in the doorway, and there were more people in the hallway beyond. I could chop them *all* to dog scraps if I got my weapon in my hand....

One-Eye held my right wrist while his partner unlocked the pin holding the clamp. To my surprise, both men stepped away. I lowered my arm and shook blood back into it. Then I lowered my hand into my pocket and brought out my weapon.

"I'll take that," said One-Eye. I gave him the weapon, which he took to the armed man at the door. He might be the only one of the three in the cell with me who was capable of using it.

The man with the key unlocked my left wrist and himself dipped the shield out of that pocket. He unlocked my waist band also while One-Eye took the shield to the fellow at the door.

I got up slowly, bracing myself against the wall I'd been strapped to. The shackles had galled the bones of both wrists and my hipbones. Nothing serious, though, and the wobbliness I felt was likely the last of the drug wearing off rather than any real problem.

I couldn't understand why I'd let the thugs take my weapon and shield. It was like a wall of frozen slush had slid over my mind when One-Eye reached for the weapon. Instead of cutting him apart, I'd just opened my hand.

"This way," said the armed man, nodding toward the door. He'd put my equipment into the satchel he carried on a shoulder strap. I walked into the hall and followed the half-dozen men there toward the room at the end. None of them were equipped as warriors, but they all carried clubs or big knives. The warrior with weapon and shield was behind me.

We came out into a chamber with a domed roof and a chair up three steps in a corner where Lang sat. Boyes and a woman who shared some features as him were on the chairs to either side on the broad bottom step. I remembered that his complaint to Jon had been that his sister Liufa and her husband Lang had dispossessed him. That had been mostly a lie, but the woman might well be Boyes's sister.

She looked terrified. She must not be controlled the way her brother was. I'd never seen Boyes show any emotion.

With the group who'd accompanied me from the cell, there were about thirty thugs in the chamber. Two or three were women. Only one other man and the guy from my cell were warriors. All were ugly, and at least half were missing body parts or had bad scars.

"Well, Pal..." Lang said. I didn't see the controller, but his hands resting on the flat arms of his chair held a weapon and shield. "*Lord* Pal. Are you ready to carry out your first mission as the Champion of Farandol?"

For a moment I said nothing—mostly to see if I *had* to speak. Apparently I didn't, so I said, "What do you want me to do, Lang?"

My tone didn't make his grin slip. I remembered the Beast saying Lang was a thing of the Waste. It seemed hard to believe.

"There's another enclave not far away," Lang said.

"A nest of robbers. Rowley's Roost, they call it. The leader styles himself Lord Charles. They raid not only among the enclaves but into Here as well."

"How do they manage that?" I said. So far as I could tell, I was completely myself, the same guy who'd boarded my boat in Dun Add—except that I wasn't carrying my shield and weapon now.

"They travel in a large band," Lang said, "just as I did when I sent Boyes to Dun Add to fetch you."

Boyes sat in his chair like a dummy. He didn't move at the sound of his name.

"Lord Charles is a warrior," Lang said. "He has two or three others. Mostly they're just filthy cut-throats."

"Like your own gang," I said.

I heard growls from the gang, but Lang just grinned again. "Exactly," he said. "I want you to wipe out the nest of ruffians, Champion. You see, you're doing what you went to Dun Add to do."

"To do that," I said, "I'll need my equipment. Are you going to give it back?"

"Of course," said Lang. "Jacques, return our Champion's arms to him."

The thug with missing fingers reached into his companion's satchel. With my weapon and shield, he approached me.

I took them from his hands and looked around the chamber. It was long odds, but not really *too* long. . . .

The frozen feeling slid back over my mind.

Lang's loud laughter rang in the chamber. Everyone joined him except for me and Boyes; and I suppose Liufa.

CHAPTER 28

The Duties of a Champion

Lang permitted me to sleep—and to eat, which was a particular mercy—aboard the boat. Baga remained in a cell. I regretted that, but just now I had as much as I could do to take care of myself.

The standard fare on Farandol's tables was meat stew. I didn't trust what the meat was. I suppose it didn't matter, but I'd still rather eat the boat's processed meals.

Buck and I were ready to leave at dawn, as Lang had ordered. I didn't need the controller to get me up, but it was nearer midmorning than dawn before the rest of the gang was gathered. They were even less impressive in good light than they had been in the throne room.

The Army of Farandol, under my command. I could only hope that Lord Charles didn't attract a better grade of soldier. That seemed likely enough, because my guide—Jacques, the thug who with One-Eye had freed me in the cell—had been one of Lord Charles's gang.

"Benlo said I was cheating at cards," Jacques said

as we tramped along the Road with the rest of the band straggling along behind us. "I slotted him before he could get his own knife out, but I took off before Charles learned what'd happened to his bum-boy. And I took all three dogs off with me so the gang couldn't make any time on the Road if they followed."

"That was quick thinking," I said. I had to depend on the man, and I've learned there's usually something good you can say if you put your mind to it.

"Scared me sober, it did," said Jacques, nodding solemnly.

"How many guards are there at the castle gate in daytime?" I said.

"Dunno," said Jacques. "One, I guess. I never had the duty myself."

"There's one at Farandol," One-Eye—that turned out to be the name everybody called him by—said. "Old Seltsy, and you've got to wake him up."

"And the gate is closed by night, like it is here?" I said. "Back in Farandol, I mean?"

"Sure, closed and barred," Jacques agreed. "And I guess there's three or four guys in the guard room overhead. They can drop the portcullis, too."

"Say, how you going to get us into the castle, hey?" One-Eye said. "You going to cut through the stone? I gotta say that your weapon didn't look like much."

I kept my temper, but it was a strain to do that. This bloody moron was criticizing as neat a piece of hardware as I'd seen even in the Hall of Champions!

But he *was* a moron, of course. I didn't need to defend my gear to him or to anybody else.

"I suppose I could if I had to," I said. "And there was nobody else around. What I figure to do, though, is to saunter up to the gate and block it until the rest of you lot come up. Jacques, you wait at the edge of landingplace. Everybody else stays on the Road where they won't be seen. When I've blocked the gate, you fetch the army."

I was wearing ordinary farm gear—floppy hat, brown trousers, and tunic with a belt of rye-straw rope. I didn't figure anybody was going to look twice at me.

"Look, Lord Charles is gonna to come at you before we get up there," Jacques said. "He's a warrior and he's got warriors, two when I was there but he was trying to hire a third one."

"He's got a woman, Jacques told me," said One-Eye. "Have you ever heard of that? Don't seem natural to me."

"It's not common," I said, "but it's natural enough. The Ancients built weapons for men only, but nothing you can point to that doesn't have some exceptions."

There were women boatmen and women Makers, though not as many as men, and there were even a few warriors. I'd been surprised when the clerk at the Aspirants' Hall had switched on my gear, but I'd seen it happen.

"Not *natural*," One-Eye repeated, though he didn't look at me. Well, he'd been a moron when he insulted my weapon. I couldn't expect him to suddenly get smarter.

"There's a branch just ahead of us," I said.

"That's it," said Jacques. "That's the Roost."

I looked back along the Road. I could see only three of the gang behind me, though one was the warrior Severin. Two more appeared as I watched, though.

"All right, Jacques," I said. "You come in but don't

come any closer than where you can watch me. One-Eye, you stay here at the fork and keep the rest of the army together. And when Jacques tells you that I'm in the Roost's gateway you come running. Understood?"

"Sure," One-Eye muttered.

"And Severin?" I said. "If I don't get back-up, then you better hope that I'm really killed. Because I'll be looking for you, and I'll tell you right now that your shield isn't going to last long."

"Don't get your bowels in an uproar," Severin said. "I never minded a fight."

He looked back. About twenty more of the gang had arrived, but the other warrior wasn't among them.

Severin shrugged and grinned at me. "Neither does Roush, but he's a slow git for all that."

I grinned back. "C'mon, Jacques," I said. "Time for me to show you folks why I'm here."

Except for the moment when I saw Lang on his chair and thought of cutting him apart, I couldn't remember the controller doing anything to me. Rooting out a nest of robbers was exactly the sort of thing I'd expected to do when I became a Champion. I hadn't expected to be doing it on the orders of a man like Lang, if he was even a man, but I was comfortable with the *job*.

The grass of the Roost's landingplace was waist high and going to seed, though there were was a well-trampled path through it. I figured I'd have chiggers in the morning, but getting to the morning was the problem right now.

There were cows on the rolling ground to the left of the castle. I wondered how big this node was. I hadn't thought to ask.

Buck and I were coming on alone. Jacques was

waiting just off the Road like he was supposed to. I was feeling pretty lonely, even though everything was going to plan.

The castle itself was two stories of stone, but there was a brick watchtower on top of that and a man in it. I heard the lookout shout something down into the castle, though I couldn't tell what the words were.

A minute or so later—I was near up to the big wooden gate—a fellow came out to meet me. He was wearing what must've been a pretty good suit once, but I doubt it'd been washed since he got it and he was a messy eater. He wore crossed shoulder belts, and I swear there must've been a dozen knives hanging from them. He held a big one in his right hand with notches in the edge like a saw.

"Whoa, buddy!" he said. "Who're you and what d'ye think you're doing here?"

"My name's Pal," I said, "and I'm here to sign on with Lord Charles."

"Are you now, bucko?" the guard said. "I suppose you think he takes just any riff-raff that stumbles in off the Road. Do you have any money?"

"If I had money," I said, stepping past the fellow, "I wouldn't be here. And I don't know who Lord Charles takes, but I figure to ask him."

I was within two paces of the gateway. My right hand was in the tunic pocket.

The gates were swung outward. A six-by-six-inch timber leaned against the wall just inside. That five-foot bar would slide into staples to lock the gates closed at night. I could see the spikes of the iron portcullis in the ceiling inward of that, ready to drop and keep the passage closed even if the gate itself was broken open.

"Hey!" the guard shouted. "You take another step and I'll cut your bloody head off!"

I brought my weapon out and turned. I had my left hand up to grab his right wrist if he tried to cut at me, but he just stared in amazement. My weapon ripped his belly, spattering blood and I suppose other things over the ground beyond him, but I could've killed him just as easily with the knife dangling from my belt—just like the one every farmer wore.

He wasn't a guard: he was a bully and a thief, or he wanted to be. But I had to get him out of the way.

I scrambled into the gateway. I wasn't thinking about what I'd done though I would be, sure enough, as soon as I had the time to.

I switched off my weapon, but I didn't have time to put it away. Gripping with my left hand and right wrist, and pushing with my booted foot, I slid the cross-bar— still upright—into the track where the portcullis would fall, then stepped further into the passage and waited with both my shield and weapon ready.

"C'mere, Buck!" I said. He came bounding to my side.

A bell was clanging in the watchtower. I figured the people I really had to worry about would be inside the castle, but I had to be ready for somebody coming from the other way too. There might be guards with the farmers and herdsmen.

All somebody'd have to do was kick the bar out of the way and the portcullis could block the passage again. That would give Lord Charles as long as he wanted to deal with me.

There was a rattle and shriek as the portcullis slid down its track—and a *bang!* as it hit the timber and stopped a good four feet from the floor. The weight of the heavy grating would make it hard to move the timber even if I weren't in place to protect it.

Three soldiers halted at the far end of the passage, ten feet from me. One had a crossbow. I saw them distorted and blurred by my shield.

"Well, shoot him!" said the man holding a broad-bladed spear. The bowman obediently shouldered his weapon and shot. The bolt's iron head sparkled as it struck the shield; it dropped to the floor.

I laughed. I wasn't sure they could hear me, but when I feinted forward as if I was charging them, they scattered away.

I backed to where I'd been standing before, just ahead of the half-lowered portcullis. I glanced behind to see if anybody was approaching from the outside end, but there wasn't. The guard was sprawled right in front of the opening, which was likely to put off anybody who wasn't *real* committed.

I'd remember in my dreams the way his eyes had rolled up. He was a nasty bully and I didn't regret that he was dead. But...

A warrior appeared at the end of the passage. "Come on!" I shouted. "I'm waiting for you!"

He doesn't have a dog, I thought. The fellow didn't come on.

Buck growled. A second warrior appeared beside the first one. Seeing through Buck's eyes, I couldn't be sure of the colors, but the new opponent wore a lighter garment.

I heard dogs barking. A third warrior—in black—appeared behind the first two. With this one were a pair of hounds and a handler who slipped their leashes and scrambled away. If they were led on leashes they couldn't be well-trained, but I no longer had the huge edge over my opponents that I'd hoped for.

I couldn't handle three warriors at once, but here in this stone tunnel I didn't have to. There was only room for one at a time to fight comfortably, though if two warriors were used to working together they could manage it.

The three argued—or more likely, the one in black harangued the other two. He was waggling his weapon in a fashion that looked more threat than encouragement.

The first two warriors turned toward me. Then my lighter-colored opponent rushed. The darker one kept a half step behind and to his right.

To Buck and therefore to me, it was all in slow motion. I stepped forward and drove the leader's stroke right, into the path of his partner. As the two of them fouled each other, I slashed for the leader's ankle, below his shield. It was the stroke I'd found that did best for me, using Buck's motion-sense to give me an advantage.

It worked this time too: the warrior toppled backward, his severed right foot on the stone floor. His partner slashed down. I took the blow on my shield and thrust for the center of his chest.

His shield was better than I'd expected—his weapon had barely flashed sparks when my own shield stopped it—but not good enough to save him. His shield failed in a bright flash, and my weapon drove on, burning a black hole through his chest and heart.

I heard my men behind me, shouting as they ducked under the portcullis, but I ignored that and lunged toward the warrior in black. He hadn't entered the passage to support his men. That didn't make him a coward: he couldn't have done them any good, and maybe he just wanted to face me where he had room to maneuver.

I jumped over the body of the warrior I'd wounded, but I tripped and almost fell. He'd lifted his torso to grab his right stump with both hands and I kicked his forehead. The blackened ends of the leg bones stuck out from where the flesh had shrunk back from the cut.

The warrior in black used my stumble to thrust. I was way out of position for blocking it with my weapon, but I'd kept my shield up. There were a lot of sparks but the shield held. I'd want to look at it when this was over because Black's weapon was a long sight better than those of his two supporters, but for now I could still trust my shield.

I cut at Black's head to see how good his shield was. He didn't recover his own weapon in time to deflect mine, and his shield was decent but not good enough for this fight.

Black retreated. There were at least a dozen people in the courtyard, but only Black was a warrior. My soldiers—Lang's soldiers—were rushing in behind me; I figured they could handle the locals.

I swung down at Black. He got his weapon up this time but wasn't able to block me completely. His shield sparked furiously, losing at least a third of its coverage.

Instead of hacking again, I thrust for Black's face. He didn't raise what was left of his shield high enough. His head burst as my weapon turned his brains to steam.

I backed to the nearest wall and leaned against it. My legs were wobbly and I was sucking in air through my mouth.

With my shoulders against the stone, I took a look around. Since nobody was near, I shut down my shield to get a better view. Yeah, there was a chance that somebody with a crossbow was going to pot me, but there was a chance that a block was going fall off the wall above and bash my brains out. You can't spend all the time thinking about how to stay safe and still live what I'd call a life.

The fight was over. Severin and Roush, Lang's two warriors, didn't have great shields, but they'd stop crossbow bolts and slow a spear-thrust to harmlessness. The Roost's fighters were surrendering now that their leader was dead.

Or they were *trying* to surrender. The Farandol troops were cutting the throats of all those who'd thrown their weapons down.

"Stop that!" I shouted, no longer feeling exhausted. "Stop killing prisoners!"

Jacques withdrew his butcher knife from the belly of the man he'd just stabbed. "The boss told us to kill everybody in the castle!" he said. "Lang did."

"Well, I tell you not to!" I said. I tried to switch on my weapon. I would've stepped toward Jacques, but the wash of cold slush descended on my mind again.

My body didn't obey my will. I put my equipment in my tunic pockets. All I could do was turn away so that I didn't have to watch the slaughter.

There was worse in the other direction.

The warrior in black tunic and tights was a man of about fifty. There was gray in his blond hair but his beard was a dark russet. Lord Charles, I supposed. He'd died quickly.

So had the warrior in walnut brown, the fellow whom I'd seen through Buck's eyes as my darker opponent. The hole burned in the center of his chest would've brought death almost before the first flash of pain from the wound. He lay well within the passage.

The remaining warrior, the first to rush me, wore yellow. She was a woman. Somebody had cut her throat, probably One-Eye since his big knife lay gobbed with blood on the stone beside her.

One-Eye was raping the corpse.

I grabbed One-Eye by both shoulders and jerked him upright. "You scum!" I shouted.

"It ain't natural!" One-Eye shouted back, meaning something different from what I would've with the same words.

I wasn't thinking. I slammed One-Eye against the stone wall of the passage. He went limp and dropped like spilled intestines when I took my hands away to reach for my weapon and shield.

I didn't draw my weapon after all. I'd flattened the back of One-Eye's skull. There was a smear of blood and brains on the stone where he'd hit.

Lang's controller would've stopped me from interfering while One-Eye was murdering the wounded warrior, but apparently it had no objection to my killing gang members after the massacre. I wondered how far I could take that. . . .

Buck smelled how I was feeling. He rubbed his head against my knee and whined.

I stroked his ears. Screams occasionally drifted from the interior of the castle.

After a while—a minute or two—I realized that my job here was finished. I clucked to Buck and we headed back to the Road and Farandol. The others would follow when they chose to.

If that was "never" I'd be pleased, more pleased than I would be with any other answer.

CHAPTER 29

A Change in Circumstances

"Lang says he'll let me out of here if I'll agree to work for him," Baga said.

I shrugged. "Maybe he will," I said, because that was the truth.

Lang had let me carry food from the boat's converter to Baga. I'd found a bowl in the castle's outdoor kitchen and scoured it with sand and dry dirt, then washed it in water. What I'd seen in the kitchen made me even less likely to want to eat anything coming from it.

"But you don't think I should, do you?" Baga said.

"No," I said. That was the truth too.

I wondered why Lang hadn't tuned a controller to Baga. Maybe the controller would interfere with a boatman's use of his boat, though it didn't keep me from using my weapon and shield normally. I didn't know whether I could work as a Maker, though. The fact I hadn't had any urge to try since I'd been captured suggested something had happened besides not being able to attack Lang.

Or maybe Lang just didn't have many controllers. I've generally found that the simplest answer is the right one.

Baga sighed. "Guess I'll stick it out," he said. He handed me back the bowl and the mug I'd brought wine in.

Jacques glowered as he locked the cell behind me. Lang had only laughed when Jacques told him how I'd killed One-Eye, but he must've adjusted the controller because I felt cold wash over me again when I'd seen Jacques kick Baga.

The controller hadn't kept me from grabbing a club from another guard and tossing it to Baga, though. Since then Jacques hadn't tried any tricks, but a broken forearm hadn't made Jacques like me any better.

I started down the corridor, planning to go back to the boat. The Beast stood at the door of an empty cell. "I came to visit you, human."

"Your controller works perfectly," I said. "I'm sure Lang would tell you so."

"If I had been concerned," the Beast said inside my skull, "the fact that Lang is still alive would have told me so. I did not doubt my skill. Sit down in this room—"

Blackness flowed from the larger blackness, toward the open door.

"—and tell me about the capture of Rowley's Roost, human."

I stepped into the empty cell. The Beast followed and closed the door behind us. I sat on the wooden bench that doubled as a bunk for prisoners.

"You see into my mind," I said. "You know what happened."

"Yes," said the Beast. "But tell me, and I will know how you feel about it."

I snorted. "About the fight, I feel fine," I said. "Neither of the first pair was as good as most folks I sparred with when I was an Aspirant. The one's shield was stiff in the center but really narrow. I found after the fight that she was a woman; maybe that had something to do with it."

"And Lord Charles himself?" the Beast asked.

"That was more of a fight," I said. "He had good equipment, not as good as mine but decent. His trouble was lack of training. He didn't respond quick enough when I did something. He just wasn't used to fighting somebody who knew how to fight. I felt good about beating him, but I had the advantages."

"And then?" said the Beast.

"Then I wished I'd never come to Farandol," I said. "Well, I sorta wished that already, or anyway that I'd known what was going on here before I arrived. This is exactly the sort of place Jon is trying to stamp out."

I remembered turning away from the massacre that I couldn't stop and seeing One-Eye on the warrior's body. I felt myself tense as I had when I jerked the *scum* off her and bashed him to death on the stone. At least I'd been able to stop *that*.

"The massacre of prisoners bothered you," the Beast said. "Even though you believe those being killed were as bad as those killing them. And as for the dead warrior—she was dead before your victim degraded her."

"The massacre bothered me," I said. "A lot. I don't

care who they were and I *know* they were the same sort as the ones from Farandol. I'd made it happen, and then I couldn't stop it."

I thought and added, "That's what really bothered me. Not that it was happening, but that I'd made it happen. *I* had."

"Is it the same sense that caused you to kill the Shade and free my kin, human?" the Beast asked. "This is a sense that I do not have and none of my kin have."

I got up and paced to the side-wall, a step and a half. "I don't know!" I said. I was angry from talking about that business, thinking about it. "I just know that it was wrong and it was happening because of me. And as for One-Eye, he was a filthy little turd and not worth burying!"

"Yes," said the Beast. "I am sure that's correct."

"The Beast I saved on the Road?" I said. "Was he part of your family?"

I felt the Beast's laughter in my mind for the first time during this conversation. "That juvenile was of a clan at feud with mine for a thousand years," the Beast said. "If I had met that pair on the Road, I would have killed the young one instead of the Shade. I am not like you, human."

I didn't say anything. I'd never given any thought to Beast families or towns; or to Beasts generally, I suppose, except to worry about meeting one on the Road.

But while there weren't any feuds like that on Beune, I'd sure read about humans getting along about that bad. I wondered if there was Beast communities more like Beune, where people—Beasts—didn't all like each other but at least everybody got along all right. Well, when they were sober.

"Clan is very important to me, human," the Beast said. "More important than you can perhaps imagine. Lang has trapped the soul of the late head of my clan in the Death Dimension, so that he cannot progress to his final fate."

I frowned. "Hung him on the wall?" I said, thinking of Palin in his dungeon.

"No," said the Beast. "Your ancestor is unwilling to die, human. Mine is dead but unable to continue his journey *in* death. Lang travels not only in the Waste but in the Death Dimension. Lang says he will release my ancestor in the future if I do as he wishes."

"Do you believe him?" I said. I couldn't imagine why anyone would, but I didn't understand anything about the situation. In particular, I didn't understand why the Beast was talking to me now.

"I believe that Lang holds my ancestor trapped," the Beast said. "My ancestor comes to me in dreams and pleads that I release him."

"That's not an answer!" I said. But I suppose it was. The Beast was saying that it had no choice, and I suppose that was true.

Instead of answering the Beast asked, "What would you do if you were freed from Lang's compulsion, human?"

"The first thing I'd do is treat Lang the same way I did the Shade," I said. If I could, of course; but I was pretty sure I could handle Lang as easily as I had Lord Charles.

"That was my expectation," the Beast said. "Lang is in the room at the end of the corridor which meets this one."

The fluid blackness extended in the direction opposite

to the staircase up. It withdrew, then reappeared from the mass. It dropped something on the floor between us.

The Beast had dropped a controller onto the stone.

It turned to the door. Well, it didn't have a face that I could see, but the whole mass rotated in the other direction.

"Wait!" I said; which was stupid, I should've just smashed the controller, but I didn't understand what was happening. "Why are you doing this?"

"What would you have done in my place?" the Beast asked.

I thought for a moment. "Killed Lang, I suppose," I said. "He's no more your friend than he is mine. But you say he's holding your ancestor and Lang is the only way to free him. And that's important to you."

"Very important," said the Beast. "Is your life important to you, human?"

"Sure it is!" I said.

"And yet you risked it to free my kin," said the Beast. "To free what to you was merely a dangerous animal. Because that was what you thought was right."

"I killed the Shade," I said. "Freeing your kin just happened. I didn't do it *to* free your kin."

"Yes," said the Beast. "You did what you thought was right. Whereas when I was faced with a choice, I chose to force you to do what you thought was wrong. I caused you to do things that anger and disgust you in a fashion that you would prefer to die rather than feel. But I have prevented you from dying as well."

"I wouldn't have killed myself," I said. But I knew that if it'd been a choice between letting the massacre happen or dying because I tried to stop it, I'd have tried to stop it.

"Then," said the Beast, "you may believe that your example has made me a better person. Or a better Beast, if you like."

It walked out of the cell. I looked at the controller, then pulled my weapon from my pocket.

The controller was an Ancient artifact. I'd rather have burned down a chapel than destroy something made by the Ancients.

I switched on my weapon and drew its tip through the controller, then back again crossways. The metal case—I think it was bronze—spit drops in all directions, and the ceramic interior shattered to dust.

I shut off the weapon but kept it and the shield in my hands. I went looking for Lang.

I'd thought briefly about fetching Buck from the boat, but Lang didn't have a dog. With a man like Lang—a thing like Lang it if the Beast was right—I didn't worry about being fair—but also, I wasn't worried about a fair fight. If Lang managed to kill me, well, I wouldn't have to watch another massacre then either.

Jacques wasn't in sight when I came out of the cell; chances were he'd ducked somewhere when he saw the Beast. I turned the corner of the corridor and started toward the far end, fifty feet away. As I did so, the door there opened and Lang stepped out. His tunic was patterned with black and white diamonds over black trousers.

"Hello, Lang," I said. "I've come to kill you."

Lang reached into a tunic pocket without speaking. His hand came out empty. I smiled and switched on my equipment.

The walls to either side became dark blurs, the

stone and the joints between individual blocks merged into featureless compression. Lang blurred also as he drew his shield and weapon from their holsters on his fabric belt.

I wondered how the Beast had gotten the controller away from Lang. Making a slave of a creature—a person—as clever as the Beast was a dangerous business.

The corridor wasn't wide enough for maneuvering, and that wasn't to my taste anyway. I went straight at him, not running but taking full strides. I thought for a moment that Lang was going to dodge down the side corridor—the basement was laid out with the castle foundations as the center of a square of corridors—but instead he raised his shield and held his weapon back to strike overhand.

He probably doesn't get any more practice than Lord Charles did....

I slammed into him, shield to shield. My weapon was high also, but I had no intention of swinging that way. Lang did and carved a shrieking, sparkling trough in the stone ceiling. I thrust, aiming at his right shoulder.

Lang jumped back, but between the shock of his weapon stalling on the stone in mid-stroke and my counterthrust, he fumbled his weapon. It bounced on the floor.

I cut at his right hand as he bent to grab it. His shield held, but he skipped back a step and now I was standing over the fallen weapon.

I thought of what I'd seen at Rowley's Roost. With our shields on Lang couldn't see my grin, but I'll bet he knew it was there. I stepped forward.

Lang tried to scramble away, but he had to face me to use his shield. I hacked at it very deliberately, slanting my strokes to keep from hitting the ceiling and walls. Bits began to fail under the punishment. It was just a matter of time....

Lang saw that too. He flung what was left of the shield at me and turned to run. I guess he was hoping to get to the staircase in the middle of the corridor. I lunged and burned across his right leg at mid thigh.

I heard the scream in my mind, a high keening like the axle rubbing in a wooden wheel. It went on and on until I stabbed again, not really picking a target because of the pain in my head from the sound.

My weapon drove into Lang's body where the kidneys would have been in a human, but there was nothing remotely human about what writhed away from my sizzling cut. Nothing.

The scream stopped, though.

I cut again, severing the appendage that I'd taken for Lang's head while he—it—was alive. I don't think it was really a head, but all in all I seemed to have killed the thing. The only way to be sure would be a fire, a huge fire.

Somebody else could worry about that. I just wanted to be gone.

I walked back the way I'd come, to Baga's cell. It was locked with a thick wooden crossbar. I could've slid it open with the heel of my right hand, but instead I cut it through to make a point.

"C'mon, Baga," I said. "We're leaving."

"Glad to hear it, boss," Baga said. He stuck his head out and looked both ways before he left the cell, though.

"It's all right," I said. "But I'll lead."

Lang's warriors might try to stop us, but I didn't think they would. They'd seen me at Rowley's Roost; Lord Charles and his warriors were all three better than Severin and Roush.

I'd seen figures scuttling away as I turned the corner at Lang's room. I thought of searching that room—I wondered what would happen to Boyes now that Lang was dead but the controller hadn't been destroyed—but I didn't want to spend the time.

"Are we going back to Dun Add?" Baga said as we entered the castle corridor.

"Soon," I said. "But first, I've got some other business to take care of. We're going to Castle Ariel. I need to talk with Palin."

Who was very likely my father.

CHAPTER 30

Castle Ariel and More Distant Places

Buck hopped willingly out of the boat as soon as Baga opened up at Castle Ariel. I'd exercised him along the Road at Farandol, but he'd still been cooped up more than he liked to be. Well, he and I both had.

The gong in the tower still echoed, though the watchman had only struck it once. He waved down at me. He was one of the soldiers who'd gone off with Garrett, though I don't believe I'd ever heard his name.

"Say, there's been a fire," said Baga. I hadn't noticed that when I'd viewed the node through the boat's eyes, but the smell of smoke still hung in the air.

Somebody'd built a fire in the rocky gorge to the left of the landingplace. I peered over the edge, frowning. It must have been deliberate because there'd only been scrub clinging to the rocks when I'd last been here.

Oh.

"It was a pyre for the body of the Spider," I said.

"My God, it must've stunk like you can't believe when Garrett came with the garrison! They must've hated me!"

"Well, there was nothing we could've done, just the two of us," Baga said reasonably. "I figure you did as much as anybody could ask when you killed the thing, right?"

"I wouldn't count on that," I said, but there wasn't a lot I could do about it now. Or earlier, like Baga had said. I started up toward the castle.

One leaf of the double gate was open. A dozen people came spilling out with Welsh in the lead. "Pal!" he shouted. "Lord Pal! *Good* to see you again, buddy!"

"It doesn't sound like they're too mad at you," Baga said in a low voice from behind me.

"Say, it's good to see you!" Welsh repeated as he led me into the castle. "Come on into the command post. Say, we didn't expect you so quick but that's fine, everything's going fine."

A soldier came running up to us with what was probably a wineskin. Half a dozen small metal cups were attached to it by light chains; they jingled like bells. "No, we'll be in the CP," Welsh told him. Then to me he added, "Say, Garrett just went out on patrol to Catermole and won't be back for a week. Are you staying that long, sir?"

They'd put the command post in the base of the gate tower. There was a bunk against the back wall; the curtain that could have concealed it was drawn back. Welsh ignored the big chair behind the desk and instead took one of the three facing it, patting the seat of another to guide me.

"Look, I'm not here to check up on you, Welsh,"

I said, feeling embarrassed. "I'm glad it's going well, though. You said Garrett is out patrolling?"

"Yeah, we've always got a squad out in one direction or another," Welsh said. The soldier with the wine skin was filling ordinary glass goblets at a sideboard against the back wall. "Me or Garrett lead them now, but when things get settled in we'll pass off the duty most of the time. You know, we've got twice the colonists moving in to the region than there were before you put us here, sir. Most to Catermole, but the country beyond the castle here's getting quite a lot too. You're going to be rich, Lord Pal! Richer."

"That's all right," I said, "but you're here to make the region part of the Commonwealth. Which you're doing. I don't really think about money."

The soldier handed us the goblets. The one Welsh got was a pale pink color while mine looked as dark as ink. I'd seen the server mix water into the one he gave Welsh.

"I'm cutting way back," Welsh said, noting where my eyes had gone. "It's, you know, being in charge that does it. I got a lot of folks depending on me."

He sipped and without meeting my eyes, added, "Garrett and Lily are making a go of it too. I won't say it's not hard; but I tell you, not all the trouble's been on Garrett's side!"

"I'm glad to hear that," I said again. I tried the wine and wished mine had been diluted too. "But I'm really here to talk to Lord Palin."

Welsh looked up. I'd surprised him. "Ah, sir?" he said. "We've got that whole dungeon locked like you told us, Is that all right? We haven't disturbed him. What's in the dungeon, I mean."

"That's exactly right," I said. I stood up. "But I'm going to disturb him now."

Welsh shrugged and got up also. "Here's the keys," he said, taking a ring of a dozen from a wall peg. "The big one's the main door. The rest are for the cells, but none of 'em are locked."

He coughed into his hand and said, "Ah, Pal? D'ye want anybody to go down with you?"

"No need," I said. "I know where the dungeon is."

I started across the courtyard. Baga was walking with me. I turned to him and said, "You don't have to go down with me, you know"

He shrugged. "Well, I'll wait in the door downstairs, I guess," he said. "Remember, I was here when the Spider came back. I don't guess anything now is going to be that bad."

A couple of the people in the courtyard or up on the battlements waved to us, but mostly they just stared—or bowed, or hid their faces like the two young women hanging clothes out to dry on a rack of poles and cords.

Somebody'd pegged the Spider's wedge-shaped head to the wall above the doorway. "It's bigger than I remember it being," I said, looking up as we passed under it. I wondered if the inside of the head had been cleaned—and how that could have been done.

"It looked plenty bloody big to me," Baga said. "And I wasn't the one it was coming for, either."

We got to the shaft. "It's just a matter of stepping in and pointing your right finger down," I said to Baga. "But if you want to wait here, that's fine."

I pointed and stepped out in the cellar. I wasn't sure whether I actually moved in the shaft or if my body went between ground level and the dungeon without going through the space in between. It didn't matter so long as everything worked.

I walked to the iron door at the end of the corridor. It had been open when I came here the first time, probably open for years or decades, but Garrett and Welsh had closed it on my orders.

Baga didn't appear in the shaft behind me. I didn't blame him.

The key turned stiffly, but it turned. The hinges were more of a problem, but my burst of anger when I felt the rust fighting me made me put a foot on the jamb and jerk hard. That pulled it half open, plenty wide enough for me to slip through.

In the cell, Palin hadn't moved. I grinned at the thought, which helped how I was feeling.

"Lord Palin?" I said. I wasn't sure what to call him. I figured that was safe. "I didn't mean to bother you again, but I need information that you're the only one I know who might have. What do you know about the Death Dimension?"

The husk of the man shackled to the wall laughed. The sound was like dead beetles rustling when the wind blew them against each other.

"I know everything about that place, man," the corpse said. "I know that I have clung to these chains for twenty years so that I am not sucked into that place and from there to my judgment."

"Sir," I said. "The ancestor of, of a friend of mine, a Beast, is held there. A thing that called itself Lang trapped him, it, there. I want to free the ancestor."

"You are a man and you say that?" said the corpse.

"I'm a man," I said. "I need to do this. The Beast,

the friend, sacrificed the most important thing there was to him in order to save me. To save my life, my *soul*. I want to give him back what he gave up for me. If I die then, that's okay. I'll pay that to free his ancestor's spirit."

Palin laughed again. *God*, that was a horrible sound. "Do you think it is as easy as you entering my mind, as you would enter an Artifact?" he said. "And we together entering the other place?"

The corpse's laughter was almost as bad as Lang's screams in my head as I killed him. "I don't think anything!" I said. "I don't know enough about the business *to* think anything. I asked you a polite question. If you can't help me, can you tell me who can?"

"For you alone," Palin said, no longer laughing, "it *is* that easy: enter my mind, and I will take you to the place you want to be. For you alone, of all the humans who are alive at this moment."

"You can do that?" I said, startled to hear his words. And embarrassed to've gotten angry because I'd thought Palin was laughing at me.

"I can take you to the spirit of the Beast which is trapped," the corpse said. "I will do that for you, Lord Pal. And perhaps for my soul as well, but for you."

I swallowed. "Thank you, sir," I said. "When can we do this?"

"You will need to make preparations to safeguard your body while your spirit is out of it," Palin said. "But as soon as you are prepared we will go, you and I."

Welsh and his troops brought everything I asked for down to the cellars, but it was Baga alone who was willing to carry the bedding behind me while I took a lighted charcoal brazier into the cell itself.

Baga kept swallowing, and he didn't let his eyes fall on Palin's body after they first accidentally flicked over it on turning the corner of the corridor, but he did it.

"Thank you, Baga," I said. "You can go out into the hall now. I'll call you if I need something."

"Yessir!" Baga said. "I'll be right out there and I won't let anybody disturb you!"

I believed that. Nobody would be coming near me and Palin until I told them it was all right, and not then for most of them. From what Baga said, the whole garrison thought Palin was a demon. I wasn't sure what he was, but he wasn't a demon; a damned soul, maybe, at least in his own head.

I stacked three blankets and a down comforter on the floor in front of the hanging corpse, then rolled myself into them. We'd borrowed the comforter from a family of six emigrating from Dun Add to Ariel. The charcoal fire would be safe enough with the door open.

"I'm ready, Lord Palin," I said. I couldn't more than twitch with the bedding around me like this, but Palin had insisted I do everything I could to stay warm. I was sure warm enough right now.

"Then enter my mind as though I were a weapon you were repairing," Palin whispered. "I am the workpiece, you are the Maker."

I don't understand, I thought, but I didn't say anything. I drifted into a trance, as I've so often done lying on the floor of our hut in Beune. This time I entered not the usual lattice but a pattern of flowing light, *living* light. It enfolded me in a prism of color.

Then I was in mottled grayness. I was naked. Beside me floated Lord Palin, exactly as I had last seen him—but freed from his chains.

The ground beneath me was streaked and fractured in different shades of gray, but it seemed as smooth as polished glass. My feet hovered above it. I dipped one leg—it moved normally—and touched the grayness with my big toe. I felt nothing, and the surface didn't show a dimple when I drew my foot up again.

I looked at Palin, which I'd managed to avoid doing pretty much. Oh, I'd seen him, sure, but you know how you do when it's somebody you really don't want to think about? Your eyes go there, but they sorta slide off and your brain doesn't let them stick.

In this place, Palin was the closest thing to normal, to sunlight and grass, that I had. His flesh had shrunk like shoe leather over his bones, but there were bare knobs at the joints where the covering had pulled away. The right hip bone stuck out also. The right ear was missing, and though the nose hadn't fallen in, it was a short, thin blade.

The hair had continued to grow. Hanks of it hung to Palin's waist, though swatches had fallen off during the years and left the skull bare. In the cell the hair had been auburn nearing a dirty blond, but here everything was gray.

"Give me your hand," Palin said, extending his right arm. His eyeballs remained; here they were as bright as if they were glass with a light behind them. "We will go to the place where the thing you wish to free is held."

"It's a person!" I said, taking his hand in mine. It was like grasping a bundle of dry twigs. "It's a person, not a thing."

"Indeed," said Palin after another rustle of laughter. "The one you wish to free is every bit as human as I am."

We began to drift over the ground as if we were spider-silk on a spring breeze. I didn't feel pressure on my body and Palin wasn't pulling me that I noticed either, but the patterns beneath us changed faster and faster.

"Do you come often to the Death Dimension?" I asked. There were no features on the ground, but occasionally I thought I saw things in the air moving. That could have been my imagination, though.

"I have never come here," said Palin. "I have spent twenty years observing this place but clinging to my chains to avoid coming to it. I do not call this the Death Dimension; I call it the Anteroom. Beyond waits justice."

"Justice for you can't be worse than your existence in that cell," I said.

"How would you know?" Palin said. He laughed.

Something ahead of us was poking up above the surface. When we got closer I saw a windowless tower resting on three thick steps. We stopped. Palin let go of my hand.

"The spirit you wish to release is in the tower," Palin said. "It cannot continue on its way because of the guardian."

"What guardian?" I said.

"Go closer."

How? I thought, because my feet didn't touch the ground when I moved them. Nonetheless I moved toward the tower, as slowly as molasses spilled onto a table.

The top step lifted from the layers on which it rested. It turned toward me. It had no eyes that I could see, but the edges of the circular "face" wriggled in the air.

The face opened into a toothless maw. It was wider across than my body was at the shoulders.

"God!" I said, and it was closer to being a real prayer than anything I remembered mouthing in chapel. I went regularly and paid my tithes because Mom would've wanted that, but I'd never been much for chapel and the priest.

I swallowed, then said, "How do I get past it, Lord Palin?"

"You fight and kill it, human," Palin said, his bright eyes fixed on the creature. "The spirit that you came to free will go on its way when the guardian is dead."

The end of the creature's body wobbled back and forth, following me. I wondered if it could strike like a snake ... though what it really reminded me of was a lamprey. I'd caught trout with lampreys attached, sucking out their flesh and life.

"The guardian's hide is tough," Palin said, "but if you pierce the hide, its substance will leak out. It will die and the spirit of the Beast will escape."

I looked around again, wondering what I was missing. I was naked and the ground was smooth as a polished mirror. There were no rocks to chip to an edge, nothing at all.

"You have your teeth," Palin said.

Ah. The creature would certainly attack me if I closed, but I didn't see any better way to deal with it. I'd said that I was willing to die to pay the Beast back, and it looked like that was what going to happen.

I strode in the air toward the creature. The head, big as a bushel measure, swung down at me.

With my left hand I grabbed the fringe of feelers around the mouth to keep from being sucked down the gullet. I tried to squeeze a roll of skin with my right. I couldn't get a grip on the slick hide but I bent my neck and bit anyway with the corner of my jaws, hoping the eye teeth would get purchase.

They didn't. The creature's hide tasted of copper. Its mouth kept pressing toward me, but I've got strong arms.

Holding the guardian off wasn't going to free the Beast. I tried again to bite, failed again, and let go of the feelers so that I could grab the skin with both hands. By holding my hands close together I was able to lift a fold and pull it taut. I bit.

Icy suction closed on the left side of my head and that shoulder. An instant later something brushed me and the mouth released. My hands held the doubled skin tightly enough that my teeth really closed on it. I jerked my head back and sideways, the way I'd seen Buck whipping a rabbit he'd caught.

Something gave. Fluid gushed over my face and hands. I dragged back the flap of skin I'd torn loose. The creature writhed, flinging me loose.

I'd shut my eyes by reflex as I worried the creature, but now I looked at it again. I'd ripped a triangular hole that I couldn't have covered with both hands. Liquid gushed from it like a split in a dam wall.

As the guardian thrashed, its shrinking body exposed a doorway in the tower which had been covered before. From the opening slid something that might have been a Beast, but it was gone too quickly for my dimming eyes to be sure.

In the guardian's maw was a bundle of sticks, halfway swallowed. It twitched. I saw leg bones from which the foot had fallen away.

Then cold squeezed in on me from all sides and my consciousness faded away.

CHAPTER 31

A Change in Direction

"*God help me!*" I shouted. I was freezing and I couldn't move when I tried to jump up and I had a splitting headache.

"Boss! Boss!" Baga was shouting. I opened my eyes and was back in Lord Palin's cell, wrapped in bedding so *of course* I couldn't jump up.

I started to unroll the blankets. The pain of my head made me gasp. It was so bad that I couldn't even scream a curse; I just froze where I was, half-lifted on my left elbow. A white glare pulsed in my head every time my heart beat, blinding me for that moment.

"Boss, what's the matter? What can I do?"

"I'm okay!" I said. "Just give me a moment."

I *wasn't* okay, but I was feeling better as long as long as I didn't move. I could imagine moving again now, which I sure couldn't when the white pain was squeezing my brain.

"Bloody hell, boss," Baga muttered. "You're cold

as Gammer Schmidt was when we dragged her out of the pond after three days!"

"Help me get out of these blankets," I said. "I need to get out, but I've got to be careful."

"Look, have a drink first," Baga said, offering me a pewter mug. I took a sip. My mouth was dry and it tasted wonderful, beer instead of wine.

I swallowed and it came back up with the little breakfast I'd had before we reached Ariel. It was as sudden as if I'd been hit in the belly with a maul. I'd managed to turn my head and I hoped I didn't spew on the borrowed comforter, but I really didn't have much choice.

I saw Lord Palin. The hands and forearms still hung in the shackles, but the rest of the corpse had fallen in bits to the floor. Some of the bones had broken when they hit the stone, and the dried flesh had crumbled like finely ground spices onto the pile.

"I got to get outside," I said. "I *got* to."

Baga frowned but he helped me get to my feet. We staggered to the door. Garrett and Welsh both stood in the hallway, their weapons and shields in their hands. I couldn't imagine what they thought they were going to fight, but they were willing.

"Lord?" said Welsh. "Are you all right?"

"Just need some air," I said. "Need it bad."

"Did you get what you needed, sir?" said Garrett.

If Garrett was here, how long have I been with Palin in that other place? Aloud I said, "I don't know. I hope so. I don't bloody know!"

I stumbled into the shaft with Baga still holding my arm. We were at ground level before I started to draw another breath.

"I shouldn't have snarled at Garrett," I said. "I don't know if I did anything at all. Except that I killed Lord Palin."

If the other place was an anteroom like Palin thought, I hope the judge on the far side saw things the way I did. But that wasn't my job.

I was taking Baga toward the outer gate. The sunlight felt good now, but the courtyard would be all shadow in half an hour. I needed the sun, not just for warmth—I was still shivering—but for the light itself. I really wanted light after being in the other place.

"Ah, boss?" said Baga as we went out toward the landingplace. He was walking beside me now; I didn't need support. "About the other fellow? Lord Palin you call him?"

"Well, what?" I said. If he didn't stop babbling, I was going to send him away...though I didn't want to be alone either.

"Well, I was just wondering what we ought to do with him now," Baga said. "I mean, just leave him or—"

"Bury him!" I shouted. "He's dead, isn't he? Dead dead dead!"

A group of people—it looked like several families together, maybe twenty folks all told—had come off the Road. A fellow had started toward us, probably meaning to ask where to go next, but he veered away when I shouted at Baga. They headed for the castle, giving me a wide berth.

"Look, Baga, I'm sorry," I said. "I'm just going to sit down here in the sun. I won't need you for a while."

"Sure, boss," Baga muttered. "I'll sit, you know, right over there for a while, I think."

I settled myself on the tall grass; I didn't even bother to check what Baga was doing.

Palin thought he'd be punished horribly if he finished dying. Whatever it was he expected, he'd believed it'd be worse than hanging in chains for eternity. He'd thrown away what passed for a life to save *my* life, while I tried to pay a debt. And I wasn't even sure that I'd done what I tried to.

I heard first a whistle, then a *whicker-whicker-whicker*. I opened my eyes. A boat landed, just this side of ours. I tried to stand but changed my mind when my thigh muscles refused to lever me up.

"Boss!" Baga said. "It's mine! It's my boat!"

The hatch opened. Stefan stepped back from the opening. Then May came out, holding her cat in her arms.

I *did* get up, using my arms to help. I got upright but I felt myself wobbling.

"Lord Pal," May said in a clear voice, walking toward me. The gong in the watchtower rang. "I'm glad to see you. I have a favor to ask. I—"

I dropped to my knees and was lucky to get my hands down in time to keep me from toppling onto my side.

"Pal, are you all right?" May said, running toward me. The cat yowled peevishly, though it landed neatly on its feet as May dropped it. Baga grabbed me by the shoulders from behind; Stefan jumped to the ground to lend a hand if needed.

"I'm all right!" I said. "Really, I'm just going to sit here for a moment. Baga, go check out your boat with your buddy there, all right?"

"Sure, boss," Baga said, though he kept looking

back at me as he joined Stefan at the hatch of his boat. They muttered briefly, then went aboard.

"Sorry," I muttered to May. "I've been really cold and I'm still getting my feet under me. But I'm okay."

I forced myself to look up and meet her eyes. I'd remembered seeing, really *seeing*, Palin for the first time in the other place.

She looked worried, and what I'd said didn't change that.

"Look," I said, "I'm safe. I can't even throw up on you, I emptied my belly back in the cell."

She giggled. "I feel reassured," she said. "You really know how to put a girl at ease."

"Well, we folks from Beune are famous for being smooth gentlemen," I said, looking at her. She was really pretty.

"Look, May," I said. "You said you wanted a favor. What is it?"

"Is there a place we can go to talk?" she said, looking up at the people coming toward us from the castle. "I mean, if you're willing to talk?"

I turned and said, "Garrett? We're okay here. If we need something we'll ask, but otherwise I'd like folks to give us some space. All right?"

"All right, everybody back inside!" Garrett bellowed. "Nobody needs to be out here! I mean now!"

Smiling a little, I looked back at May. "I'll talk to you," I said. "But I'd rather not get up again for a while, if that's all right. And the sun feels good."

"Yes, of course," May said. She was carrying a light cape in her hands. She moved beside me so that she wouldn't block the sun and arranged it on the ground. She sat cross-legged.

She looked sharply at me, then put her fingertips on my forehead. They felt warm.

"I'm all right," I repeated, keeping a grip on my temper because I really wasn't all right. She'd seen me shivering, I guess.

May stood, whipped the cape off the ground and laid it over my shoulders. She sat down again. "No," she said, "you're not. This is a bad time, but it's the time we have. Pal, I'd like you to come back to Dun Add and be Lady Jolene's Champion. That is, if you can. Are you sick?"

"I just got out of a bad time," I said. "I'm not sick, I'll be fine. But I don't understand what you're saying."

May crossed her hands primly in her lap and looked down at them for a moment. She was wearing a dark green dress of heavier material than her usual clothes in Dun Add.

"Please just listen to me," she said, raising her eyes to mine again. "You won't approve, but just listen."

I nodded. I guess my face looked pretty hard, but I can't help that.

"Lord Clain and the Consort are having an affair," May said, watching me closely. My expression didn't change. "They're discreet, but that's the truth. Just as Lord Baran said, though that had nothing to do with what happened between his friend Berenice and her page."

"Go on," I said. That was what Garrett and Welsh had told me too, though I didn't see what it had to do with me.

"Lord Clain is a very attractive man," May said. "Any woman might want him for a lover."

My lips twitched then. I didn't mean them to, but I felt them do it.

"I asked you to hear me out!" May said.

"Go on," I repeated. "Sorry."

I was responsible for how I lived. Maybe it was a good way, maybe it wasn't, but it was my business. The same was true for everybody else. Including my real mother and father, I now saw.

"Any woman would," May said; she'd said "might" before, "but Clain isn't interested. He's never touched any woman but Jolene since I've been in Dun Add. They're in love."

"Go on," I said. I didn't know what to think about all this, but that could wait until I understood what "all this" really was. Which I certainly didn't do so far.

"Another of the Consort's maids, Ziga," May went on. "She was a little thing—long black hair and a triangular face. Maybe you remember her?"

"I don't," I said. "Go on."

I didn't look at the maids of honor. Mostly I hadn't been in places where I'd see them, but I didn't pay them much attention regardless.

"Well, Ziga *really* wanted Clain," May said. "We all knew that, but you know, it wasn't anybody's business but hers. And Jolene's, I guess, but Jolene just kind of laughed about it. She never said anything to Ziga and she didn't send Ziga away. I told her—Jolene— she was being cruel, but like I say, she just laughed."

"It seems cruel to me too," I said. Just plain nasty, though I didn't say that. "But go on."

"Somebody sent Jolene a bottle of port," May said. "One of the Champions, we figured—it was good vintage. There wasn't a note with it. Jolene doesn't like port, but she thought it might be a way to mend fences with Baran, you know the things he's been saying about her. She sent it to him."

She shrugged. "I could've told her it wouldn't work," she said. "Baran's seat is Caledon, and his head is as hard as the rocks of his estate. Still, why not try? Baran told the messenger to take it back to the slut, pretty much as I figured, only his friend Lord Gismonde said he'd willingly drink it in honor of the gracious woman who'd sent it."

May shivered. "Which Gismonde did," she said. "And the port was poisoned. And Gismonde died. So Baran's saying Jolene poisoned his friend and demands trial by combat. And Ziga hanged herself, so *we* all know what happened but we can't say anything without everybody knowing why she was trying to kill Jolene. And nobody else will stand up for Jolene because they all think she did it. And she *didn't*."

"Well, Lord Clain will be her champion," I said. What a bloody awful mess. "That may look bad, but he'll do it anyway."

I didn't bother saying that Clain would be a much better champion than I would. I certainly remembered the rap he'd given me in the Aspirants' Tournament, and that was just at twenty percent power.

"There must be a dozen people gone off trying to find Clain," May said. "Jolene sent some, Jon sent some; I know that some of the other girls sent messengers too. But this boat arrived in Dun Add with a delegation from Roughpuff and I hired it to find you."

She took a deep breath and added. "The boatman, Stefan, knows you. I told him I was your friend and I think that's why he was willing to leave Dun Add right away. I apologize for the lie."

"It doesn't matter," I said. I was feeling a dizzy spell

coming over me. "Look, why me? Even if you can't find Clain, there's better people than me out there."

"I could tell you the truth," May said. "I could trust you to be fair. Jolene's a slut, if you want, but she didn't poison Gismonde. Or try to poison Baran!"

"I didn't call anybody a slut," I said. I was shivering so bad that I was slurring words. "I was going back to Dun Add anyway, I've finished here."

And I'd finished at Farandol, which was the task the Leader had set me. *A lifetime ago*, I thought. It was a lifetime: Lord Palin's life.

I lurched to my feet. The sun had gone down, and the sudden chill went straight to my bones.

"I need to get warm," I said, trotting toward my own boat. So long as I took short steps and didn't change speed, I thought I could make it.

I was running down a tunnel with gray walls, the edges of my vision. All the color washed out, and the walls narrowed. I stepped through the hatch and the tunnel went black. For a moment I could feel hands supporting me.

Then there was nothing.

I woke up with all the bedding and spare clothes on top of me in my compartment, and a warm body huddled against mine. May was in the bed with me.

I slid out. Buck came out of his compartment and nuzzled me gratefully, whining.

"Pal, I was afraid," May called. "You were so cold even with the blankets over you."

"I meant to raise the temperature in my compartment," I said. "But I guess I fell asleep too soon."

"You passed out, you mean," May said, joining me

in the hall. Except that she was barefoot, she was wearing the same clothes as she had when we'd been talking outside Castle Ariel. "Pal, what *happened* to you? Baga isn't sure."

"I'm not sure either," I said. "Something attacked me. It's dead now but it seems to have screwed me up worse'n I thought."

Baga was leaning against the bow console; we were under way. I frowned.

"I told Baga to take us all to Dun Add," May said, following my eyes. "You'd said you were finished where we were—Catermole?"

"Castle Ariel," I said. I realized I might never have told Baga my name for the place we'd captured.

"There are doctors as good as anywhere on Dun Add," May said. "And your friend Guntram is there, he knows a lot of things. Maybe about what happened to you."

"That's possible," I said. Not about what happened to me—I was pretty sure that I was the only living person who'd been in the place Palin had taken me. But I trusted Guntram to fix me better than I trusted any of the doctors I'd seen in Dun Add. Anyway, it'd be good to see him again.

"Just a moment," I said. I dropped into a brief trance to enter the boat's controls, then returned to Here and closed the door of my compartment.

May was watching me doubtfully. "I raised the temperature in that room to ninety degrees," I explained. "In case I have another of these attacks."

May's face went hard and she turned her head. She didn't speak.

"What you did was very smart," I said. "Without your body heat, I don't know if the covers would've been enough. But now that I'm awake again, I'm doing what I meant from the beginning."

"I just didn't want you to think..." she said. She didn't finish that, and I didn't want her to.

We had plenty of room for three people and Buck—and May's cat, if she didn't sleep with May. The boat wasn't designed for people to socialize, though.

I opened another compartment and sat on the bed with my knees out in the corridor, then patted the end of the bunk closer to where May stood.

"I'll sleep in another of the compartments if I'm all right," I said as she carefully lowered herself onto the bunk. "The warm one's just if I get the chills again."

"Pal, how did you make the compartment warm?" May said. "Are you a boatman? Baga said that wasn't possible."

"I'm a Maker," I said. "I think all the Ancients must've been Makers and boatmen and maybe warriors too, given how much we find from them even after thousands of years."

I felt old ideas running through my head again. These were things I'd thought about ever since I was a kid, as soon as I learned about Makers and that I was one.

"I don't know what happened to them, to the Ancients," I said. "I wonder if it's going to happen to us. We don't even know enough to know what to be afraid of, May!"

May looked at me cautiously. *She thinks I'm crazy, but she doesn't want to say that.* I smiled with my lips and said, "Well, there's probably nothing at all. But if there is, I think it'd be best if we were all united in a Commonwealth. The Leader is doing that."

"I used to have dreams," May said, turning her face away from mine. "I laugh at them now, but I've got a very nice estate on Danalaw."

Then she said, "I wonder if I'd be happier if I went back to dreaming."

I don't think she was talking to me.

I had another attack of the chills on the next day and ducked into the warmed compartment. In the times I was conscious, I wondered how long this was going to go on. I knew the answer might be, "As long as you live," and the wash of despair made me feel even worse.

I was weak as a kitten when the spell passed. "I'm not going to be much use to you in Dun Add if this goes on," I said to May as we sat on the edge of the other compartment. She was petting her cat, I was rubbing Buck behind the ears.

"I hope it stops," May said, and it wasn't just words. She really sounded worried.

"Chances are, somebody will've come back with Lord Clain by the time we reach Dun Add," I said. "He can handle Baran."

What I was really thinking, though, was what it'd be like to have these spells for the rest of my life. If the creature in that other place had bitten my leg off, I wouldn't expect it to regrow. I'd been there in spirit, so my body wasn't harmed, but the harm to that spirit might be just as permanent.

"I didn't mean that," she said. She wasn't looking at me. "I'm sorry you've been hurt."

"That comes with being a Champion," I said. "I hope I'll get over it."

"My uncle was a Champion," May said to the closed door of the compartment I was keeping warm. "He's retired from a hurt shoulder but his son's an Aspirant now. Do you know him? Lord Parry?"

"I met him, I guess," I said, trying to place the name. "I don't know him well."

"Parry was eliminated in the first round of the Aspirant's Tournament," May said. "He's a nice boy, but he's not in your class, Pal."

She looked at me and said, "You're really very good, Pal."

I started to say, "I've got good gear," which is true; but it'd also be a lie if I meant it for an answer to what May'd said. I could beat Parry any time, every time, and the difference wasn't the hardware.

"Thank you," I said. And that was all I said.

"My father is the Count of Baygen," May said, to the other compartment again. "We do all right, but Baygen isn't big and I'm the third daughter. My uncle introduced me to Jolene. She liked me and took me into her suite."

She swallowed but didn't look around. "It was very exciting," she said. "A lot better than marriage to the sort of man my pittance of a dowry would attract. I've never seen the attraction in slopping hogs. I met interesting, powerful men, and some of them were rich. Very rich."

I didn't know what to say. *Nothing* was what I wanted to say, but she'd take that as well, bad.

I said, "I've never much liked hogs myself."

May nodded sharply. "I think I'll lie down for a bit," she said as she rose. "Since you're all right."

Baga brought us onto the landingplace at Dun Add a few hours later.

CHAPTER 32

Getting Ready

The figure of light standing in front of Guntram's door looked nearly human, but the ears and eye-sockets were almost perfectly round and the hands each had three slender fingers and thumbs that stuck out at right angles while at his sides.

"Good morning, Lord Pal," the figure said in a soprano voice. "Master Guntram asked me to send you in directly that you arrived."

Guntram had been friendly as you could ask to everyone I'd seen him talk to; I hadn't been able to understand why people at Dun Add seemed frightened as well as respecting him. I wasn't afraid of the new doorman, but it startled me. I suddenly had a notion of why Guntram did frighten people who weren't Makers.

"Thank you, ah, servant," I said as I opened the door. It was silly to speak, I guess, because I knew that the figure wasn't even material—let alone able to be pleased by my politeness. Mom had driven into me that it was always right to be courteous, though, and I didn't see any reason to make exception for people who weren't really people.

I closed the door and took a moment to look for the projector. It stood on the end of the shelf to the right of the door, a set of three spindles of different-colored crystal, joined at the top. I recognized the chartreuse one as a scrap from my own collection, though it'd been extended on both ends. I hadn't had the faintest notion of what it could be used for.

I came out of my trance and searched for Guntram. His head rose above the top of the workbench in a corner across the room. "Pal!" he said. "I'm glad to see you. Are things going well?"

"Well, yes and no, sir," I said, weaving toward him through the stacks and tables. "I was able to straighten things out on Farandol, but I seem to have gotten hurt. I hope you can maybe help me."

As I spoke, I realized that I hadn't really fixed Farandol, just gotten rid of Lang. It still needed a proper government and, if Jon really wanted, a garrison. I hadn't seen any sign of the Road there in the Marches being dangerous, but I hadn't done any patrolling because I'd travelled by boat.

Except for going to slaughter the people in Rowley's Roost. I winced, but I'd paid off Lang for what I'd done there.

Guntram was looking at me closely. "Yes," he said. "There certainly is something wrong with you, Pal. Come over to the couch."

"I'm not sure that it'll work for this, sir," I said, following as he bustled to the corner. "My spirit was in another place, and a thing there fought me. I came off best, but it was a fight and no mistake."

"I've been playing with the couch since you provided me with a series of subjects to test it on," Guntram said. He sounded brightly cheerful, but I don't know how the injured warriors who'd come to him would've taken being called "subjects." "I've been entering the mechanism while it's working, and I think we can work on your current trouble. Enter it along with me, as when we were working on the boat together."

Guntram had moved a chair with arms near the couch since I was here before. He sat in it.

"Can I—" I started. And stopped, because Guntram wouldn't have suggested that if I couldn't do it. I lay down carefully on the couch and dropped into a trance. Guntram was waiting for me in a bundle—a basket, maybe—of strands of light, completely different from the artifacts I was used to. There were no angles in this—in me.

I hadn't learned about this capacity of the couch when you were last here, Guntram said. *I learned by observing as the couch healed physical wounds.*

Guntram was a presence with me, but I didn't see a little figure. I wasn't a present figure either.

Fortunately, Guntram continued, sounding to me just like he always did, *the couch had created an image of you when you used it before, so all we have to do is to return the new image to the form and color of what you were previously.*

I spent a moment looking at amazing curving knots. The colors were toward the blues and purples to start out, but as my viewpoint travelled along the pattern we slipped into bands of green and almost immediately reds and oranges. The fibers in the brighter colors were thinner and often ragged.

Here is the damage, Guntram said. A web in fine gray formed over a section of the bright portion, enclosing and sometimes tucking in the broken ends. *Now, if we fill it back according to the previous pattern, matching the hue to that of the threads to which it's attached . . .*

One of the strands turned yellow, then green and on into darkening blues. I chose another strand and concentrated on it. Normally I would have been encouraging material from trays nearby to move and resettle itself onto the workpiece—down at the crystalline level.

There was no material damage here to repair. I was transferring energy into the pattern from—somewhere. I suppose from the couch itself, because there was nothing else around. It reminded me of guiding water into irrigation channels, row by row, as farmers in the south of Beune did in dry months.

The strand I was working on darkened slowly. I found it worked better for me to start with a considerable length and build it back gradually. Guntram worked on shorter sections at a time, bringing them down to indigo at the edge of violet in a smooth process. He worked so quickly that the intermediate stages were barely visible.

Technique apart, Guntram was simply better than I was. That didn't bother me. There were things I was better at than Guntram was, but none of them involved skill as a Maker.

I later figured that we'd worked eighteen hours solid, both of us. I didn't have any notion while it was going on. I'd never have been able to work that long in a single run on normal stuff, but because of *what* we were doing I didn't feel tired the way I'd have done if it'd have been a shield I was rebuilding.

As for Guntram, well . . . there was nobody like Guntram. I don't doubt that Louis could turn out weapons that were more powerful than the originals of the bits he started with—Guntram said he could, anyway—but Louis would never have figured out the structure of what we were doing now.

I wouldn't have either. But I could learn, and I had a good teacher.

I think we've repaired the damage, don't you? Guntram said.

I drew back my focus and looked at the pattern rather that the series of little bits. Everything I could see was a uniform dark indigo, more consistent— particularly the strands Guntram had worked on—than the portion that hadn't been damaged to begin with.

"Thank you, Guntram," I said. "Thank you, sir."

Then let's get something to eat, said Guntram. Together we withdrew.

We ate in Guntram's quarters, stew that quiet servants brought in more quickly than I'd have expected them to be able to bring it up from the refectory on the ground floor. I wondered if there was a little kitchen nearby on this floor—just for Guntram. He made folks in Dun Add nervous—no question. But they honored him anyhow, and they all seemed to like him.

It made me think about me and my neighbors in Beune. It's not really a bad way to live, if you weren't the sort who needed a lot of people around all the time. I didn't know enough Makers to be able to guess if they all—we all—were like that.

I emptied my beer—they had beer for me—and poured myself another mug. "Guntram?" I said. "Do you think they'll find Lord Clain before the Consort's champion has to fight Lord Baran?"

"If Clain hasn't been found thus far," Guntram said, "it's because he's deliberately put himself out of the way. Clain is as committed to the Commonwealth as Jon himself is, or Louis. This ... difficulty must embarrass him greatly. I think he's gone somewhere that people from Dun Add wouldn't be able to call him back easily."

He looked at me. "Clain would come back to save Jolene if he knew the situation," Guntram said. "I don't doubt that in the least. Even if he believed in his heart that it would be better for the Commonwealth if she died."

"That's an awful thought!" I said. "Do you believe that, Guntram?"

"I didn't mean to offend you, Pal," he said with a lopsided smile. "I don't really believe in anything, I'm afraid. Certainly not enough to sacrifice the life of a gracious lady to support that belief."

"Sorry," I said, embarrassed at flying hot because a friend had told the truth. I had another sip of beer—just a sip; the speed I'd gulped the first one might have had something to do with being snappish. "Guntram, what do you think about trial by combat?"

He shrugged. "I think the practice has been very good for the Commonwealth," he said. "It has repeatedly replaced a probable war with a fight in which one or at worst two men die. Whether it's been good for the individuals involved depends on circumstances, of course."

"And justice?" I said.

"Justice is the province of God," Guntram said. "I won't speculate on that."

I drank more beer. It was sharper than the ale I was used to, but I could get used to it.

"Guntram?" I said. "Do you think I could defeat Baran? I know, you're not a warrior, but you've seen a lot of combats."

Guntram poured himself a little more wine. "We'll work on that," he said. "I have some ideas."

After dinner we went down to the practice hall together. Guntram configured a machine to duplicate the techniques of Lord Baran as gathered from every time Baran had used the hall himself.

The machine whipped me solidly three times running before I called it quits for the night.

I was up early the next morning. I hoped I was done with those dizzy spells, though I couldn't be sure until I'd died without it happening again.

Which would be soon enough, if I didn't do better against Baran in the flesh than I was managing with his image on the machines. I did two more trials first thing after I got up, and I got hammered both times.

Guntram was taking notes. I didn't ask what they were about.

After I showered, I went back to Guntram's quarters and put on one of my good outfits: the blue one, I decided. It was the one I'd worn when May took me out to the Consort's garden. I don't know if that was an accident or not. I was pretty confused when I tried to think about anything except what was right in front of me, so I just focused down on that.

"Guntram," I said, "I need to talk to the Consort."

"I see," said Guntram. "Do you want me to come with you? I don't know where she is at present, but I'm sure I could learn."

"I think it's better just me," I said. "And I'll ask May. She'll know, and she got me into this."

I went out and walked down to the Consort's suite, nodding to servants I met on the way. Some of them met my eyes and muttered, "Lord," but mostly they just scuttled by with their heads turned away. It wasn't anything about me, they just didn't expect to be noticed by Champions.

I really wanted to get out of Dun Add. Wanted to go back to Beune, I might've said, but that wasn't really true. I'd done a good thing at Castle Ariel and maybe a better one in the other place, when I'd freed the Beast's ancestor. I couldn't have done those things if I'd stayed in Beune.

But I now was in Dun Add, so I'd do my duty here.

The guards at the cross-corridor watched me coming toward them. I wondered what I'd do if they told me to take myself off, but I said, "I need to see Lady May," as firmly as I could manage.

"Of course, milord," one said. He actually bowed to me.

They think I'm somebody, I realized. That bothered me just about as much as being sent away because I didn't belong here would have, but this was better for what I wanted to do.

I rapped on the door. "It's Pal," I called. "Hoping to talk to Lady May."

I was wondering how long to wait before I knocked again—and at the back of my mind, wondering what to try next if nobody answered at all—when the door jerked open. "Pal, come in!" May said. She closed the door as soon as I'd slipped through.

Fabric-covered wooden frames had been unfolded in front of the bay windows, making the large entrance hall much dimmer than I'd expected. My eyes took a moment to adapt; the corridor was much brighter because of the south-facing windows on the top tier.

Counting May, I saw four women. One held the long-necked banjo that I'd seen before, but she wasn't playing it. Another lay on the stone floor, snoring. She'd been holding a goblet, but it had fallen from her hand, denting the rim slightly. It was empty. On a round table stood decanters, some of them nearly empty also.

"Lord Pal, I'm glad to see you," May said. She glanced around at her companions. "We're all glad to see you. We've been, well, dismayed by what's been going on, but if there's anything we can do, just ask. *Please* ask."

The other two women were watching us hard, but they didn't say anything. The one with the banjo leaned it against the chair beside her.

"Well, what I want..." I said. "What I need, I think. Is to talk to the Consort. I can't be her Champion unless that's what she wants."

"Yes, of course," May said, turning at once to a wall-hanging of a dragon—some creature, anyhow—embroidered on maroon plush. She moved it aside and I saw behind it stairs going up instead of a stone wall. Over her shoulder she called, "She's up in the tower."

I followed May's slippers up the staircase inside the thick walls of the castle. Every ten feet or so there was a slit window that let in plenty of light for us.

The slippers were pale green, like May's dress. She had nice little feet and sturdy calves, though they were nice too.

At the top we came to a little landing and a wooden door. May knocked on the door while I waited two steps below and leaned my head forward so that I could watch.

"Jolene, open up," May called through the door. "We need to talk to you."

Nothing happened. May made a sour face and took a small brass key from a pocket I hadn't noticed. Before she could fit it into the lock, the door opened.

"Come in, dear, come—" Jolene said. Then she saw me and twitched back. "Who's that!"

I almost didn't recognize the Consort. She was wearing the night dress that she must've slept in. Her hair was mussed and her face looked puffy. She hadn't been drinking, though, or at least not so much that I could hear it in her voice.

"Jolene, this is Lord Pal," May said. The Consort hadn't tried to slam the door shut, but May was pushing against it just in case she did. "He's agreed to stand as your Champion at the trial by combat, but he wants to talk with you first."

"Him?" said Jolene, really looking at me instead of just seeing a man on the landing when she expected May alone. "What's happened to Clain?"

I wondered if she remembered that we'd met. No real reason she should have, of course.

"We don't know what's happened to Clain," May

said. I was pretty sure I heard exasperation in her voice, but she kept it buried pretty deep. "Lord Pal has generously left his estates to help you, Jolene. Can we please come in so that we can talk?"

"Oh, it's just so *wrong*," the Consort said as she turned and flounced away from the door. She didn't invite us in, but May waved me through and followed, closing and locking the door behind us. "*I* didn't poison Gismonde! I *liked* Gismonde!"

She led us onto what turned out to be a balcony. The view toward the hinterlands north of the castle made me jerk back when I started through the door after her. I'm not exactly afraid of heights, but there's no place in Beune you could get as high up as the top of this castle.

I stepped out after I'd caught my breath. "I guess you could say we're even now, ma'am," I said. "You hadn't expected me, and I—"

I swept my hand up the valley.

"—hadn't been expecting this."

Jolene had sat down in a chair where there was a silver goblet on the little table beside it. There were two other chairs on the balcony, but May didn't take one and I kept my shoulders firmly against the stone wall behind me.

The landscape of hedged fields and blotches of forest seemed a very long way down. Occasionally I saw people moving. Small people...

The Consort looked at me blankly. She had no idea what I was talking about; she was completely lost in her own dark misery, and the rest of us were just shadows drifting around the fringes of her awareness.

"We all hope that Lord Clain will return in time to

stand for you, dear," May said, slipping into the chair nearer to the Consort. "But you know that messengers have returned from all the obvious places and there's been no sign of him as yet."

She put her hand on Jolene's elbow. "Dear, I think we have to consider what will happen if Clain *doesn't* arrive in time. My friend Lord Pal—"

Jolene turned with a vicious expression. "Look at him!" she snarled. "He'd have no more chance against Baran than one of the potboys would! Where is Clain? Why doesn't he come?"

I kept my mouth shut and I think my face pretty calm. Given the way practice had been going, I'd do better against Baran than a potboy would—but not enough better to save the Consort's life. Or mine either one, but I was here by choice.

More fool me, I was thinking; but I kept my mouth shut.

"Jolene, you're being impolite!" May said, sharp as a branch cracking. "Clain isn't here because he doesn't know about the situation. Lord Pal *is* here, purely from a sense of justice. He owes you *nothing*, and the least you owe him is to be polite!"

Jolene didn't say anything for a moment, but I saw her tighten up. She sat straight and patted her hair with both hands. "I must look a fright," she murmured; talking to herself, I suppose.

She stood gracefully and turned to face me. Her face didn't look puffy anymore, though I'd swear she was thirty years older than she'd been the first time I saw her up close.

"Lord Pal . . ." she said. Her voice was as smooth as an organ note. "Our friend May is quite correct.

My situation has caused me to be ungracious to a man to whom I owe a great debt. I trust that May will pay that in the fashion I cannot."

"Ma'am!" I said, and I stopped because there was no place I wanted to go with the subject. No place at all.

"Jolene, Lord Pal is here because he's a brave gentleman and he believes you're innocent!" May said. She'd risen when her mistress did; now she slid sideways to put herself between Jolene and me. "He's always behaved as a courteous friend to me and nothing more. He's a *decent* man, dearest—as hard as it is for people like you and me to believe that sort of man exists."

"Of course, dear," Jolene said calmly. She urged May aside gently with her arm, then curtseyed to me. "Lord Pal," she said, "this really hasn't been my day, has it? I'm deeply grateful for the kindness you're showing to a woman whom you scarcely know. And who"—she gave a rueful smile—"has been behaving in a fashion to convince you that she's unworthy of the consideration, I fear. Forgive me, please. I am honored by your kind offer, and I humbly accept it."

She smiled again. It was as sad an expression as I've ever seen on the face of a person who wasn't crying. "Believe me," she added, "I've learned a great deal about humility in these past few weeks."

I bowed. I wasn't very good at it. "Thank you, ma'am," I said. "I just needed to be sure I was doing what you wanted."

I sidled to the door off the balcony. "And ma'am?" I said. "Believe me, I want Lord Clain to show up even more than you do."

May was through the door right after me. The

Consort didn't leave the balcony while we were still in the tower room. I closed my eyes and took a deep breath. I didn't open them again until May shut the door behind us.

"Pal..." she said. She spoke softly, but the door was thick—and so was the one at the bottom end of the staircase. "I'm so sorry that happened. Jolene is trying very hard, but she hasn't been herself since all this started. And it's getting worse."

"She's in a hard place," I said. "She's doing the best she can, I guess. We all do, pretty much."

"Pal, we're not all as strong as you are," May said, even quieter than before. She was looking toward one of the slit windows. It was high in the wall, so all she'd be able to see through it was clouds and sky. "But knowing you makes us, some of us, try to be as good as we can."

"I'm not strong," I said, starting down the stairs. "I'm a kid from Beune, about as deep in the sticks as you can get, and I'm scared. But I said I was going to do this, and I am."

"Yes," said May as I opened the door at the bottom of the stairs. "Of course."

CHAPTER 33

Various Maneuvering

I'd got what I wanted from the Consort, so I suppose I ought to have felt good. I didn't, not even close. I thought about going down to the practice room to work out what I was feeling, or maybe just go somewhere private to mope.

I wasn't really sure *what* I was feeling. Nothing that was going on was clear or good. Everything was like swirls in muddy water.

Finally I decided that for me to crawl into a hole wasn't going to help the problems that made me want to do that. Instead I'd do something else that I didn't want to do. I couldn't get more miserable than I felt right now.

I walked out of the castle and through the town down to the landingplace. Baga and Maggie were living aboard my boat and taking care of Buck. I came out every day and went up the Road, searching for artifacts.

There was more than you'd think close in to Dun Add like this, though everything I'd found so far was diddly stuff, so worn that I doubted it'd be any more use even to Guntram than pebbles from a stream bed. Mostly I was keeping my eye in, but there was always a chance of something more interesting; and besides, I'd seen Guntram do things with scraps that were as impossible as weaving cobwebs to me.

"Baga, the master's here!" Maggie called. She was hanging out wash—some of it mine—on a line strung between the boat's stern and a post I'd set for her. Baga had been willing, but he didn't have the experience in ordinary farm chores that I did, and he had blessed little talent for them either.

Buck came bounding through the hatch and was rubbing hard against my legs when Baga followed. He looked a bit muzzy. "Sorry, boss," he said. "You're earlier today than I expected."

He'd been drinking the night before—been drunk, pretty clearly. Sitting at landingplace must be pretty boring, and I didn't give Baga much to do. More muddy ripples.

"Baga, do you know where Lord Baran lives?" I said. "I've heard he's got a bungalow in Dun Add, but I don't know where."

"Yessir, it's out on the west road," Baga said. "I asked around when we got here since it seemed you might want to know. You want me to take a message to him?"

"I'd like you to guide me, actually," I said. "I need to talk to him."

"You bet!" said Baga, brightening obviously.

"Lord Pal?" said Maggie. "Can you wait just a

moment while my husband changes into clean clothes? For seeing another noble, you see."

"Sure," I said. "But I want to get this over, Baga."

He popped back into the boat. I didn't care what he wore—I doubted Baran would even see my servant, let alone bother about what he looked like. But Maggie cared, and there were stains from last night—or past nights—on the tunic Baga'd come out wearing.

"Thank you, your lordship," Maggie whispered.

I nodded to her. There were lots of little things that made people happy. I wished I'd been better about doing them all my life, but I was sure trying now.

Baga was out quick. He'd taken time to splash his face with water as well as change clothes. He waved back at Maggie as we and Buck set off up the slope.

We didn't talk much till we'd reached the castle and turned left. Close in, the buildings were pretty shabby— shops and lodging for castle servants, I figured—but before we'd gotten a half mile out from the castle, there were some really nice places.

I was trying to go over what I'd say to Baran, but I didn't know the big Champion well enough to imagine how he'd respond. Well, I could only hope.

"Boss?" said Baga. "Did you know that a lot of folks are saying that you're Guntram's son?"

I'd thought I'd been pretty well numbed when the Consort blithely assumed that May was my mistress, but I stutter-stepped at this new thing. I was really pretty lucky that I hadn't fallen on my face.

"Whyever would they think that?" I said. "I'm from Beune, *you* know that!"

"Sure, I tell them," said Baga. He didn't sound concerned. "But you're staying with him in the castle, and most folks in Dun Add are, you know, scared about him."

"I haven't met a nicer man in Dun Add than Guntram is," I said. "And I don't know anything about Guntram's family, except that it has nothing to do with me. We're just friends, and I count myself lucky for that."

"So he's not your father, then?" Baga said.

I decided to laugh instead of getting mad. "No, Master Guntram is not my father," I said.

A few years ago I didn't have any doubts about my parentage. Since I met Marina and Lord Palin I'd had a *lot* of doubts, because I didn't trust either one of them. It didn't really matter; I was who I was, not who my parents were. I was better off not thinking about it, though.

"This next one on the right is Lord Baran's, boss," Baga said. He gestured.

I was glad of the change of subject, but the "bungalow" was what I'd call a palace. There was a round turret on the left corner facing the street and on the right a turret with eight sides and windows on three levels. One of the two panels of the high front door was open. I could see people in the hallway beyond.

I patted Buck. "Stay out here with Baga," I said. I squared my shoulders and walked up the front path between chestnut trees that hadn't had more than started to grow. They must've been planted when the house was built.

"Yes ... ?" said the servant who got up from a chair in the entranceway. The sleeves of his tunic were slashed green and white.

"I'm Pal of Beune," I said. "I need to speak with Lord Baran, if you please."

"Do you indeed?" the servant said. Several more servants were peering toward us, men and women both. They all wore the same sleeve colors.

"He's *Lord* Pal, the Champion of Beune, you bonehead!" Baga roared from right behind me. He hadn't stayed in the street as I'd intended.

The servant's face didn't change, but his tone softened noticeably as he said, "One moment, Lord Pal. I'll inform my master. Ah—are you expected?"

"No," I said. "But it's really important that I talk with Lord Baran."

I expected the servant who'd greeted me to send the boy lurking behind a sideboard displaying plate, but instead he trotted up the big staircase himself. He was brisker than I'd expected in somebody so chubby. I looked around at the furnishings while other servants stared at me silently. I was glad Baga had changed clothes after all.

There were two sets of deer horns mounted on the wall beside the staircase, both of them big, and over the transom itself was a *huge* pair—twelve feet across. Those were broad and shovel-shaped, like no antlers I'd ever seen before.

"Lord Pal?" called someone from the top of the stairs—Lord Baran, when I looked up. "Come up if you must see me. I don't believe we've met, have we?"

"No sir," I said. I climbed the stairs, waiting to speak more till I'd reached the top. With Baran was a Champion whom I'd seen but didn't know by name.

"Lord Baran?" I said. Both Champions were bigger than I was. Baran himself was at least six feet six, bigger even than Clain. "My business is private. I'd appreciate a few words with you alone."

"Private about what?" Baran said. I won't say he growled, but I've sure heard friendlier voices.

I was already standing as straight as I could. "Sir," I said. "About your charges regarding Lady Jolene."

"Well, I didn't expect that," Baran said. His voice was friendly enough, but from his face he was thinking about pulling my head off. He looked at his companion. "Did you, Monroe?"

"Throw him out," Monroe said. He looked at me like I was something he was about to wipe off his shoe.

"No, we'll listen to him," Baran said. "Kid, you say what you've got to say here and now, or I'll see if I can toss you through the front door from up here. If I miss the first time, I'll keep trying till I get it right. Okay?"

"Sir," I said. This was a bad spot, but I hadn't expected it to be a good one. The only choice was to bull on through.

"Lady Jolene is Lord Clain's mistress," I said. There were probably a dozen servants listening besides the other Champion, but there was no help for it. I didn't suppose it was going to surprise anybody. "One of Jolene's attendants, Lady Ziga, had offered herself to Clain and been refused. In jealousy, Ziga attempted to poison Jolene. Jolene passed the poisoned wine on to you in complete innocence."

I swallowed. "I'm not defending Jolene's behavior," I said. "But she didn't try to kill you or anyone else. It was really bad luck. And Ziga's hanged herself."

"So I guess I ought to drop my prosecution because the slut is completely innocent, is that it?" Baran said, still quiet.

"Jolene is innocent of trying to murder anybody,"

I said. *And she's not a slut*, I thought, but I didn't say that. "So yes, you should drop your prosecution."

I hope I sounded calm. I was looking Baran in the face as I spoke, and his expression would've been a good enough excuse for me to sound rattled.

"Are you really so stupid that you believe this pack of lies the slut came up with?" Baran shouted. "Or are you having it off with her yourself and that's why you're here? Sure, that's it: it's your mouth but it's really Jolene's pussy talking!"

"I'd've thought Jolene could find a better replacement for Clain than this wimp," Monroe said. His expression hadn't changed from the first time he looked at me. "Of course, I don't guess she stops with one, right?"

"Sir," I said to Monroe. "I'm not sexually involved with the Consort or with anyone else."

I turned to Baran and said, "I hoped that if you learned the truth, you'd step back from a monstrous injustice. I still hope that."

I've heard "Soft words turn away wrath," but it's never been true in what I've seen. Somebody who's bellowing mad—or drunk, and they go together pretty regularly—isn't going to listen to anything you say, quiet or not. They're just hearing their own crazy anger. Still, I wouldn't have to remember that I'd been a screaming madman myself.

"Well, you're bloody wrong!" Baran said. "Tell your whore that if she can't find somebody to meet me at the trial, I'll have her burned alive! And if somebody'd done that sooner, maybe Gismonde wouldn't be dead with froth on his lips, you hear?"

"I understand, Lord Baran," I said. My voice was

trembling but I doubt anybody but me noticed that. I started to turn but paused instead and added, "As for finding somebody to meet you at the trial, the Consort has already done that. I'll be seeing you in two weeks time, sir."

I went down the stairs, half expecting Baran and his buddy to come after me. They didn't, and I made it out the door. Buck whined, but I was barely aware of him or Baga as we headed back to the castle.

I whispered, "I *really* want to win this one."

"I've been studying your matches on the practice machines," Guntram said as we stared at my weapon, lying on the worktable between us. "Baran's equipment is simply more powerful than yours. It's bulky and heavy, but that doesn't handicap Baran because he's very strong. I don't think you'd be able to handle his gear for any length of time. Ah—I don't mean to sound insulting."

"I'm not insulted," I said. I wasn't seeing muddy swirls when I thought about the future, now. I was remembering Baran bellowing in my face—and having to bend down to do it because he was so *bloody* big. "I wouldn't be insulted if you told me I couldn't fly back to Beune right now by flapping my arms."

Though that was looking more and more like the best idea I'd come up with yet.

"Well, I don't think the situation—" Guntram said.

Somebody knocked on the door. I jumped. Nobody'd bothered us since I'd gotten back from Castle Ariel. Guntram hadn't gotten a lot of visitors when I first came to Dun Add, but the new greeter out in the hall was about as good as an iron grating for keeping everybody away. Folks in Dun Add thought it was a demon, Baga said.

"Come in...?" Guntram called. I got up and headed for the door. I wasn't sure the visitor would be able to hear through the thick panel.

The door opened before I got there. The man who stuck his head in was in his late thirties but already balding. He was one of the Makers in Louis's stable, but I hadn't ever heard his name.

"Master Guntram?" he said. "Master Louis sends his compliments and asks that Lord Pal visit him in his private chamber as soon as possible."

The fellow spoke to Guntram, but when he'd finished speaking he nodded to me to show that he wasn't ignoring that I was standing in front of him.

Guntram rose from his chair also. "Certainly, Brian," he said. "We'll be there at once. Did Louis say what he wanted us for?"

"Sir," Brian said with a grimace. "I'm very sorry, *very* sorry, but my master wants to see Lord Pal alone. He's sent all of us away for the rest of the afternoon. Truly, none of us have any idea why he's done that. No idea."

"Well, then I'd better be off," I said. "Guntram, I'll be back, well, when I'm back."

"Lord Pal?" Brian said. "You remember where the Master's chambers are, don't you?"

"Sure," I said, frowning. "Down one flight and right around two corners. But aren't you coming with me, Master Brian?"

"Lord, I'm very sorry but I have orders not to come near the chambers until tomorrow morning," Brian said. I didn't doubt the truth of what he said, because he obviously wasn't comfortable about it.

"Leave your weapon with me, Pal," Guntram called. "I'll get to work while you're gone. That is, if you're willing to do that?"

"I trust you, sir," I said. I took out my shield and laid it beside the weapon. Light as it was, my tunic felt *wrong* without both of them in the pockets to balance each other. "I've done a lot of dumb things in my life—"

Most recently, I'd agreed to fight Lord Baran.

"—but I'm not so dumb that I don't trust you."

I headed for the nearest staircase. Brian went the other way; deliberately, I suppose. The attendants at each cross-corridor weren't there today. I didn't know what was going on, but I wasn't exactly worried. I would've been worried if I hadn't had the fight with Baran on my mind.

I knocked on the door to Louis's chambers. Nothing happened for a moment. I was wondering if I ought to knock again when Louis himself pulled the panel open.

"Come in, come in," he said. I'd never known him to sound gracious; he didn't now either. "I'm sorry about the secrecy, but we decided it was best."

I stepped into the big workroom, which was just as empty as Brian had said. Artifacts—weapons and shields, all that I saw—lay on the tables in various stages of repair. At least one shield was being created from three pieces, none of which was big enough for me to imagine making anything useful out of it.

"Come into my private office," Louis said. He saw where my eye had caught. He said, "Brian is showing off. It's skilled work, but the result isn't going to be better than we'd issue to the regular army. Still,

I want my people to stretch themselves, and I hope next time Brian will do so in a more useful fashion."

I followed Louis to his office at the far end, thinking of the image greeting people who approached Guntram's door. Louis would never have built the doorman because he wouldn't see any point in it.

There wasn't any point, not really. I could never work with Louis.

We entered the private office. Two more chairs had been moved there, crowding the space a lot. The Leader stood in front of the one he'd just risen from.

"I'm glad you could make it, Lord Pal," Jon said. "Sit down, won't you?"

I took the seat he pointed to. As soon as I settled, I wondered if I was supposed to have waited until Jon himself was down. Nobody seemed to notice.

"I'm told you're acting for Lady Jolene at her trial," Jon said.

"Yes sir," I said, suddenly feeling cold inside.

"I can't have any public part in it," Jon said. I'd thought Jolene had aged thirty years since I first saw her. So had her husband. "The justice of the Commonwealth has to go forward. The worst thing is that I be seen to intervene as a person and bring about an unjust result."

"Sir," I muttered. I *was* afraid now. If when I arrived on Dun Add, Jon had asked me not to get involved with his wife's trial, I suppose I'd have obeyed. Jolene was nothing to me, and Lady May shouldn't have been anything. I'd sworn to serve Jon and the Commonwealth, and I truly believed that anything Jon did, it was because he thought that was best for the Commonwealth.

But now I'd given my word. I wasn't going to go back on that, no matter who I made angry.

"Unofficially, though..." Jon said. His eyes seemed to drill right through the front of my skull. "Is there any help we can give you? Louis and myself, that is."

I didn't know what to say. After a moment I realized that my mouth had opened; I shut it.

Jon didn't notice. He was looking down into his clenched fists. To his hands he said, "The Commonwealth needs Lord Clain. Clain believes in the Commonwealth, believes in what we're doing. It's not just how strong he is as a warrior that lets me go on, it's how strong his belief is."

Louis was nodding. I could see the shape of his skull through his short blond hair.

"But the Commonwealth needs me too!" Jon said. "Maybe after we've got Mankind united it won't, but it does now. And I need Jolene!"

He raised his hands to his face and then—may God help me!—he started crying.

I looked away. I'd never been so embarrassed in my life, not even when May was screaming abuse at me in the Consort's Garden.

I said, "Sir, I'll do the best I can." I wasn't sure the words had really come through my lips.

"I have the highest regard for my teacher Guntram's skills," Louis said. He leaned toward me, trying to ignore Jon the same as I was. "Even so, Lord Pal, I wonder if you'd mind my taking a look at your equipment?"

"Of course!" I said. "Sir, Guntram'd be the first one to say that there's nobody alive who can do more with fighting equipment than you can. Only—"

I didn't know how to say the next part, so I met Louis's eyes and just said it. "The thing is, sir, Guntram knows *me*. If you said one thing and he said another, I'd probably go with him. I don't mean to insult you."

Louis gave me a slow smile. "I begin to think that Lady Jolene may survive this wretched business after all," he said. "I'll talk with my friend and mentor Guntram. We'll see what we can come up with between us."

"Thank you, sir," I said. The Leader had stopped snuffling, so I glanced at him, hoping that I could get out now.

Jon gave me a wan smile. "You have my prayers and best wishes, Lord Pal," he said. "I'm sorry to have shown you the strain I've been feeling."

"You have the whole Commonwealth on you, sir," I said as I got up. I was deciding to take what Jon had said as an excuse to leave. "I'll do my best."

"Lord Pal?" said Jon, rising also. "Will you give me an honest answer if I ask you a question?"

If I'd been the sort who lied when it was handy to, I'd just have said, "Sure." But I wasn't, so I stood there a moment with my mouth open before I said, "Yes sir. If that's what you want, sir."

"Do you think I'm a fool to let this trial go ahead?" Jon said. "I could end it in a number of ways, as you must know."

"Sir," I said, nodding as I looked for words. The Leader was the most powerful person in the Commonwealth; the most powerful human being alive.

I took a deep breath. "Sir," I said, "I'm a Maker. Not like Louis, not even like Master Brian, I guess, but I'm a Maker."

The Leader nodded, but from his frown he didn't see where I was going. Louis had no expression at all.

"Sir, you're the Leader," I said. "But if you tried to tell me how I should modify an artifact, I'd ignore you because you don't know anything about what a Maker does. And I *sure* don't know how to lead the Commonwealth."

Both men grinned. It was the happiest I'd seen either of them since I came in.

I went back to Guntram's room. I was feeling a lot better too, though I couldn't really have told you why.

CHAPTER 34

Final Arrangements

When I got back to Guntram's quarters the next day after sparring with Morseth on the jousting ground, the inhuman—and unreal—doorman said, "Good afternoon, Lord Pal. Master Guntram hopes you'll go straight in, as he and Master Louis may be working when you arrive and unable to hear your knock."

"Thank you, sir," I said to the round-eyed image. No matter what it was, not a "thing" at all and for sure not a person, I'd still rather be polite. It didn't cost anything.

I opened the door. Louis was just getting up. Guntram turned when the hinge squealed; he was standing beside the couch he worked on. My weapon lay on the table between the two Makers.

I took off the rig holding the gear I'd borrowed from Louis while the two Makers worked on mine. Morseth had beaten me once, but we drew the second match and I didn't feel too bad about it. I still felt the clout Morseth had given my right wrist—at full power he'd have taken my hand off—but the healing couch would take care of the bruising. And it hadn't kept me from facing him again right away and coming off better than I had before.

"How did the equipment perform?" Louis said. He looked groggy from his recent trance, but he was still thinking about his regular duties. I'd gone off to spar three hours earlier, and I suspected that both Makers had been under ever since I'd left.

"It's heavier than I'm used to," I said, "and that made me a bit slower than I should've been." I massaged my wrist with the fingers of my left hand. "Once in particular. But it's good gear, and the shield Brian put together is a *lot* better than you gave it credit for being, sir."

"I'm surprised to hear you say that," said Louis, frowning. "The core elements hadn't fused, and I wasn't able to correct the problem when I went over it myself."

"That was an advantage in a fight, sir," I explained. "The portion of shield that takes the initial blow twists and sends the stroke into the parts beside it. Lord Morseth has very good equipment, and he was getting really frustrated."

I grinned. Morseth being peeved had been an advantage to me also.

"The downside is that I didn't know how the blow was going to turn me either, the way I would if it'd been a straight-on block," I said. "I wouldn't trade for my own shield, but once somebody got used to it he could do pretty well, I'll bet."

"This has something to do with the modifications

we've made to your weapon," Guntram said. "But perhaps you'd rather have something to eat rather than discuss it immediately?"

What I'd really have liked to do was to give my wrist an hour on the couch—it was throbbing worse and worse since I'd climbed the stairs—but I didn't mind a little pain if I was going to learn how I might be able to face Lord Baran. These two men were the best hope in the human universe of my doing that. Which didn't mean that they'd be enough.

"I'd love to hear what you've done," I said, pulling a stool closer to the Makers' benches. "I *need* to know."

"We butchered it," Louis said, grimly. He glared at the weapon. Around it sat flat trays of materials too finely divided for me to tell what they were.

Louis looked over at me again. "Guntram says you helped him fashion this," he said. "You did a *bloody* good job. I couldn't have bettered it on a good day, and now—"

He gave an angry shrug.

"We can rebuild it after the trial," Guntram said to his former pupil. "We have to get Pal through the trial first, though."

He turned to me and said, "Pal, you know that weapons can either thrust or slash. Most of them are biased toward thrusting, because it's more effective."

"Sure," I said. I thought of my original weapon, the one I'd rebuilt from a rock drill. I didn't think even Clain could have survived a thrust from that one, but of course I could never have gotten close enough to Clain—or anybody competent—without being chopped to doll-rags.

"But from observing your jousts," Louis said, "we've

noticed that you prefer to use the edge. Are you aware of that?"

"Well, it works out that way," I said. "I've been using Buck's brain to predict the motion of the other guy's weapon and deflect the stroke with my own. Getting a little jump, I guess. And because I'm slashing to turn his stroke away, it's generally easier to slash when *I* attack."

"Yes," said Louis. "Your weapon was almost perfectly balanced between thrusting and slashing. What we have done is to adjust it so that ninety percent of the effort goes into slashing and only a tenth toward the thrust."

"So long as you're able to anticipate Lord Baran's blows," Guntram said, "you'll be able to turn them. He won't be able to weaken your weapon by repeated hammering—yours is as strong as his."

"This would be *terrible* design for ordinary use," Louis said, disgust obvious in his tone. "I would never let something like this out of my shop. But as my teacher said, it's the only way we could find that might allow you to survive the trial. And thus allow the Consort to survive."

He shook his head. "And without Jolene, whatever I may think of her personally," he went on, "I'm very much afraid that the Commonwealth will have lost its center. Jon hasn't been able to work since this whole *foul* business blew up."

"Do you think Baran will be willing to give up the prosecution if we fight through the day?" I asked. Guntram had said that my weapon would take a full day's hammering by Baran. I wasn't at all sure that *I* could take that, but at least I wouldn't be around to know if I failed.

Louis shrugged. "If the first day is inconclusive,"

he said, "the Leader can halt the proceedings. He's done that before."

"I see," I said. That might work. I was sure as I could be that Baran wouldn't willingly accept a draw, but not even he could expect to fight the whole Commonwealth. Any two of the Champions together could handle Baran. Though they wouldn't stand up for Jolene, they'd surely support the Leader giving a proper order.

"I suppose it's obvious that you can't actually defeat Baran," Guntram said. "We're just making it possible for you to survive."

Louis snorted and said, "Well, lightning might strike Baran during the match. Are you religious, Lord Pal? You could pray for that to happen."

"Sir, I'm not that religious, no," I said. "I'll just keep practicing until the match, using the weapon like it is now."

I felt myself smiling. "During the match, I'll probably pray," I added. I felt better for making a joke, even a pretty feeble one.

"Now, I believe," said Guntram, "we should all have something to eat and drink."

To my surprise, I wasn't noticing my wrist anymore—not to speak of.

I had a chance of survival after all. For somebody who'd been living under a death sentence from the time I first fought the image of Lord Baran on a practice machine, that was a major improvement.

I'd spent a long time in the steam room, then had dived into the plunge bath. I didn't swim—I'd never learned to on Beune—but I splashed around a little. I walked into the waiting room of the bathhouse at the southeast of the castle. Baga was there as I expected—I'd told him to come back after he'd carried Buck down to the boat.

I didn't expect Maggie, but she was there too. And I *really* didn't expect Lady May to be with them, which she was.

I stared at the three of them, figuring I had to say something but not having a clue about what that was. Baga said, "Ah, boss—"

That was all he got out before Maggie stepped in front of him. She took a deep breath and said, "Lord Pal, her ladyship here—"

She nodded. May actually stood in back of her, but I got the idea.

"—came to the boat to bring you some clothes. I brought her up here myself, but we left the clothes in the boat. Buck'll be all right till you get back there."

Buck pretty much slept all the time there wasn't somebody with him, putting him through his paces, so I didn't doubt that he'd be fine. I hadn't been planning to go straight back to the boat, but there was no reason I shouldn't.

"All right," I said. "We can head there now. I want to talk to Guntram about today's session, but that can wait a bit."

"Lord Pal . . ." said Maggie, her voice sharp. She was looking at—glaring at—her husband. "Baga and me are going to stop in at the Swan Tavern. You know where that is? The south end of Castle Street, near to landingplace. When you're done with your business at the boat, you can stick your head in and tell us. It's right on your way."

"Well, there's no need for that," I said. I hadn't looked straight at May yet, and so long as I kept talking to Maggie I wouldn't have to.

"There's every *bloody* need if my husband knows what's good for him," Maggie said. "Baga, we're going to the Swan *now*, you hear."

"Yes, dear," Baga muttered, his head down. They went out together.

"I thought we could sit out in the shade of your boat," May said. "And I brought a leather ball along with the suit. We could throw it for Buck."

I gestured her to the door and followed her out, past the goggling attendant. God knows what he was thinking about the visit of a Lady to the bathhouse. I wasn't sure what I was thinking about it either.

"Buck doesn't chase things," I said as we started down one of the lanes that run toward landingplace alongside Castle Street. "He's been trained out of it for work. We can rub his ears, though. He likes that."

I grinned. "He's got kind of a nose for artifacts out on the Road, too," I said. "I don't know how he does it, sees them in the Waste or sniffs them or for all I know hears them. I guess if you wanted exercise, we could go up the Road looking for artifacts."

"I think rubbing Buck's ears is exercise enough," May said. She looked straight at me as we walked along. She said, "Pal, are you all right? You don't look..."

"I'm tired," I said, smiling again. "*Very* tired. I just spent six hours on the machines. But believe me, I couldn't have done that if I weren't in good shape."

"Oh," said May, looking away again. "Ah, is it going well? The practicing? That is, if you don't mind...?"

"I don't mind," I said. I was actually kinda glad

to talk about it with somebody besides Guntram and Louis. They made me think about doctors talking about a patient; a really sick patient.

"I'm practicing against a machine that fights the way Baran does," I said. "Ah, I don't suppose you'll be talking to anybody who'd go to Baran with the story—or even that Baran would care. But, you know, I'd rather that he didn't know that."

"I won't tell anyone," May said. "Even Jolene."

She hadn't objected that *she* wouldn't do anything like that, or object to my tone or any of those things I'm used to people saying when I warn them about something. May was really a lot nicer—and smarter— than most of the people I'd met.

"So I'm trying new tactics, to wear him down," I said. I didn't mention the changes to my weapon because I didn't figure it'd mean anything to May. "I lost—I would've been killed—after two hours in the first run today. In the second run I lasted four hours, but I was starting to come apart and it wouldn't have been long. Guntram asked me to stop so that he could work on my shield. He had some ideas."

"Fighting for four hours is really good, isn't it?" May said.

"It's a lot better than I've been managing," I said. "I've got another week to practice. And Guntram and Louis are polishing my equipment. Anyway, after that I took a hot bath. It's not just getting clean—a dry shower in the boat would do that even better. But for the muscles."

"Jolene is really lucky to have you, Pal," May said to the path at the end of the cobblestoned lane. "I'll make sure she knows that, though I won't tell her any of the details."

"If the Consort is *really* lucky," I said, "Lord Clain will arrive before the trial."

And I'll be even luckier, I thought, but I didn't say that. If Jolene and her household could be happy for a week, that was a good thing.

We came onto the landingplace. Buck saw me right away and came bounding over to us. He doesn't jump up, but he rubs my legs hard enough sometimes that I have to step back or he'd knock me over. Despite the six hours we'd spent at the practice machines, this was one of those times.

"Hey, it's okay, boy," I said as I rubbed him. "I'm back. Heavens, you'd think I'd been gone for a year."

"He's worried about you," May said.

"Well, I'm still around for now," I said.

Baga and Maggie had set up a table and bench outside the boat, since they were living here while we were in Dun Add. I patted one end of the bench and walked down to the other end.

I hadn't really thought about what would happen to Buck if Baran killed me. I mean, back in Beune I always knew that I could die—plenty of people have gone into the Waste looking for artifacts and not come back—but I didn't think about it.

Now I had to think about it: there was a better than fair chance that I was going to be killed when I fought Baran. I wasn't near as good as him, and he was going to be coming at me with all he had—not for me, he didn't care about me, but because I was in the way of him getting the Consort.

Let him bloody have her!

But I didn't really feel that way. I'd become a Champion to help bring justice, Justice, to Mankind, and it wouldn't be just to let Jolene die for something she hadn't done. For all that I didn't much like her, and her having an affair with Lord Clain seemed to be going a long way to tearing up the Commonwealth.

I'd been rubbing Buck behind the ears. He'd flopped his head in my lap when I sat down. I realized I hadn't said anything for a while and looked up. May was watching me, but I wasn't sure about her expression.

"Maggie said something about clothes?" I said. "I didn't know what she meant, but I forgot to ask with all the rest going on."

"Lady Jolene sent you a suit," May said. She smiled, but it kinda lost shape after a moment. "Maggie and I set it in your chamber, but—would you like me to bring it out and show you?"

"Sure," I said. "But I wasn't expecting anything like that."

May whisked into the boat. Buck turned his head to watch her, but he didn't trot after her like I thought he might. She was back in just a moment, carrying a bundle of white cloth and a small packet wrapped in paper.

She put everything on the table, then unfolded the top piece of cloth into a tunic of shiny white material, picked out with gold buttons and gold-embroidered flowers and hummingbirds. I stood and stepped closer, though I didn't touch it because I'd been petting Buck.

"Is this silk?" I said, looking up at May. "It's lovely."

"We made it ourselves," May said proudly. "The Consort's attendants. Jolene bought the material. It gave us something to focus on, which was good— especially for Emma. She was Ziga's best friend. She didn't expect anything like this, of course."

"It'd have been simpler if Ziga had just hung her-self right off," I said, saying the words I was thinking. From the way May winced, I guess I should've kept my mouth shut.

She squeezed out a smile and said, "We thought you could wear it for the trial. That is, if you want to. We just wanted to..."

May didn't know where to go with the sentence, so she let it trail off.

"Thank you," I said. "And thank the other ladies. And Lady Jolene, of course."

"You needn't worry that it won't fit," May said. "We were all brought up to be *ladies*, you see. We sing and play instruments, and we do needlework."

She coughed. "It's cut a little loose," she said. "For the purpose, you know."

I nodded. "Thank you," I repeated. The white was going to be a mess if Baran cut me open, but that wouldn't hurt me. Or anybody, I supposed.

"There's another thing," May said. She turned and folded the tunic back on top of the trousers. Without facing around again, she continued, "You know that it's traditional for a warrior to wear the favor of the Lady he's fighting for?"

"I've heard that," I said. The literature we got in Beune made jousts a lot more romantic than the real-ity of the fights I'd been in, but they pretty much all talked about the Lady's favor.

"It wouldn't be proper for you to wear Jolene's favor at the trial," May said, still not looking at me. "Because she's the Leader's Consort, you see. Even if Lord Clain had returned, he wouldn't wear her favor."

"I see that," I said. Actually, I was glad to hear

it. I guess everybody in Dun Add knew about Clain and Jolene, but it still wasn't right to rub the Leader's nose in it.

"But we were thinking, we girls you know," May said. "That a friend, a close friend of the Consort's, could give you a favor and that would be all right. We didn't want you to go out and have it look like nobody cared about you. Because we all do. We care really a lot."

"That would be nice," I said. I got the words out without choking but I swallowed hard afterwards. Buck was whining but I ignored him.

May opened the paper packet and faced me, holding out the muslin sleeve of her light blue sundress. "Would this be all right?" she whispered.

"I would be honored to wear it," I said. "I'll hope to be worthy of it."

May set the sleeve on top of the suit and clutched all the fabric to her chest. "I'm glad," she said. "I'll take these back to the castle and have them delivered to Master Guntram's chambers when I'm finished. I'm a very good seamstress."

Then she said, "You'll want to wash up now."

She strode off briskly. "Don't forget to stop at the Swan," she called without turning her head.

I watched her until she disappeared among the horse chestnuts. I thought about the first time I'd met her. Then I went into the boat to wash my hands.

CHAPTER 35

The Trial

The sky was overcast, but it was a muggy day and already hot by mid-morning. Things were supposed to have begun by now, but there was some administrative problem.

I really, *really*, wanted to be out on the field and able to do something. The longer I sat on a chair under a marquee, though, the less time I'd need to stand up to Baran's attack. This was better.

Anyway, I didn't have a choice. We'd get going when the Sergeant of the Court said so.

"More to drink, boss?" Baga asked.

I glanced at the mug on the side table and saw it was still half full of ale. I opened my mouth to snarl at Baga not to bloody badger me when I was tense enough already. Then I remembered Baga was nervous too, and screaming at people didn't help. It certainly wouldn't make me calmer.

"No," I said, getting to my feet. "But I'll stretch my legs a bit."

I'd planned to speak with Guntram—mainly to get away from Baga and his fussing—but when I looked toward him, I saw Garrett and behind him Welsh trotting up from landingplace. They had dogs with them as well as a pair of attendants who held the animals when the warriors—my vassals—approached.

"Garrett!" I called. "Welsh!"

I started toward them, then decided I shouldn't move from under the marquee. I was pretty sure it'd be an hour before they got things going, but it'd be my luck that they'd call the trial and I'd have to run an extra hundred yards to meet Baran. I waved, but right now I'd let my friends do all the walking.

As the defender, I'd been placed on the north side of the field. Baran was on the south. Ordinary folks from Dun Add were mostly on my side because it was nearer the town and the castle, but I could see forty or fifty of the Champions clustered around Baran's marquee. Most of the Champions who weren't with him watched from the east end, where the Leader and his court officials were.

Lady Jolene sat at her husband's side. That was proper, but I probably wasn't the only person watching who thought it looked funny. Where else should Jolene be, though?

The Consort's servants and her Ladies stood beside her seat. I couldn't make out faces from where I was, but one of the women wore a blue sundress with only one sleeve. I smoothed the muslin which loosely covered the white silk of my own right sleeve.

Welsh and Garrett were breathing hard when they

reached me. "What're you fellows doing in Dun Add?" I said. I didn't figure it was bad news or else they wouldn't both have come. Unless it was *really* bad news.

"Guy from Dun Add came to us looking for Lord Clain," Garrett said. He was puffing from the recent run, but he looked a good deal better than he had when he led settlers out to Castle Ariel.

"What would Clain be doing out in the sticks with us?" Welsh said. "But the thing is, the guy was a messenger from the Leader. He said that unless they got Clain back in time, you were going to be fighting Lord Baran. So we come to find you."

"Didn't get here any too soon, did we?" Garrett said. "Well, we made bloody good time anyway. We figured you might need a couple sidemen, but you seem to have that covered pretty well."

I stepped forward and hugged them both at the same time. I hadn't dreamed that they'd come if they heard about the trial.

"Bless you both," I said. "Bless you for coming all this way."

"Well, you're our lord," Welsh said. "It's our duty."

"Who is this lot?" Garrett asked, looking past me toward the dozen attendants standing under the marquee with me. Most of them were eyeing me and the warriors, but nobody was crowding closer. "I don't recognize any of 'em except the Makers. And Baga, of course."

I looked at my supporters and smiled. "Guntram," I said, "you know my vassals Garrett and Welsh, but Louis and his aides may not. Garrett—" turning my head toward him and Welsh again "—*all* of my supporters here are Makers. Master Louis very kindly agreed to stand with me and to bring his staff."

"You're one of our own, Lord Pal," said a young fellow named Feeney or Sweeney.

"Sirs?" said Brian to Garrett and Welsh. "Lord Pal is our hero. Warriors like you take what we make for them and maybe you appreciate it, but you don't *understand*. And us, we're like the servers who bring you dinner. But Lord Pal, *him* you all notice."

"I think they're getting ready," called one of Louis's people. "The Sergeant and the trumpeter 're walking out."

"Well, we'll be getting out of the way, then," Welsh said. "Since you don't need us after all."

"I needed you two showing up more than you'll ever know," I said. And more than I'd dreamed, though I didn't say that aloud. "Hey look—can you take orders from a Maker?"

"I guess we've taken your orders pretty well, haven't we, Pal?" Garrett said.

I laughed. "Look," I said. "Louis is in charge of my staff. You do what he tells you, right?"

"Right," said Garrett, and he and Welsh both gave me big grins.

The trumpet sounded a fanfare from the east end of the field. Buck and I turned and moved to the front of the marquee. Everybody made way for us.

"The trial of Lady Jolene of Leys for murder will now commence!" the Sergeant called through a megaphone. He and the trumpeter stood twenty yards in front of the Leader and his Consort. "The Prosecutor is Lord Baran ben Joos, in red."

There were a lot of cheers from the other side of the field. Baran, with a white-furred wolfhound, stepped onto the field and waited.

"The defendant is represented by Lord Pal of Beune, in white and blue!" the Sergeant called. I stepped forward and took a deep breath. I had my weapon and shield out, but neither Baran nor me switched on yet.

There were cheers, including from some of the general spectators. Many had cheered for Baran too. They were looking forward to the fight, not backing me.

The trumpeter blew a long single note, then with the Sergeant trotted toward the east end, getting off the field. I switched on, entered Buck's mind, and walked toward the center of the field.

There was a slight breeze. I couldn't see individual grass blades through Buck's eyes, but the surface rippled and swept past us again and again. It was like sitting on a tethered boat in a windstorm, watching the water approach and rush past.

Baran was a black figure to me now. He was taking full strides, not running but clearly looking forward to swatting me out of the way.

I think he must've expected me to try circling, but my footwork's never been very good. I went straight for him.

Baran swung a trifle sooner than he should have, a quartering stroke aimed down at the left side of my neck. Buck saw it coming before a human would've noticed movement. Instead of letting my shield take it, I met Baran's weapon in the air and deflected it down into the sod to my right front. Baran jerked back, recovering the weapon.

The first time I'd fought Baran's image on a practice machine, we'd had an exchange like that. The image's shield was low and I'd thought I had the opportunity I needed: my weapon was already up, so I'd struck over the shield at the point of the image's left shoulder.

Its shield blocked my stroke, and its weapon thrust through the middle of my thigh. Baran was *extremely* strong. Even when he looked like he was out of position, he wasn't. He could whip his massive shield about like it was a flyswatter.

Now I just shifted my leading foot—the right—a little forward. Baran's blow had rocked me back, even though I'd redirected it.

Baran swung again, this time down from straight overhead. My weapon was in position almost before Baran's arm started to move. Again the stroke hissed into the ground, leaving a smoldering black scar when he withdrew the weapon.

Everything had gone as planned; but though I'd caught both strokes, I felt them. They hit me like tall pine trees which toppled slowly but slammed the ground like thunder.

"Aren't you going to fight, you coward?" Baran shouted. I waited. He thrust and I slid his weapon past the left side of my shield.

Sparks showered away each time our weapons made contact. The spectators were certainly getting a show. I'd seen matches where both parties moved in slow circles around a center, like partners in a leisurely country-dance. I was willing to fight, but I wasn't counterstriking.

Because Baran would kill me if I took the fight to him. It was that simple. I *couldn't* match his strength and the power of his equipment.

After the thrust, Baran started using his size to grind away at me. He stepped close and struck. When

I caught the blow he stepped in again and struck again. I gave ground each time.

I didn't try to disengage, but I couldn't hold him. That would be like trying to push a plow-ox backward by main strength. I managed to slant to my left so that he was driving me toward the east end of the field instead of the shorter distance straight into my marquee, but that wasn't much of a victory.

Baran fought for every inch, though. I couldn't stop him, but he knew he was in a fight. He snarled, "You coward, you bloody coward!" each time before he stepped into the next blow. I met each one in a rush of sparks, and I gave back because I had to.

The trumpet called. I was barely aware of it. Blackness covered me, the same blinding darkness that Guntram had projected over my first duel with Easton. I switched off my weapon and shield and fell to my left knee.

The first round was over. We'd been fighting for fifty minutes, and there'd be a ten-minute break before the next round.

An instant later the blackness vanished. I heard spectators crying out in surprise. Baran, with his shield still live, stood two paces away. He stared toward the Sergeant and the trumpeter, who continued to blow. Only then did Baran switch off his own equipment.

Baga and a group of Makers reached me first, carrying a skin of wine, buckets of water, and towels. Garrett and Welsh were right behind them with their shields up and weapons in their hands. They didn't switch off their shields until Baran shut down.

Baga unstoppered the wineskin for me and held the nozzle to my lips. I sloshed the first swig around my mouth, then swallowed the next two cautiously and waved Baga back. The wine was mostly water, but even so I didn't want a lot of liquid sloshing around in my gut when we got back into it.

Two Makers rubbed my face with wet towels and my torso through the thin silk. Two more were working on Buck, and they'd poured a half inch of water into a pan for him to drink from. I reached over and scratched the base of his spine; his tail wagged.

Guntram had joined us. "I wasn't sure that Baran was going to stop for the trumpet," he said, "so I took a hand."

"If he struck me after the time call," I said, "he'd forfeit his prosecution."

"You would be dead," Guntram said.

"That's not much of a threat the way I feel right now," I said. That must have been why Garrett and Welsh ran up armed, too: just in case.

I opened my eyes—they'd been closed. Baran was twenty feet away, surrounded by his supporters. I caught only fleeting glimpses of him, but the bright red of his tunic and breeches had darkened with sweat.

He felt my eyes on him. "Bloody coward!" he shouted. "I don't care how far you run, I'll catch you and cut you to collops! Maybe I'll toss the pieces onto the pyre when we burn the slut you're serving! What do you think of that?"

I think you're an uncultured barbarian. I didn't say the words or any words, just closed my eyes again.

"I really don't care much about the Consort," said Guntram. I opened my eyes and looked at him. He was smiling. "I would not regard it to be a fair exchange if she were to live because you died."

He turned slightly to the man kneeling beside him. "Louis believes in the Consort's importance to the Commonwealth," Guntram added, "but of course Louis believes in the importance of the Commonwealth."

"So do I," I said, realizing for the first time that Louis was here, in a trance viewing my weapon. "But that's not why I'm fighting Baran. Jolene isn't guilty and it wouldn't be right to execute her."

"'Justice' is another concept that I've never fully understood," Guntram said. "But I accept that others whom I respect feel as you do."

Louis come up from his trance and shook himself. "How has the weapon felt when you use it?" he asked.

"It seems at full strength with no falling off," I said. "It gets a little warm, but only a little. My forearm, though, that gets hot every time I take a blow and it's getting worse."

"Yes," said Louis with a shrug. I hadn't expected him to be concerned. "That's not to be helped, I'm afraid. The energy has to be dissipated somehow. If it's any consolation, the same thing is happening to Baran. And your shield?"

"It's only taken a few blows that I've deflected into it," I said. "I really haven't noticed any problem. How does the weapon look from inside?"

I could have checked it myself, but I was in no mood to go into a Maker's trance. Besides, I was logy for a bit after a trance, and that was the last thing I needed now.

"It's in perfect condition," Louis said happily. "And having watched you fighting, I'm not sure that our changes limited the weapon's general usefulness as much as I feared that they would."

He looked at Guntram and said, "Teacher, I've never considered Lord Baran one of my more reflective clients. I think if he were, however, he'd be getting worried."

Guntram smiled. "I don't think Baran is reflective either," he said. "I'd be very interested to examine *his* weapon, though. I think we did a better job on Pal's than we realized."

The trumpeter blew a two-note call. I quickly took another drink, then turned the mug upside down so that Baga wouldn't dither wondering if I wanted more. I got to my feet and only then bent to pick up the weapon and shield where I'd dropped them on the grass while I rested.

"C'mon, Buck," I said as he lurched to his feet also. "No rest for the weary. We've got a lot more hours of this yet, if everything goes right."

My supporters were scampering off the field. Well, Guntram and Louis were walking off with dignity. They'd be clear before the call to resume, though.

I looked at Baran. He snarled, "You bloody coward! Your mother must be ashamed to have raised a coward who won't fight!"

I grinned at him. My mother *hadn't* raised me. And if she was who I thought she was, she didn't think either that I was a coward or that I wouldn't fight.

I didn't say any of that. I figured that my smile would get home to Baran better than anything I said.

I walked around Baran, keeping the same ten feet away that we'd been while resting. My right arm tingled; the silk sleeve was still damp and that felt good.

"What're you doing?" Baran said. "What are you *doing*?"

I was putting myself between my opponent and the east end of the field, giving myself the longest distance to retreat in. Which I'd be doing for the next fifty minutes.

I glanced toward Jon and his court. A woman near the Consort's seat was waving her bare arm.

The trumpeter blew a single blast. He and the Sergeant rejoined the court. I faced my opponent and switched on my equipment.

Baran came at me fast, like I thought he would. He brought his weapon up and straight down with all his strength, a blow that would've burned my shield out in a spectacular overload if I hadn't skidded it to the right with my own weapon—as usual. Believe me, I felt it all the way to my toes, though.

Without moving from where he stood, Baran brought the weapon around for a second, identical blow, like I was a tent stake he was trying to drive into the ground. I deflected it again, this time to my left. That changed the stress on my right arm, but I had to time it perfectly or Baran would cut me in half the way he was trying.

He buried the point in the ground, withdrew, and bloody *hell!* swung overhead and down a third time. I slanted it to the side again, but my right arm ached to the shoulder and the sleeve of my tunic was stiff and dry. I wouldn't be surprised to find the silk had started to sear. My forearm was in an oven.

He had me. The next stroke and I was going to go down. Baran was too strong for me and too determined. Guntram and Louis had built me weapons to match Baran's, but the component they hadn't fixed—me—was about to fail.

"You bastard!" Baran shouted. "You sniveling coward!"

I waited for the blow that would finish me. My arm hurt like never before. The next time Baran hit me my flesh would burst into flame. It was over.

Instead of hammering down again, Baran strode forward and banged his shield against mine, his weapon out at his side. He drove me back a step, but when I feinted an over-arm blow—the first attack I'd made today—Baran jerked backward instead of meeting the stroke with his own weapon.

Baran's weapon arm was hurting just as much as mine was. He was unwilling to take that fourth crashing swing, because he was afraid that if he did, he'd drop his weapon and run screaming.

Baran was afraid.

I don't know what he imagined. He knew Makers were helping me. Maybe he thought they'd somehow made me magically invulnerable.

All I'd done was to stand and take whatever Baran flung at me. He didn't understand the equipment, so he was giving it all sorts of powers that it didn't—couldn't—have. As Louis had said, the energy had to dissipate somehow.

Baran came at me again, but he thrust more than he cut, which he mostly hadn't been doing. I continued to slant his weapon away, sometimes absorbing the last of the attack with my shield. I had to retreat, but he wasn't driving me back as steadily as he had in the first round.

But Baran was still making the running, no question about that. I responded to his attacks, but I didn't dare attack myself or even counterstroke. Baran was favoring his right arm because he'd burned himself when he tried to hammer his way through me, but he was still a lot stronger. My only advantage was that Baran didn't realize how bad he'd hurt me with those three blows.

The trumpet called. I backed away and was glad to see that Baran did also. I switched off, dropped my equipment on the grass, and knelt. I bent over to breathe easier. My right arm throbbed and my lungs were burning.

My supporters arrived at a run. I slurped more watered wine, not a lot but I was really dry.

"Keep wet towels on my right arm," I croaked, sticking it out in the breeze. A Maker and Welsh were already wrapping it. The flesh had started to swell, though Baran hadn't really stressed me after that first flurry.

"You're all right, boss?" Baga said, sounding worried.

I set the mug down. "I wouldn't've been if he'd hit me one more time like at the first," I said.

I looked at Guntram. "The practice machines show you the moves," I said. "They don't get the way the fight wears you down, though."

Guntram nodded. "This is an unusual fight," he said. "If you don't mind, I'll modify your shield?"

"Go ahead," I said. I was too wrung out to have an opinion on anything. I trusted Guntram's judgment, but I couldn't imagine what he planned to do.

I sipped more wine with my left hand and looked around for the first time since the previous break. Louis bent over my weapon, in a trance. Garrett was trickling water onto the towels around my right arm with a determined look on his face. Buck lay upright, panting; two Makers worked on him with wet towels, and a third poised to pour more water into his drinking pan at carefully measured intervals.

I had a simple job today: fight Baran. The people here on the field around me didn't know what they ought to be doing, and they really wanted to do *something*.

We weren't quite back to mid-field. Baran hadn't driven me near as hard in the second round as in the first. He was in the middle of his own handlers; I got only occasional glimpses of his red outfit.

Guntram was right about this being an unusually long fight. Even the assault on Rowley's Roost had been over in five minutes, and I'd faced three separate opponents. Before now, the longest match I'd had was when I was sparring with Lord Clain and didn't know it was him. That had lasted twenty minutes, and afterwards I'd felt like I'd been rolling a boulder all afternoon.

Thought of Clain made me look toward the Consort. I wondered what was going through her mind now. My handlers weren't the only people who couldn't do much but watch and worry.

May was waving again. Her favor was plastered to my arm with wet towels, but I knew it was there.

Louis and Guntram came out of their trances at the same time. Louis said, "From inside your weapon shows no signs of wear. Have you noticed anything in use?"

"No," I said. "But the heat from fighting almost cooked my arm."

I glanced at the dripping towels and wondered if I'd gotten permanent injuries already. It was probably too early to worry about that. At present, a crushed skull continued to be a more realistic concern.

"I've adjusted your shield's resistance," Guntram said when I turned my eyes to him. "It's now biased with eighty percent resistance to vertical strokes or thrusts in the central six inches."

"That's what he's been attacking," I said. "But I've been deflecting him every time, right?"

Guntram shrugged. "I expect you'll continue to deflect him," he said. "But concentrating on where he's concentrating seemed a good idea."

"Right," I said. I looked again at Baran. He sat with three other champions; one of them was Wissing, like Baran himself one of Jon's inner circle. Baran saw me and, though his lips twisted in what was probably a curse, he didn't shout abuse this time.

I wondered what strategy Baran's buddies were offering. It seemed to me that all he had to do was keep up what he was doing already. He was wearing me down, and before long I was going to stumble as I backed away. It was all over then.

The trumpeter sounded his two-note call. I got to my feet. My thighs ached, my calves ached, my knees ached. I shook my right arm as Welsh stripped the towels off. The elbow bent normally; I hadn't been sure that it would.

"Come on, Buck," I said, knuckling his spine between the shoulders. He lurched to his feet as I picked up my shield and weapon.

I felt dizzy as I straightened, but the feeling passed while I worked at staying upright. I saw Baran staring at me. I raised my arms up to head height, then grinned at him.

Baran growled a series of words at me, ending with bastard. "Bastard" was true, but the adverbs he'd put in front of it weren't. I lowered my hands and equipment, continuing to grin.

God knows I wasn't feeling cheerful, but Baran wasn't God. I figured that if he thought I was as fresh as I'd been to start with, he was less likely to repeat the sledgehammer attack that had almost beaten me at the start of the second round.

Baran came at me hard, swinging hard and trying to close. I fended the blows off without great trouble. My right arm wasn't showing any immediate danger of giving out on me, which I'd been afraid it might.

On the other hand, Baran had recovered also. By closing he couldn't take full swings, but I was going back faster.

I worried about backing away under pressure. I didn't have any choice, but a stumble would be the last mistake I made. The field was in good shape, but it wasn't a dinner table. A divot or a gopher hole could kill me.

I knew we were getting close to the east edge of the field, though I didn't dare glance around to make sure. I wasn't sure what happened if Baran forced me across the limed boundary. Perhaps we just turned around, but it could mean that I forfeited the bout. It hadn't occurred to me until now to ask about that.

I decided to play safe by shifting around to my right. I wasn't sure whether I'd be able to manage that, but I needed to try. The trumpet might sound time at any moment...but "might" meant also "might not."

Baran pushed forward and swung. I took the blow overhead and shuffled right.

Baran shouted and swung down again, moving sideways also to block me. I guided the stroke away to my right.

Buck yelped and I was no longer in his mind. The world showed in full color through my own eyes. Buck writhed on the ground, twisting to reach the stump of his severed left hind leg.

It's my fault!

And it was, but I'd be joining Buck soon, so it wouldn't be on my conscience long.

Baran had injured Buck by accident. He might have done a number of things next. One of them was to send away his own dog and fight me as equals again. That would've been an act of high courtesy that would have him talked about with approval in romantic accounts of the fight.

And maybe on another day, in other circumstances, Baran would have done that. I didn't like the man, but he was a respected member of the group closest to the Leader. That wouldn't be true if Jon and Clain thought he was dishonorable.

But Baran really hated the Consort, and he thought she'd murdered his friend. Also I'd scared him, pushed him hard when he'd come into the trial expecting to brush me out of the way. He wasn't concerned about his fame in years to come. He was going to end the fight.

Using his dog's agility, Baran came at me from my left quarter. I couldn't get my weapon around in time to meet an attack from that angle. All I could do was raise my shield as I turned widdershins. Baran brought his weapon down in another of his smashing overhead cuts.

I had just time to shift my shield slightly before Baran's weapon met it. He rocked me back and I felt a surge of heat, but my shield held.

"For Buck!" I shouted. I swung down at Baran's head, a blow just like his. His shield was high to cover him. My weapon struck at the top center, and Baran's shield blew itself apart in a white flash and a shower of burning fragments.

Baran's wolfhound yelped and pirouetted away, snapping at bits sizzling on his white fur. Baran fell onto his back, trying to fling away the ruin of his shield. Some of the device had melted onto his flesh.

"Yield!" I shouted. "Yield or I'll bloody kill you!"

Baran rolled forward and came up on his feet. He lunged toward me, raising his weapon. I stepped into the attack, swinging. My weapon caught him at the base of his neck and slanted deeply down into his chest.

Baran toppled backward. He was still in one piece, but his head and right arm were dangling loose on tags of muscle.

"Yield!" I said again, but my world was turning gray. The gray darkened into black. I was toppling also, and that was the last thing I knew for quite a while.

CHAPTER 36

Life Goes On

Bright sunlight was coming through the glass of the windows, but for a moment all I was sure of was a white blur through which ghosts drifted. I shouted in surprise and sat up for an instant.

I hurt all over, but what really threw me down again was the rush of nausea. I turned onto my side and stuck my head over the edge of the bed. Thank goodness, the spasm passed as soon as I got my head down again.

"Here you go, boss!" Baga said. "I'm getting you some wine!"

My stomach roiled again. I wanted to object, but I was afraid to open my mouth.

"Baga, you get Master Guntram *now!*" Maggie said. "And you stay there with Buck until he comes back."

Then, apparently to somebody in the doorway, she added, "Yes, he's awake, but nobody can come in except his friend Guntram, you hear?"

"How's Buck?" I croaked. I didn't lift my head, but I turned it so that I could see something besides the floor. That was covered with rugs instead of the replaceable straw mats that I'd seen in most rooms of the castle.

"Master Guntram is caring for him," Maggie said. She held a cloth so that I could see it; water dripped from the corner. "Would you like me to wipe your face, milord?"

"Please," I said. I was feeling enough better that I lifted my torso slightly, though I didn't try to sit up again.

"Master Guntram said that you would want Buck to have the couch rather than you," Maggie said as she mopped my cheeks and brow carefully; she kept her left hand under the cloth to catch drips. "The Leader's doctor gave you something on the field so that you'd sleep, and he poulticed your arm."

Then she said, "It was terrible the way they cut your wonderful tunic off. It was a *crime*."

I closed my eyes again. "I can get another tunic," I said. "I'm glad Guntram's taking care of Buck."

It was a relief to learn that Buck was alive. Seeing him injured had . . . well, it was good that I'd had a way to let out what I was feeling.

I remembered Baran's shield failing and smiled. I remembered Baran dying also; I remembered *killing* Baran. I didn't smile at that, but I was glad that Jolene was safe.

"Where am I, Maggie?" I asked, lifting myself till I was sitting. I was on a feather bed; I'd have liked something firmer. My stomach stayed where it ought to.

"You're in the Consort's apartments, milord," Maggie said. "She insisted, she did. You're in the room of one of her ladies who left her a bit ago."

I felt my face stiffen, but then I smiled. "Was the lady named Ziga, Maggie?" I asked.

"I really don't know, sir," Maggie said. "I can ask one of the girls if you like. I told them all that Baga and me were going to take care of you because it's our rightful *duty*."

"I'll have a little of that wine, Maggie," I said. Since I'd come away from Beune, everything I'd seen was people in pyramids, somebody at the top and everybody else scrambling to get on top instead. Or at least to get off the bottom. "And don't bother asking about whose room it was. It doesn't matter."

"Sir?" Maggie said from the serving table near the door. "There's beer too, a little cask. Lady May brought it, in case you'd rather?"

"You know," I said, "I think I *will* have the beer if it's there. And I probably wouldn't turn down a mug of soup."

"At once!" said Maggie. She placed a silver goblet of what turned out to be ale carefully in my left hand, then scurried out of the room. I heard her giving orders to people outside.

I looked around the room. The walls were hung with velvet tapestries showing women dancing with wild leaps and arm gestures. The figures were simplified and woven in pastels which contrasted sharply with the dark green background.

I wondered what sort of woman Ziga had been. If this was even her room, of course.

The door opened. Guntram came in. I started to

get up but caught myself and instead said, "Guntram! How's Buck doing?"

"Quite well, considering," Guntram said. "The leg is reattached, but he won't be able to use it as well as he did in the past."

"You put the leg back on?" I said in amazement. I'd been relieved when Maggie told me that Buck hadn't died on the field—been put down, most likely. I hadn't dreamed that he wouldn't be three-legged for the rest of his life.

"Well, the couch did," Guntram said. "The muscles were burned back some distance on both sides of the cut. The damage is being removed but it can't be repaired. Of course, without the searing, all the blood would have drained out."

"I've known plenty of people who limp," I said. "I'm glad that Buck's in that good of shape. It's cheap at the price, I suppose."

I thought about the fight. I had a few vivid memories—the time I'd almost missed catching Baran's stroke and his weapon had swept down within a finger's breadth of my right elbow; how I felt as I saw Baran's weapon start to descend the third time as he tried to smash me flat—but I didn't have a connected memory of the whole trial.

"It wasn't Buck's fight, though, you know," I said. "He shouldn't have to pay for it."

Guntram shrugged. "It wasn't your fight either, Pal," he said. "You're certainly paying for it, though. And you could have been killed."

"I chose it, though, Guntram," I said. "It was for justice."

Guntram smiled. His smiles always looked sad to

me. He said, "Dogs don't need philosophies, they just fight. It seems to me that men do the same, though they usually come up with reasons. Justice is a good one."

"I wouldn't have come to Dun Add if I didn't believe in justice," I said. I wasn't arguing, just sorting out how I felt.

"I'm glad you did come here, Pal," said Guntram. "I wasn't bored—who could be bored with so many wonderful things to find?—but you certainly brought me out of the pattern I had been living in."

I thought about the fight as I drank more of the ale. I said, "Oh, Guntram? The way you changed my weapon, you and Louis, saved my life. But can you change it back before I go out again?"

"Yes, you're not going to have to fight Lord Baran again," Guntram said, smiling slightly. "And in fact Louis is already working on it. I'll look over what he does, but I don't think there's anything I could do with fighting tools that Louis couldn't do better and faster."

Guntram shook his head. "I don't think you realize how hard it was for Louis to adjust your weapon as we did, Pal," he said.

"I bloody well *do* know how tricky that was," I said. "I'm not much of a Maker beside the two of you, but I hope I'm good enough to judge that."

"No, that's not what I mean," Guntram said. "Of course that was a task, but it was easy enough to see what had to be done when we were in the weapon. The problem for Louis was to be willing to do that to an artifact which he considered a nearly perfect balance of factors. Your life depended on it, but I'm afraid that—"

Guntram's smile was as broad as it ever got.

"—while Louis likes and I think respects you, Pal, he's really more committed to his art than he is to any human being. I don't mean to offend you."

I laughed. "I'm not offended," I said. "Louis wouldn't be as good as he is if he didn't—care about good workmanship. And I'm glad he's changing the weapon back to being the way it ought to be."

I looked at the window—there was nothing for me to see out it from my angle—and said, "Guntram. Thank you and Louis. I couldn't have fought Baran without the way you adjusted my equipment. You beat Baran, not me."

"That's a little strong, don't you think?" Guntram said mildly. "If we'd laid the equipment on the field, it wouldn't have beaten Lord Baran. And if you'd been even slightly less skilled, Baran would have killed you anyway. I was watching, remember. Besides—"

He smiled again.

"—Baran would have been much less effective if he hadn't been using what Louis assures me is as good a set of equipment as he's ever made. He's amazed and not altogether pleased that you overloaded Baran's shield with that last blow. Though he's happy about the result, of course."

He pursed his lips and said, speaking to the memory rather than to me, "Your next to last blow."

Someone tapped on the door. I called, "Come in," expecting Maggie to appear with the soup.

The door opened. It was a pottery mug of soup, but the Leader was carrying it. He saw Guntram and said, "Hello, Master. Louis tells me that we have you partly to thank for the good result in the trial."

"Partly, yes," Guntram said, getting to his feet. "Pal, don't push yourself for a few days. Right now, I'll get back to Buck. Jon, things are well on your end?"

"Never better, Master," Jon said, bowing to his foster father. From the Leader's expression, if "never better" was the truth, things for him were usually very bad.

When Guntram went out, Jon turned to me. I set the empty goblet on the floor and took the soup in my left hand.

"How's your right arm?" Jon asked, frowning.

I held it out to the side and wriggled the fingers. "It's bandaged to the shoulder so the elbow doesn't bend very well," I said. "Other than that, it's all right. It sort of throbs when my heart beats, you know."

"I'll send Master Melchior over to change the bandage when I return," Jon said. "I'm surprised you're not on Guntram's healing couch. There's still some who're afraid of it, but you've used the couch before, haven't you?"

"The couch is occupied," I said. "I don't need it and he does."

I didn't explain who "he" was. To me—and maybe Guntram, or else he was just doing what he knew I'd want—it seemed the right choice, but I wasn't sure anybody else would think giving the couch to a hurt dog made sense.

I drank some of the soup, beef and vegetable. It was warm, but not so hot that I had to be careful about how fast I drank it.

"Well, you know best, I suppose," Jon said. His tone meant that he thought I was a fool. "I assure you that my Consort is very grateful to you. She has property of her own, you know, and I believe she intends to transfer something to you—but I shouldn't have spoken, she'll want to give you the details herself."

"Sir, tell her that's really not necessary!" I said, louder than I wished I'd been when I remembered I was talking to the Leader. More calmly I said, "Look, tell her another nice suit like the one I ruined in the fight, that'd be wonderful."

"I believe there will be a suit. Suits, in fact," Jon said. His expression was as close to cheerful as I'd seen it since I came back to Dun Add. "My understanding is that each of Jolene's ladies is sewing one, and there's something of a competition going on."

I closed my eyes. "My Lord," I muttered. "Sir, I was just standing up for Lady Jolene for justice's sake. Nothing else."

Jon snorted. "I believe you," he said. "I don't know how many other people will, but Master Guntram raised me. He does things because they're the right thing to do, in his mind. Nothing else matters to him. Eh?"

"Yessir," I said. "That's Master Guntram."

I'd been wrong to think that everybody I knew was trying to climb a pyramid. Guntram wasn't that way . . . and I surely wasn't.

"Well, Master Guntram sees right and wrong as being a great deal clearer than a ruler is able to," Jon said. "I respect him for it, of course."

He'd been frowning down at the back of his hand when he spoke. He raised his eyes to me and said, "I suppose you see things that way too, Lord Pal?"

"Yessir," I said. "I suppose I do."

He shook his head, looking down at his hands again. "Well, the Commonwealth needs people like you two," he said. Looking up abruptly, he said, "Lord Clain is back, by the way. I'm afraid the business of government hasn't been kept up to date in the absence of my Chancellor. It's my fault, but I couldn't seem to concentrate."

Jon cleared his throat and went on, "He and my wife are trying to put things in order right now. I'll join them shortly, but I wanted to see you as soon as you were awake and thank you. I'm sure Jolene and Clain will be up to see you before long. Clain arrived in the middle of the trial. He was most impressed by your performance, Lord Pal."

"There wasn't much to be impressed by," I said. "I just kept deflecting Baran's strokes. I didn't swing at him until I'd lost my temper."

"Lord Pal," Jon said in a harder voice; the voice of the Leader. "I have no idea how Makers like you and Louis and Guntram work. And I realize you may think that I'm a fool in certain ways—"

"Sir! No sir!"

"—and it may be that you're right," Jon continued. "But I *am* a warrior. It was Clain and me and nobody else worth mentioning who cleared Dun Add of the bandits all those years ago. We were just boys, then, but we did it."

"Yes sir," I said.

"I *watched* the trial," Jon said. "You didn't make a false move. You never let Baran get a stroke home until you traded blows there at the end. And when you did, he went down. *Don't* tell me that there was nothing impressive about your performance!"

I cleared my throat and stared into my soup mug. It was empty. "Thank you, sir," I said to the mug.

"Yes, well," Jon said, mildly again. "Have you thought

of what you want to do next, Pal? When you're recovered, of course."

"Well, sir," I said. "I'd like you to send me where I'd be most help. You know, the usual thing. For a Champion."

"So?" said Jon. "There's a vacancy on my Council, you know. Two of them, Gismonde and now Baran. I'd be pleased to have your observations on the matters that come before me, Lord Pal."

I looked hard at the Leader. He was really serious.

But he shouldn't be.

"Sir," I said. "Leader. I don't want to stay in Dun Add, I'd *hate* it, and I don't know anything about it either. But mostly I'd hate it. There's plenty who'd be good at it, but I'm not one. Say, you should ask Master Guntram!"

"I have asked him," Jon said with a lopsided smile. "Years since. And got much the same answer, except that Guntram doesn't mind Dun Add so long as people leave him alone. Which they generally do, unless he takes them under his wing. As he did you..."

The smile changed but I couldn't have sworn just how.

"And before you, Guntram fostered me, you know."

I laughed. "I don't guess Guntram taught you how to build the Commonwealth, sir," I said. "And he *sure* hasn't taught me anything like that."

I thought of Jon as a young warrior, and Jon now: his face worn, his eyes sad and tired.

I remembered Rowley's Roost, cutting through the warriors of Lord Charles and then taking down Charles himself. The woman at Rowley's Roost had her shield built the way mine had been when I beat Baran, almost all the power focused on resisting a vertical slash in the center. I'd put her down by taking her foot off, and One-Eye had murdered her.

It was the right thing to do at the time, even if the thing calling itself Lang hadn't compelled me. Now, though, I'd like to talk to that warrior about her shield, whether she'd gotten it that way or if she'd had it modified and who had done that for her.

I couldn't talk to her because she was dead.

I met the Leader's eyes, set in a face twenty years older than its real age. He'd been like *me*. I'd rather be dead like the woman at Rowley's Roost than to live the life that the Leader did.

"Sir," I said. "Send me out to the Marches, send me the places nobody else wants to go. That's what I wanted to be a Champion for. I want to make all of Here to be a good place for people."

Jon clenched his hands and grimaced as he rubbed the knuckles together in front of himself. He looked up fiercely. "I used to think it was that simple, Pal. It isn't. Whether or not you believe that, it really isn't!"

"I believe you, sir," I said. "But it can be that simple for me. The Commonwealth has you and Louis and Lord Clain to do the hard things here in Dun Add. Send me out to the edges of Here to bring them into the Commonwealth."

Jon stood up. "Yes," he said. "That seems to be the best choice for now. Ah, Lord Pal? I understand you'll need a dog?"

"Yessir," I said. I looked out the window and swallowed. "I'll be going out to Beune first off and see if Demetri's bitch Colleen has littered recently. She was Buck's sister, and I figured..."

I let my voice trail off. I hadn't really "figured" anything. I just wanted things to be back the way they were a year ago, and this seemed like a way to go in that direction.

"Well, in the interim," Jon said, "would you accept a collie sired by my own dog? Clain's dog is from the same sire."

"Sir," I said. I was blushing. "Sir, I'd be honored."

"Then I think I'll get back to my own business," Jon said. "And leave you to yours."

He nodded and opened the door.

I don't have *any business*, I thought.

Baga stood a moment in the doorway. "Well, come in," I said. "How's Buck?"

Baga stepped aside. Behind him stood Lady May. She wore a white frock today. It was embroidered with golden hummingbirds like the ones on the suit I'd fought in.

"May I?" she said.

"Yes," I said. I swallowed.

"I..." she said. Her face had been as smooth as the velvet ground of the tapestries. It suddenly broke up. "Pal, I thought you were going to be killed. I did!"

I swallowed again. "I did too," I said. "But somebody had to stand up for the Consort. That was more important than how it worked out."

"No it wasn't!" May said. "It was me who got you into it and it would've been my fault!"

"Stop," I said. I closed my eyes. "Just stop. That's not what I want to talk about."

I settled my mind, then opened my eyes again. "Lady May." I swallowed. "*May*. The Leader just told me that I know what's right and what isn't. And that's true. I don't want it not to be true. But you see, that doesn't always mean that I *am* right, just because I think I am. Sometimes I've been a real prig."

I didn't want May to speak but I thought she might. She didn't. She stood there with her face still as velvet again.

"May, I'd like to see more of you," I said. "A lot more. If you'd like that."

"I'd like that very much," said May. She took a step toward the bed, then turned.

"Baga?" she said. "You may close the door now. We'll call you when we need you."